THE GREATER WAR 1912–1923

General Editor
ROBERT GERWARTH

The Great War and the Transformation of Habsburg Central Europe

PIETER M. JUDSON
TARA ZAHRA

Great Clarendon Street, Oxford, OX2 6DP,
United Kingdom

Oxford University Press is a department of the University of Oxford.
It furthers the University's objective of excellence in research, scholarship,
and education by publishing worldwide. Oxford is a registered trade mark of
Oxford University Press in the UK and in certain other countries.

© Pieter M. Judson & Tara Zahra 2025

The moral rights of the authors have been asserted.

All rights reserved. No part of this publication may be reproduced, stored in a retrieval system, transmitted, used for text and data mining, or used for training artificial intelligence, in any form or by any means, without the prior permission in writing of Oxford University Press, or as expressly permitted by law, by licence or under terms agreed with the appropriate reprographics rights organization. Enquiries concerning reproduction outside the scope of the above should be sent to the Rights Department, Oxford University Press, at the address above.

You must not circulate this work in any other form
and you must impose this same condition on any acquirer.

Published in the United States of America by Oxford University Press
198 Madison Avenue, New York, NY 10016, United States of America

British Library Cataloguing in Publication Data
Data available

Library of Congress Control Number: 2025937309

ISBN 9780198804000

DOI: 10.1093/9780191842306.001.0001

The manufacturer's authorised representative in the EU for product safety is
Oxford University Press España S.A. of Parque Empresarial San Fernando de Henares,
Avenida de Castilla, 2 – 28830 Madrid (www.oup.es/en or product.safety@oup.com).
OUP España S.A. also acts as importer into Spain of products made by the manufacturer.

Links to third party websites are provided by Oxford in good faith and
for information only. Oxford disclaims any responsibility for the materials
contained in any third party website referenced in this work.

Acknowledgments

We have always wanted to write a book together, and Robert Gerwarth gave us that opportunity by commissioning this book for his Greater War series at Oxford University Press. Along the way many life changes, from Eloisa's birth to Covid, kept us from making many promised deadlines. We are grateful to Robert and to our editor Cathryn Steel for their enormous patience.

This book is neither an exhaustive account of the war nor a definitive one. It can't replace a book like Manfried Rauchensteiner's or Alexander Watson's in their extraordinary detail and attention to the military aspects of the War. Inspired by the foundational work of Maureen Healy, we wanted to write a book that shifted the focus from those important military campaigns to document the remarkable daily-life experiences of the citizens of empire and of the occupied regions during the War years.

We benefited enormously from the veritable explosion of innovative scholarly research in the past decade about every imaginable aspect of Austro-Hungarian society in the First World War, especially the new research on the end of empire and its consequences. Ironically, there is more original material available today on this subject than there was for the centenary of the outbreak of war in 2014. We are grateful to the many scholars who generously shared their ongoing research with us during the writing of this book, and we apologize to those whose important studies we could not include because they were published after we had finished the manuscript.

At a crucial moment in the writing, we benefited from a manuscript workshop with Claire Morelon, Máté Rigó, Leonard Smith, and Miloš Vojinovič. Doina Anca Cretu, Claire Morelon, Jan Rybak, Tamara Scheer, and Rok Stergar graciously shared work in progress, shared documents they had discovered, and pointed us to crucial sources. Seth Koven and Belinda Davis generously supported the project from the start and made critical suggestions for two of the chapters. The work of Gábor Egry and his team at the NEPOSTRANS ERC project was foundational for our thinking regarding the period 1918–23. Eric Phillips proved a most valuable research assistant and sleuth. Others whose work and suggestions contributed substantially to our thinking include Pamela Ballinger, Peter Becker, Ágoston Berecz, Isaac Bershady, Marco Bresciani, Laurence Cole, Mark Cornwall, Krisztian Csaplar-Degovics, Gábor Egry, Francesco Frizzera, Elisabeth Haid, Maureen Healy, Ke-Chin Hsia, Ivan Jelačić, Rudolf Kučera, Hannes Leidinger, Michael Miller, Iris Rachamimov, Dominique Kirchner Reill, Stephanie Reitzig, Nancy Wingfield, and Larry Wolff.

We could not have undertaken this project without the loving support and needed distraction provided to us by our families, Charles, William, and Eloisa.

During the writing of this book, we lost some dear colleagues, friends, and family. We dedicate the book to the memory of an inspiring and fearless historian of Central Europe, our friend Heidemarie Uhl, who died in August 2023.

Contents

List of Figures and Maps	ix
Maps	xiii
Introduction: The Great War and the Transformation of Habsburg Central Europe	1
1. Why War? Austria-Hungary, Europe, the World, 1900–1914	7
2. Mobilizations	31
3. The Fortunes of War: Occupation Regimes	56
4. The Empire in Camps: Refugees & POWS	78
5. Entitled Citizens: Empire, Citizenship, and the Welfare State	103
6. Revolutions	119
7. The Enduring Empire	152
Conclusion: Continuities, Legacies, Memories	181
Index	185

List of Figures and Maps

Figures

1.1 Franz Joseph observes army maneuvers at Groß-Meseritsch/Velké Meziříčí in 1909. Chief of General Staff Franz Conrad von Hötzendorf explains the course of the maneuvers to the emperor and to Archduke Franz Ferdinand, heir to the throne. 9
Source: Austrian National Library: https://onb.digital/result/1120CD34

2.1 Hungarian reservists march to their barracks through the streets of Budapest after being issued their rifles upon mobilization. 32
Source: Alamy: https://www.alamy.com/reservists-march-through-budapest-1914-image68845341.html?imageid=EE554A36-EF2E-40E3-8331-DC27F1AF8AC1&p=291611&pn=4&searchId=29ffeeea737ce4e415a3cc559e1d6572&searchtype=0

2.2 Der Wehrman at the Přerov/Prerau train station. Wehrman statues appeared throughout Austria-Hungary beginning in 1915 and became focal points for patriotic demonstrations. 49
Source: Herder-Institut: https://www.herder-institut.de/bildkatalog/iv/257529

2.3 Women making munitions during World War I in the Bohemian Škoda arms factory. 50
Source: Alamy: https://www.alamy.com/women-making-munitions-during-world-war-i-in-an-arms-factory-in-austria-hungary-automated-translation-image446963121.html?imageid=6FE56375-C114-452F-95F3-08CEBDD3AD67&p=1760052&pn=1&searchId=4bd20e541ccedf238662732b8a1aa03a&searchtype=0

2.4 A 1917 war bond poster in Hungarian. To the left, a group of civilians throw gold coins onto the ground. To the right, a group of Austro-Hungarian infantrymen aim their rifles. The text reads "The homeland is defended by our civilians at home, [and] our soldiers at the front. Subscribe to the war loan at the Hungarian Discount and Exchange Bank." 52
Source: Imperial War Museum: https://www.iwm.org.uk/collections/item/object/2340

3.1 Ski troops cross a beam bridge. 57
Source: Imperial War Museum: https://www.iwm.org.uk/collections/item/object/205081847

3.2 Austro-Hungarian troops in a trench. 58
Source: Imperial War Museum: https://www.iwm.org.uk/collections/item/object/205268360

3.3 The recapture of Lviv/Lwów/Lemberg, June 22, 1915, with a double portrait of Germany's Kaiser Wilhelm II and Austria-Hungary's Emperor-King Franz Josef I.   59
Source: Herder-Institut: https://www.herder-institut.de/bildkatalog/index/pic?id=a13755110ea9f4be466e6122d3c75d9c

3.4 Austro-Hungarian troops in front of a burning village in Poland, 1916.   60
Source: Herder-Institut: https://www.herder-institut.de/bildkatalog/index/pic?id=0b7e43eef0c29579317ccbaabfeb71f8

4.1 Refugee barracks under construction in Mitterndorf, 1914–15.   82
Source: Austrian National Library: https://onb.digital/result/11135634

4.2 Life inside a refugee camp in Landegg, 1914–15.   82
Source: Austrian National Library: https://onb.digital/result/11135656

4.3 Refugees outside of a camp in Gmünd, 1914–15.   83
Source: Austrian National Library: https://onb.digital/result/1113566F

4.4 Women learn to sew in a refugee camp in Grieskirchen, 1914.   83
Source: Austrian National Library: https://onb.digital/result/10BA4FA5

4.5 Inspection of refugees in the snow at a camp near Salzburg, 1915.   84
Source: Austrian National Library - https://digital.onb.ac.at/rep/osd/?1127A50B

4.6 Street in a refugee camp in Porhlitz/Pohořelice Moravia, 1915.   84
Source: Austrian National Library: https://onb.digital/result/1127A7F7

4.7 Advertisement for an exhibition of handicrafts made by Austro-Hungarian prisoners of war, 1917.   95
Source: Austrian National Library: https://onb.digital/result/11310A3C

5.1 Wounded soldiers taken off a train.   107
Source: Austrian National Library: https://onb.digital/result/1124272F

5.2 Vienna breadline in Ottakring district, 1915.   109
Credit: Polizeifotografie (1914–1918) (Fotograf), Warteschlange vor Anker-Brot-Verkaufsstelle (Ottakringer Straße), 1915, Wien Museum Inv.-Nr. 41233/4, CC0 (https://sammlung.wienmuseum.at/objekt/105843/)

5.3 A Favoritenstraße Breadline in Vienna, ca. 1918.   111
Source: Austrian National Library - Wien 10, Favoritenstrasse 128, ca. 1918 https://onb.digital/result/10BBB021

5.4 "Brothers in America! Why don't you join our army?"   117
Source: Herder-Institut: https://www.herder-institut.de/bildkatalog/iv/257522

LIST OF FIGURES AND MAPS   xi

6.1 Emperor King Charles and Empress Queen Zita.   125
    Source: Alamy: https://www.alamy.com/emperor-charles-i-of-austria-
    1887-1922-with-empress-zita-museum-private-collection-author-
    anonymous-image407166738.html?imageid=FA8498D6-4C57-423D-
    B28C-109EA8D40D3F&p=697458&pn=1&searchId=
    fdc378b4692bf5944052f6d28daa654d&searchtype=0

6.2 Emperor King Charles inspects the Polish Legion, 1917.   126
    Source: Austrian National Library: https://onb.digital/result/10D3E45

6.3 Italian POWs, 1917.   134
    Source: Wikimedia Commons: https://commons.wikimedia.org/wiki/
    File:Italijanski_vojni_ujetniki_po_bitki_pri_Kobaridu.jpg

6.4 Signing of the Treaty of Brest-Litovsk, March 1918.   141
    Source: Austrian National Library: https://onb.digital/result/110DF798

7.1 German nationalist demonstration in Vienna, 1919.   155
    Source: Austrian National Library: https://onb.digital/result/10BCE75B

7.2 Removing German signs in Prague, 1918.   159
    Source: https://commons.wikimedia.org/wiki/File:Removing_german_
    signs_in_1918_from_Rosicky.png

7.3 Proclamation of Hungarian Soviet Republic, 1919.   165
    Source: https://www.alamy.com/march-1919-the-proclamation-of-hungarian-
    republic-now-turned-over-to-hungarian-bolsheviki-apparent-from-the-
    dispatches-received-of-the-proclamation-of-a-new-hungarian-government-
    inviting-the-workmen-and-peasants-of-bohemia-serbia-rumania-romania-
    and-croatia-to-form-an-armed-alliance-against-aristocracy-landowners-and-
    dynasties-that-cout-kayrolyi-provisional-president-of-the-republic-has-turned-
    the-country-over-to-the-bolsheviki-anger-over-the-decision-of-paris-peace-
    conference-and-thereby-plunging-these-people-into-a-war-against-the-
    entente-image227004129.html?imageid=E53FEF14-81D3-453D-
    B40E-B28CAAB9CA1F&p=307105&pn=1&searchId=
    9a026ba3869d1abc16f258252223499c&searchtype=0

7.4 Romanian troops enter Budapest, 1919.   166
    Source: https://archive.org/details/outlawsdiary02tormuoft/page/n7/
    mode/2up?view=theater; https://commons.wikimedia.org/wiki/File:Tropas-
    rumanas-ocupan-budapest-1919--outlawsdiary02tormuoft.png

Maps

1 Austria-Hungary in 1914   xiii
2 Regions Occupied and Administered by Austria-Hungary During the War   xiv
3 The Successor States to Austria-Hungary in 1925   xv

Maps

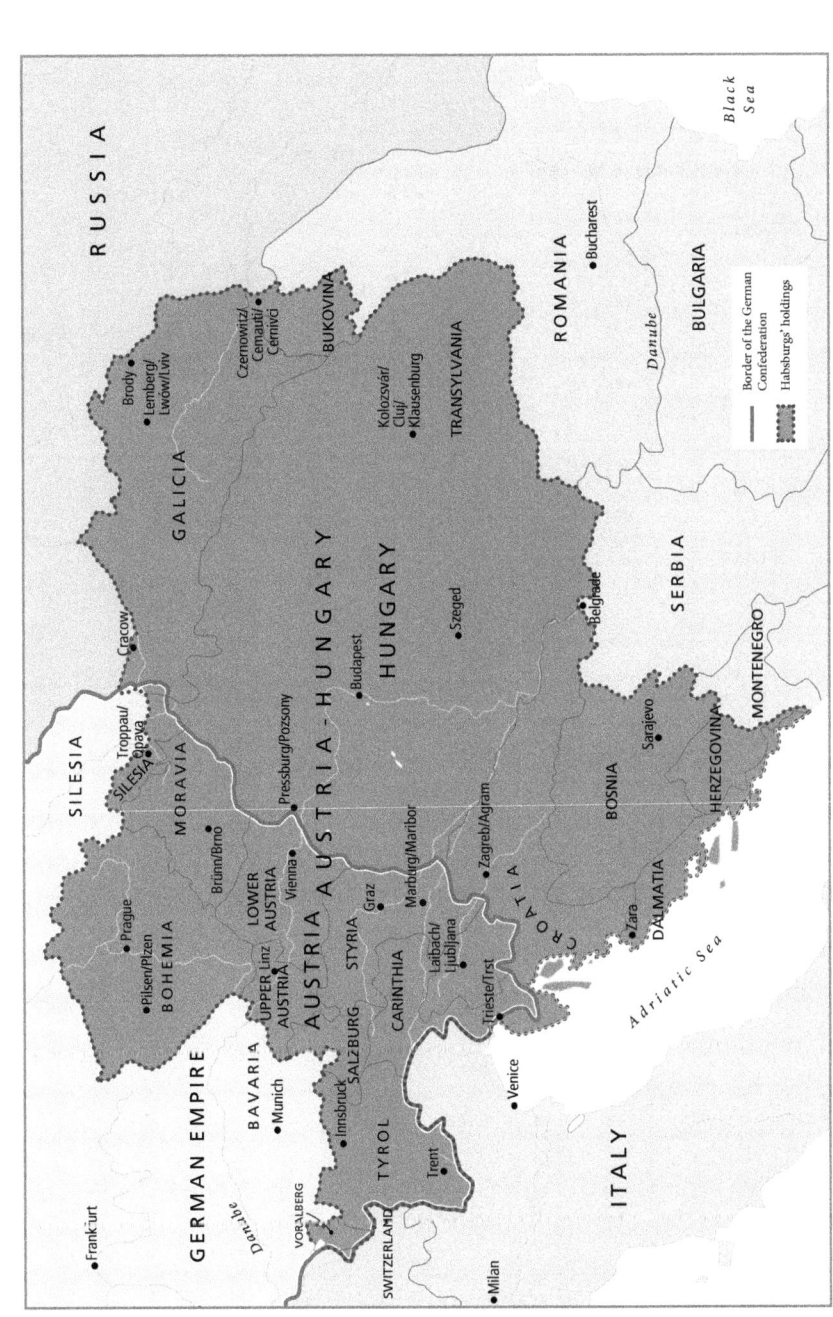

Habsburg Empire, 1914

Map 1 Austria-Hungary in 1914

Habsburg Empire, 1918

Map 2 Regions Occupied and Administered by Austria-Hungary During the War

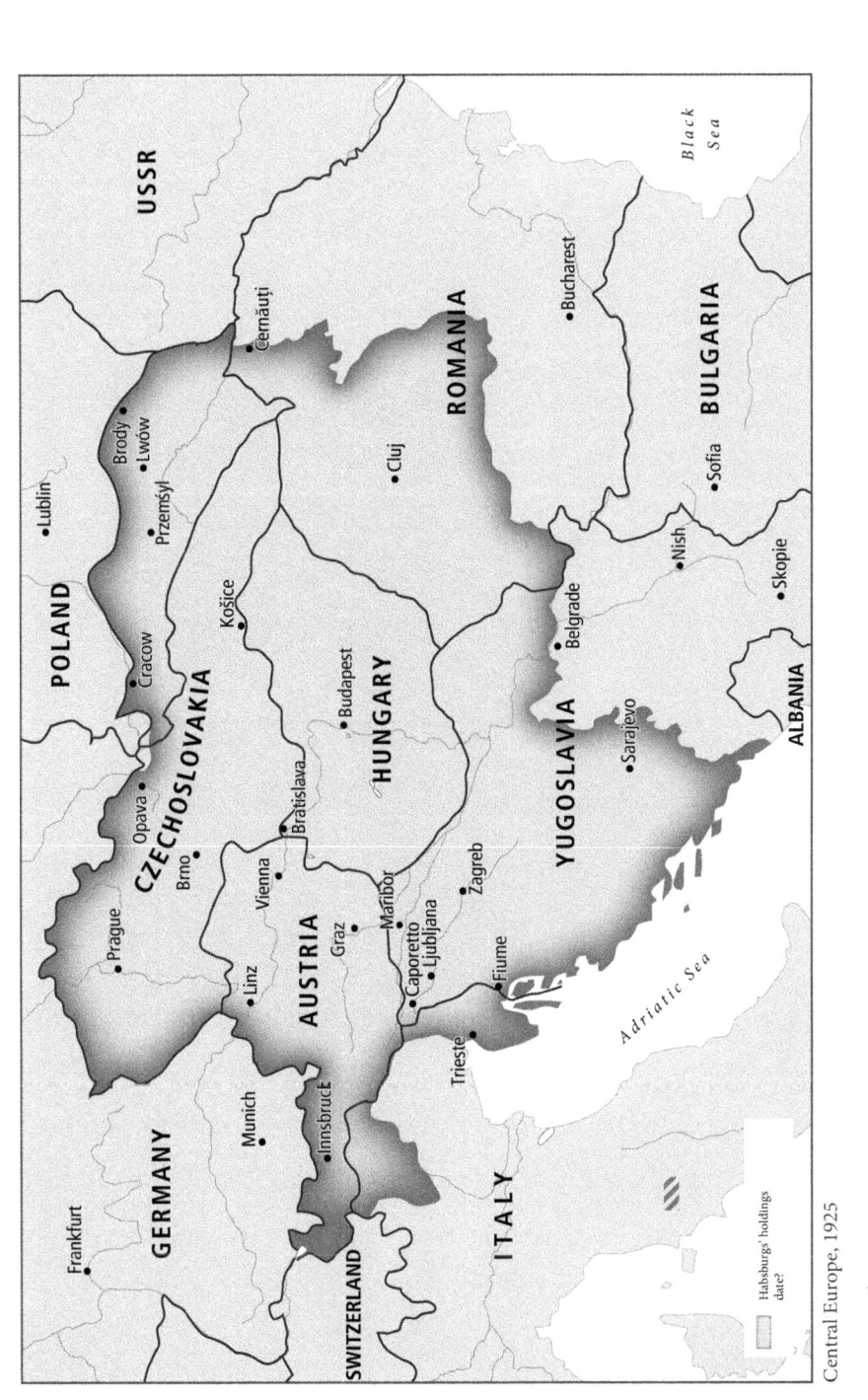

Central Europe, 1925

Map 3 The Successor States to Austria-Hungary in 1925

Introduction

The Great War and the Transformation of Habsburg Central Europe

Sarajevo, June 29. "As the news about the fateful day...spread throughout Vienna, and the terrible events became known in all their painful details, it was as though a storm sailed through the Monarchy...as though History had written the gruesome title of a new chapter with a blood-red pen," reported the *Neue Freie Presse*.[1] The Archduke Franz Ferdinand and his wife Duchess Sophie von Hohenburg had been shot dead that morning as their open car processed through the streets of Sarajevo. The couple reportedly grasped each other before slumping into unconsciousness, their last breaths overlapping.

The world's eyes were on Austria-Hungary on June 28, 1914. But both inside and outside of Austria, few could imagine the dramatic consequences of the events in Sarajevo. The popular shock and anger that greeted the assassination in the Monarchy did not mean war was a likely or necessary outcome. Nor, as the *Manchester Guardian* opined, was it "to be supposed, that the death of the Archduke Francis Ferdinand will have any immediate or salient effect on the politics of Europe."[2] The *Guardian*'s words now seem remarkably naïve, and yet standard histories of the First World War still tend to treat the events in Sarajevo as an almost absurd pretext for what later became understood as a supremely senseless war.

Even at the time, many European elites saw Franz Ferdinand's assassination as a shocking but ultimately highly localized crime involving some desperate Balkan terrorists in the hinterland of an almost oriental empire. Violence, they believed, was to be expected in the Balkans. Austria's own *Neue Freie Presse* characterized the assassination as a "Balkan murder" (*Balkanmord*), a "bloodthirsty" act of senseless barbarism.[3] For this very reason it could hardly concern the rest of Europe. These attitudes help to explain why following its declaration of war on Serbia, Austria-Hungary itself disappears from most historical accounts of the war, only to reappear again in time for its critical and allegedly inevitable collapse

---

[1] "Erzherzog Franz Ferdinand. Der Thronfolger Und Seine Gemahlin Ermordert," *Neue Freie Presse*, June 29, 1914.
[2] "Trials before Austria," *The Manchester Guardian*, June 29, 1914.
[3] These connotations of alleged "Balkan barbarism" rest in part on the memory of the 1903 murders of Serb King Alexandar and Queen Draga. Christopher M. Clark, *The Sleepwalkers: How Europe Went to War in 1914* (London: HarperCollins, 2012), 3–14.

in 1918. As it turned out, the very idea that Austria-Hungary's collapse was somehow necessary and even inevitable became a founding ideological claim crucial to the legitimation of the successor states that replaced the Empire.

If, however, the Habsburg Monarchy was not in a dire condition on the eve of the war, then war itself can no longer be treated as a mere postscript to its biography. Instead, the war also becomes a constitutive factor in the Empire's dissolution, in the domestic relations that structured society in the successor states, and in the birth of the world order institutionalized by the Paris Peace Conferences. Both the experience and outcome of the First World War in the Habsburg Monarchy held implications that also extended far beyond its borders, and beyond the lives of its 48 million citizens. For one, the Empire's collapse spelled the demise of an organizational ideal and set of practices that remain powerfully compelling in today's Europe: the idea of a polity legitimized by something other than the principle of national homogeneity. Additionally, the Empire's dissolution and the creation of new self-styled nation-states, justified in a language of anticolonial nationalism, made it possible for Imperial and colonial subjects around the world to imagine a post-Imperial world. It empowered them to make their own demands for national self-determination and democracy, and it created an international order in which nationally homogenous populations came to be seen as a prerequisite for modern, democratic states. At the same time, and according to the very same logic, the Empire's dissolution inaugurated a century of ethnic cleansing, creating thousands of refugees and stateless peoples. The unmixing of populations was often justified by the notion that population transfers were a "humanitarian" solution to the "problem" of a diverse society. The fate of these refugees was overseen by new international institutions that cut their teeth in the crumbling Monarchy.

This book tells the story of the Habsburg Monarchy's last war and the emergence of a new postwar world. It reconstitutes contemporaries' experiences and sense of contingent and multifarious possible outcomes of the conflict triggered by events in Sarajevo. Few imagined much less predicted Imperial collapse. It was never an inevitability.[4] We attend to the outer rings of the Empire—places like Silesia, Dalmatia, Galicia, Bukovina—as much as to its capital cities, integrating diverse regional experiences into a common, overarching narrative.[5] We do not,

---

[4] Pieter M. Judson, *The Habsburg Empire: A New History* (Cambridge, MA: Harvard University Press, 2016). For a review of literature on the Habsburg Empire during the First World War up until 2014, see John Deak, "The Great War and the Forgotten Realm: The Habsburg Monarchy and the First World War," *The Journal of Modern History* 86, no. 2 (June 2014): 336–80.

[5] We build on the excellent work of other scholars whose research has focused on the experience of war in particular regions or cities. See Maureen Healy, *Vienna and the Fall of the Habsburg Monarchy: Total War and Everyday Life in World War I* (Cambridge: Cambridge University Press, 2004); Claire Morelon, *Streetscapes of War and Revolution: Prague, 1914–1920* (Cambridge: Cambridge University Press, 2024); Rudolf Kučera, *Rationed Life: Science, Everyday Life, and Working-Class Politics in the Bohemian Lands, 1914–1918* (New York: Berghahn Books, 2019); Tamara Scheer, *Zwischen Front Und Heimat: Österreich-Ungarns Militärverwaltungen Im Ersten Weltkrieg* (Frankfurt am Main: Peter

however, write the history of "the Czechs," "the Germans," or "the Poles" during the First World War. Instead, this history takes seriously the complex Imperial loyalties of Austro-Hungarian subjects, while considering the extent to which the war created and fragmented new forms of loyalty, activism, and political imaginings. This book is also not an attempt to write the military history of Austria-Hungary during the war, something that has already received adequate attention in some excellent and comprehensive histories.[6]

We argue that the Empire's internal collapse in 1918 was not evidence of the inherent fragility of multinational polities. At least initially, citizens with diverse national loyalties participated in the war effort with at a surprising degree of patriotism. But both patriotism and enthusiasm for war quickly eroded, not only because of the immense material and human sacrifices citizens were called upon to make, but because the state turned against its own citizens. In many localities, the military quickly took control from civilian bureaucrats, suspending civil rights and imposing its own autocratic vision on the population.[7] Civilian and military administrators alike also turned against individuals or groups that they perceived to be disloyal to the Empire—merely by virtue of the languages they spoke. This had severe consequences, as newspapers and associations were censored or banned, and "suspect" individuals were denounced, interned, and prosecuted

---

Lang D, 2009); John Deak and Jonathan E. Gumz, "How to Break a State: The Habsburg Monarchy's Internal War, 1914–1918," *The American Historical Review* 122, no. 4 (2017): 1105–36. There are also many excellent new edited collections examining wartime experiences in different parts of the Habsburg lands during and after the First World War. See for example Ernst Otto Bräunche and Sander-Faes, Stephan, eds., *Städte Im Krieg: Erlebnis, Inszenierung Und Erinnerung Des Ersten Weltkriegs* (Ostfildern: Thorbecke, 2016); Wolfram Dornik et al., eds., *Frontwechsel: Österreich-Ungarns "Grosser Krieg" im Vergleich* (Wien: Böhlau Verlag, 2014); Judith Devlin, John Paul Newman, and Maria Falina, eds., *World War I in Central and Eastern Europe: Politics, Conflict and Military Experience* (London: I.B. Taurus & Co, 2018); Tamara Scheer and Nancy M. Wingfield, "Habsburg Home Fronts during the Great War," *European Review of History: Revue Européenne d'histoire* 24, no. 2 (March 4, 2017): 171–5.

[6] See especially Manfried Rauchensteiner, *The First World War and the End of the Habsburg Monarchy, 1914–1918*, trans. Alex J. Kay and Anna Güttel-Bellert, Revised and expanded edition (Wien: Böhlau Verlag, 2014); Alexander Watson, *Ring of Steel: Germany and Austria-Hungary in World War I* (New York: Basic Books, 2014).

[7] There has been a great deal of new work on the wartime military regime, including its administration of occupied territories, from which we draw. See Scheer, *Zwischen Front Und Heimat*; Jonathan E. Gumz, *The Resurrection and Collapse of Empire in Habsburg Serbia, 1914–1918* (Cambridge: Cambridge University Press, 2009); Watson, *Ring of Steel*; Clemens Ruthner and Tamara Scheer, eds., *Bosnien-Herzegowina und Österreich-Ungarn, 1878–1918: Annäherungen an eine Kolonie*, Kultur—Herrschaft—Differenz, Band 24 (2018) (Tübingen: Narr Francke Attempto, 2018); Stephan Lehnstaedt, "Two Kinds of Occupation? German and Austro-Hungarian Economic Policy in Congress Poland, 1915–1918," in *Other Fronts, Other Wars? First World War Studies on the Eve of the Centennial*, ed. Joachim Bürgschwentner, Matthias Egger, and Gunda Barth-Scalmani (Leiden: Brill, 2014), 197–217; Elisabeth Haid, "Galicia: A Bulwark against Russia? Propaganda and Violence in a Border Region During the First World War," *European Review of History: Revue Européenne d'histoire* 24, no. 2 (March 4, 2017): 200–13; Milan Ristović, "Occupation During and After the War (South East Europe)," *1914–1918—Online International Encyclopedia of the First World War*, 2014, https://doi.org/10.15463/IE1418.10481; Isa Blumi, "Albania," *1914–1918—Online International Encyclopedia of the First World War*, 2014, https://doi.org/10.15463/IE1418.10197.

on flimsy grounds. The principle of equality before the law was abandoned when the complaints of German or Hungarian speakers were dismissed as innocent grumbling, while the same complaints from someone speaking or writing in Czech, Italian, Serb, or Ukrainian, for example, were considered treasonous.

Rather than writing the history of an ending, we also suggest that Austria-Hungary during the First World War was the birthplace of experimental and revolutionary ideas, institutions, and modes of statecraft. Even as jubilant nationalists in the Habsburg successor states tore down the Imperial eagles from government buildings in 1918, at the same time they quietly built on and perpetuated crucial Imperial institutions, laws, and cultural and social practices. Indeed, leaders of Czechoslovakia, Poland, Yugoslavia, and other Habsburg successor states loudly insisted that they were the architects of a radical new world of nation-states, but many of the changes they took credit for had already occurred long before the war ended. These changes included the devolution of state authority to local and regional governments and nationalist associations. Despite the suspicion directed toward "suspect" national groups, such as Czechs, Italians, and Serbs, nationalists of all kinds actually gained authority during the war by stepping into the vacuum created when Imperial authorities could not adequately provide for the population. If we imagine a world in which the Empire did *not* collapse, the war itself would still have been an enormous turning point in the region's history and in world history, as a result of new experiences of conscription, occupation, and hunger, which in turn bred new institutions and practices, from the refugee camp to the welfare state.

The story does not actually begin with Franz Ferdinand's untimely death, however, but rather with the domestic and regional challenges produced by the Austro-Hungarian annexation of Bosnia-Herzegovina in 1908 and the subsequent Balkan wars of 1912–13. The extreme tensions around these events shaped much of the nationalist paranoia and bloodshed to come, but also some of the institutions that revolutionized Austro-Hungarian society. The Balkan Wars escalated into the first great clash of European empires on European soil, becoming a testing ground for policies of ethnic cleansing and nationalization.

Subsequent chapters pay close attention to the social and cultural history of the Empire during wartime in relationship to its political, economic, and military history. By thinking across scales in each chapter—from the local to the Imperial to the international, we seek to demonstrate their close interconnections. By thinking across regions, we seek to demonstrate fundamental commonalities of the war experience that otherwise can be seen as highly diverse depending on the local setting. Across regions and at different levels of society we investigate the mobilization of women, workers, and children for (and ultimately against) the war effort; the crisis of provisioning, the perceived breakdown of the family and rise in juvenile delinquency; the mobilization of a culture of patriotic paranoia fed by censorship and rampant denunciation; the birth of new forms of social welfare along with new understandings of citizenship and social rights.

Austria-Hungary's citizens encountered one another in unprecedented ways during the First World War, a result of new experiences of conscription, occupation, flight, and internment. These trans-Imperial encounters, officials hoped, would strengthen a sense of shared belonging and loyalty to the Empire. In reality, they often had the opposite effect, accentuating or creating new regional, local, religious, and national antagonisms. As occupying armies traversed its eastern territories in 1914 and 1915, and as the military moved some populations from frontline areas to the hinterlands, hundreds of thousands of refugees flooded the Empire's cities and countryside. Government officials attempted to manage the logistical, political, and social crisis created by mass population displacement by setting up camps to accommodate a range of different populations, from refugees to suspect populations to POW laborers. But in doing so, they once again highlighted differences among citizens, by sorting refugees based on their social class, religion, and nationality—and treating these groups differently and unequally. The refugee crisis especially bred mistrust and resentment between and among the Empire's citizens. Urban dwellers in Prague and Vienna resented refugees who competed for scarce food, housing, and energy. Refugees were greeted with no less antagonism in rural areas, where they were interned in camps that were seen as breeding grounds of disease and crime.

The war bred other new divisions as well. Rural people resented the city folk who crowded onto trains intent on raiding farms for their provisions; Austrians resented Hungarians who they believed were hoarding food supplies for themselves. POWs displaced far into the Russian interior feared that they had been abandoned by the state, while paranoid military officials worried that their soldiers were being turned against their own government. Citizens denounced their neighbors for violating rules such as "meatless Monday," or for uttering disloyal words in pubs, on trams, or in cinemas. These experiences and encounters deepened mistrust among the Empire's citizens and between citizens and state officials, fraying the Empire at its seams.

Nor does the story end with the Armistice of November 4, 1918, since clearly the war had no definitive end point in East Central Europe.[8] Wartime conditions continued for months—sometimes years—with the persistence of hunger and disease well beyond 1918, ongoing struggles to define the borders of new states

---

[8] Robert Gerwarth, *The Vanquished: Why the First World War Failed to End* (New York: Farrar, Straus and Giroux, 2016); Maureen Healy, "Civilizing the Solider in Postwar Austria," in *Gender and War in Twentieth-Century Eastern Europe*, ed. Nancy M. Wingfield and Maria Bucur (Bloomington: Indiana University Press, 2006); Maureen Healy, "Introductory Remarks: Space, Chronology and the Habsburg Home Fronts," *European Review of History: Revue Européenne d'histoire* 24, no. 2 (March 4, 2017): 176–84; Paul Brian Miller and Claire Morelon, *Embers of Empire: Continuity and Rupture in the Habsburg Successor States After 1918* (New York: Berghahn Books, 2019); Marcus M. Payk and Roberta Pergher, *Beyond Versailles: Sovereignty, Legitimacy, and the Formation of New Polities After the Great War* (Bloomington, IN: Indiana University Press, 2019); Mark Cornwall and John Paul Newman, *Sacrifice and Rebirth: The Legacy of the Last Habsburg War* (New York: Berghahn Books, 2016).

and to control their populations, in the violence perpetrated by paramilitary and revolutionary groups on civilians, and in the effort to create new European and global orders.

The significance of the Habsburg Empire's Great War (and last war) thus extended far beyond the borders of the Empire itself. In many ways, the challenges that tested Austria-Hungary resembled those that brought other societies to the brink of collapse between 1914 and 1918. These included the tasks of mobilizing labor, resources, and troops on a massive scale; feeding soldiers and civilians despite crushing shortages; and providing for the health and welfare of disabled veterans who returned or of families left behind by fallen soldiers. As the war dragged on with no clear end in sight, Europeans across the continent increasingly turned on their neighbors, resented perceived inequalities of sacrifice, and blamed military and political leaders for leading them into what seemed like a fruitless war of mass death.

In all these ways, the Habsburg Empire was not unique. But the Habsburg Monarchy did face unique challenges thanks to its Dualist structure and multinational character, the vastness and diversity of its territory, the untrammeled power of its military elite, and its exposure on multiple fronts. Nevertheless, the Empire was not defeated by its diversity, but it was seriously weakened by the abandonment of its commitment to the rule of law, to its traditional promise to treat subjects from different linguistic, national, and confessional backgrounds equally. The collapse of the Empire, and of the multinational ideal it represented, may have begun with the death of an heir on the edge of Europe, but its consequences would radiate across the continent and the world for decades to come.

The Great War and the Transformation of Habsburg Central Europe. Pieter M. Judson & Tara Zahra,
Oxford University Press. © Pieter M. Judson & Tara Zahra 2025. DOI: 10.1093/9780191842306.003.0001

1

Why War? Austria-Hungary, Europe, the World, 1900–1914

On July 28, 1914, a handful of elite men in Austria-Hungary—among them Emperor/King Francis Joseph (1830–1916)—took the Empire to war with the neighboring state of Serbia, ostensibly as punishment for Serbia's alleged role in the Sarajevo murders. This fateful choice started the First World War. Austria-Hungary's military leaders originally hoped—with little reason—that this war might remain a purely local one, confined to two neighboring states. From the very start on July 28, however, this hope proved completely unjustified and illusory. Within a few days and weeks of Austria-Hungary's war declaration, Russia, Germany, France, Great Britain, Japan, and the Ottoman Empire had joined the hostilities. Other greater and smaller powers subsequently joined the conflict: Italy and Bulgaria in 1915, Romania in 1916, Greece and the United States in 1917. Although most of the fighting took place in Europe, the war touched the Middle East, Asia, Africa, Australasia, and the Americas. Europe's global empires took the opportunity to attack each other's colonial holdings and eventually, to mobilize millions of colonized peoples for the fight. Austria-Hungary had unleashed a world war.

As with other great powers, Austria-Hungary's 51 million citizens had had no say in the choice to go to war. Nor had the hundreds of elected politicians in Austria, Hungary, and Bosnia-Herzegovina even debated the decision. Nevertheless, in the first few days of the July crisis, at least according to newspaper articles and personal reminiscences, the decision to go to war appears to have been popular or at least accepted across Austria-Hungary. This, even though so few people had participated in making the decision, and no one could yet imagine the terrible ways in which this war would profoundly shape their everyday lives. Historians interpret these newspaper accounts of enthusiastic crowds eager for war in all the belligerent societies with some skepticism, since this apparent excitement was hardly universal in each society.[1] More importantly, this excitement did not last very long, as the realities of war came into sharper focus for most people within a matter of days. Austro-Hungarians and their counterparts across Europe may

---

[1] For a nuanced analysis of popular responses to the outbreak of war in one Austrian provincial city, see Laurence Cole, Marlene Horejs, and Jan Rybak, "When the Music Stopped: Reactions to the Outbreak of World War I in an Austrian Province," *Austrian History Yearbook* 52 (May 2021): 147–65.

have harbored strong feelings of patriotism toward their homeland and a determination to sacrifice, but this hardly counted as enthusiasm for war. In this book we will return often to the question of popular attitudes toward the war, what war meant to local societies, and how its meanings changed over time. Much of our story focuses on how the war changed the everyday lives of Austro-Hungarians, and how in turn women and men themselves transformed the very meanings of the war for their own benefit.

This chapter investigates how the anxieties of a few elite men in the Army High Command, in the Foreign Ministry, and in the circles closest to the ruler produced a war that deeply affected and was itself transformed by the everyday experience of ordinary people. The military leadership and some in the Foreign Ministry feared that Austria-Hungary was rapidly losing its status as a great power and sliding into political irrelevance even in its natural region of influence, southeastern Europe. In their anxiety, they pointed to two culprits to explain the Empire's declining great power status: Serbia, and Austria-Hungary's own ongoing domestic political liberalization. Their dual goal became to reestablish Austro-Hungarian hegemony in southeastern Europe by crushing Serbia, and to impose an apolitical domestic unity on the Habsburg population by establishing an authoritarian regime.

To understand these goals, as well as the distinctive elements of the Austro-Hungarian war experience, we need to identity the structures and institutions that help to explain the first apparent paradox our story addresses: how was it possible that a liberalizing society which had mobilized increasing numbers of people into politics at every level of governance over the past half century, nevertheless could be taken to war by the erratic decisions of a handful of individuals? The highest levels of the military command, among them military Chief of Staff Franz Conrad von Hötzendorf (1852–1925), along with Emperor/King Francis Joseph (1830–1916), decided that Austria-Hungary would declare war. The Foreign Minister Count Leopold Berchtold (1863–1942) also agreed to war, and the Austrian and Hungarian governing cabinets ratified and implemented the decision. But neither the two cabinets nor the elected Austrian and Hungarian parliaments played any role in taking this decision. The Austrian Parliament was not even in session at the time. The two ill-fated prime ministers of Austria and Hungary, Counts Karl von Stürgkh (1859–1916) and István Tisza (1861–1918), both fated to die at the hands of assassins, exercised little to no influence on the decision to go to war. In fact, as we will see, although Tisza originally opposed the possible war, calling it contradictory to Hungarian interests, he quickly acquiesced to the decision after receiving certain assurances. And with few exceptions, the same narrow circle of elite military men would maintain an outsized influence over political and strategic decision-making until the final months of the war. Ultimately, it was their political anxieties and their narrow worldviews that rushed Austria-Hungary

Figure 1.1 Franz Joseph observes army maneuvers at Groß-Meseritsch/Velké Meziříčí in 1909. Chief of General Staff Franz Conrad von Hötzendorf explains the course of the maneuvers to the emperor and to Archduke Franz Ferdinand, heir to the throne.
Source: Austrian National Library: https://onb.digital/result/1120CD34

into war, shaped most of the Empire's disastrous wartime decisions, and were in a very real sense responsible for the Empire's collapse in October 1918.

Austro-Hungarian Statehood and the Military

How was it possible that a liberalizing society which had mobilized increasing numbers of people into politics at every level of governance over the past half century, nevertheless could be taken to war by the erratic decisions of a handful of individuals? Structurally and politically, what gave them the opportunity to do so?

As a dual state, Austria-Hungary was a different kind of polity by most European standards.[2] A political settlement in 1867 had created two independent

---

[2] Another dual state in Europe, Sweden-Norway, had recently separated into two states in 1905.

states out of the former Austrian Empire, whose ruler was simultaneously Emperor of Austria and King of Hungary. The two states had very different constitutions, different administrative systems, and different governing institutions. They did not share a common citizenship and their citizens enjoyed different civil rights. Austria's constitutional laws of 1867 included a detailed bill of citizens' rights and created a representative parliament that, after reforms in 1897 and 1906, was elected by universal and equal manhood suffrage.[3] Hungary's constitution, like the British, was unwritten. Its laws guaranteed citizens' rights, but in Hungary, thanks to the large size of non-Hungarian speaking populations, the ruling Magyar elite kept the franchise highly restricted until 1918.

What bound the two states together was their common Habsburg ruler, a common foreign policy, a common military, and a common economic division of the state debt.[4] Still, as we will see, it was not Austria-Hungary's dual nature itself that enabled the military to act independently of the politicians in 1914. Rather, it was the relationship of the military to the two states' liberal parliamentary institutions.

When he negotiated the 1867 settlement, Francis Joseph had insisted on maintaining personal control over foreign and military policy. These two areas remained technically under the monarch's personal supervision and outside any direct constitutional oversight.[5] There were only two ways that political parties and politicians in the two parliaments could hope to influence military or foreign policy. The first was through the right to interrogate the respective Joint Ministers for Foreign Affairs and Defense. The second way to influence policy was through their right to review the common military budget. In fact, over the five decades following the 1867 settlement, the two parliaments regularly cut military budget requests, and this explains why in 1912 Austria-Hungary budgeted a mere 2.6% of its GNP for the military, as compared to Russia (4.5%), France (4%), and Germany (3.8)%.[6] Budgetary politics indirectly forced the General Staff to cut back on several ambitious projects, ranging from the renovation of decrepit fortresses on the Russian frontier to the provision of troops with the latest equipment. Budgetary battles also embittered military leaders toward their civilian counterparts and ensured that each group generally viewed the other with suspicion. In every other way, however, the emperor king jealously guarded his prerogative to control the military and remove it from civilian influence. This contrasted

---

[3] Officially the constitution was known as "fundamental laws." The 1897 reform enfranchised most men over the age of 21 but kept a curial voting system that privileged property owners. The 1906 reform ended curial voting.

[4] Delegations chosen by the two states' parliaments negotiated the changing specifics of these arrangements, but never face to face, always through formal written communication.

[5] Günther Kronenbitter, "Die Akteure der Macht: Politische und militärische Kriegsvorbereitungen," in *Die Habsburgermonarchie 1848–1918*, vol. 11/1/1, *Die Habsburgermonarchie und der Erste Weltkrieg*, ed. Helmut Rumpler and Anatol Schmidt-Kowarzik (Vienna: Verlag der Österreichischen Akademie der Wissenschaften, 2016), 81.

[6] Statistics quoted in Clark, *The Sleepwalkers*, 217.

with the ability—however weak and rarely used—of legislatures in France and Britain[7] to assert civilian control over the military and instead resembled more the extra-constitutional situation of the military in Germany.[8]

Military officers in turn saw themselves as responsible to a different code of conduct outside the legal norms that governed Austrian and Hungarian civilians. As István Deák has argued, the demands of maintaining the strict code of military honor—whose violation frequently resulted in demotion and punishment— often required behaviors of officers that contradicted civilian and even official military law, especially regarding dueling. This led often to problematic legal situations when officers found themselves away from military barracks and sought to maintain their honor in civilian company, usually by fighting civilians. Civilian authors, journalists, and politicians in turn, regularly complained about, and even satirized, the degree to which the military—especially its officers—behaved as a caste apart from the Habsburg social order. In society, the constitutional independence of the military worked visibly in more ways than simply in the two parliaments' inability to call military and foreign policy to account. Austria may have had a long governing tradition of the *Rechtsstaat* or "Rule of Law," anchored in provisions for equality before the law articulated in the 1811 General Civil Code, but Austria-Hungary's political and judicial institutions exercised no voice when it came to foreign or military policy. Legal, judicial, and administrative institutions could not contain the bad behavior of officers, and officers considered it normal that they functioned according to laws apart.[9] This separation from society helps to explain the willingness of the Military High Command to go to war in 1914 without consulting with or considering the politicians.

One of the most—if not the most—influential actors in stoking enthusiasm for war in the period before 1914 was the above-mentioned chief of the general staff, Franz Conrad von Hötzendorf. Appointed to the position in 1909 thanks to his reputation as a master tactician, Conrad's ambitions soon showed him to be much more than that. Tasked with improving Austria-Hungary's military preparedness, he saw himself equally responsible for advancing Austria-Hungary's global influence as a great power. He understood this task in terms of a close connection between military and foreign policy, and this tendency to see his role so expansively—and

---

[7] Clark notes that in Britain and France, with more parliamentary oversight of the military, nevertheless during the period around 1914 restructuring of the military concentrated greater power in the hands of the chiefs of staff and created greater military independence from political control. Clark, *The Sleepwalkers*, 222–3.

[8] An insightful analysis of the comparative constitutional situation of the military in Germany is Isabel V. Hull, *Absolute Destruction: Military Culture and the Practices of War in Imperial Germany* (Ithaca: Cornell University Press, 2005).

[9] See István Deák, *Beyond Nationalism: A Social and Political History of the Habsburg Officer Corps, 1848–1918* (New York: Oxford University Press, 1990), especially 126–38. On the military in general after the introduction of universal conscription, Christa Hämmerle, *Ganze Männer? Gesellschaft, Geschlecht und allgemeine Wehrpflicht in Österreich-Ungarn (1868–1914)*, Krieg und Konflikt, Band 16 (Frankfurt New York: Campus Verlag, 2022).

to tread on other's areas of expertise—caused his downfall in 1911. The Chief of Staff constantly bombarded the ruler with memoranda and lectures that sought to influence foreign policy, so the emperor/king eventually replaced him as chief of staff with someone far more cautious toward the Foreign Ministry and its prerogatives. Nevertheless, in the winter of 1912, amid the Balkan crisis we discuss below, Francis Joseph returned Conrad to the position of Chief of General Staff. In fact, it was the ill-fated heir to the throne, Archduke Francis Ferdinand, who argued to have Conrad restored as Chief of Staff.[10]

The high diplomats of the joint Foreign Ministry also saw themselves as very much responsible for improving Austria-Hungary's global position. In terms of personnel, this Ministry was one of the last government bastions of the court aristocracy that had dominated the bureaucracy a century earlier.[11] When Francis Joseph appointed Count Alois Lexa von Aehrenthal Foreign Minister in 1906, Aehrenthal pursued a more activist policy than had his more cautious predecessors. He sought both to raise the Empire's global status, but equally to produce greater internal domestic unity by conjuring notable foreign policy successes. Like Conrad and his circle, as we will see, Aehrenthal too believed that a more vigorous foreign policy could achieve greater political unity within an empire whose politics often centered on nationalist conflicts. To aristocrats wary of losing their social status to democratization as well as to many foreign observers alike, those domestic nationalist conflicts created an impression of social disunity and sometimes even of an impending Imperial collapse. Aehrenthal, as we will see below, was the architect of Austria-Hungary's surprise annexation of the formally Ottoman provinces of Bosnia Herzegovina in 1908, territory coveted by both the Ottomans and Serbia. After his early death from leukemia in 1912, Aehrenthal's more vigorous foreign policy exploits inspired many of the younger diplomats who remained influential at the Ministry. Many of them agitated to continue an energetic foreign policy to restore Austria-Hungary's international importance under Aehrenthal's more cautious successor, Count Leopold Berchtold.

An Empire in Europe

If many elite members of the General Staff and Foreign Ministry wanted to raise Austria-Hungary's international prestige, why did they see war specifically against Serbia as necessary, and why now in 1914, when such a war risked provoking Serbia's ally Russia?

---

[10] On Francis Ferdinand's role in advising on military matters, see Kronenbitter, "Die Akteure der Macht," 84.

[11] William D. Godsey, *Aristocratic Redoubt: The Austro-Hungarian Foreign Office on the Eve of the First World War* (West Lafayette, IN: Purdue University Press, 1999).

To understand why Austria-Hungary started a war in 1914 we need to examine Austria-Hungary's changing role as an Imperial state in Central and southeastern Europe. We need especially to consider how Austria-Hungary's military elite related to the demands of this Imperial role as these demands changed significantly in the decades before the war. The next sections investigate the recent history of Austria-Hungary in the Balkans, and especially the rise of an obsession with Serbia and the alleged dangers this small neighbor posed to its Imperial survival.

Austria-Hungary had long played a key role in the global system of strategic alliances. Although hardly as economically influential as Great Britain or Germany, or as territorially vast as Russia, Austria-Hungary remained an important international broker in nineteenth-century Europe. Because it did not rule overseas colonies, it was not directly involved in the kinds of colonial conflicts that pitted Britain against Russia in Afghanistan, against France in Morocco, or that pitted Italy against the Ottoman Empire in Libya.[12] Even as a second-rank European military power, however, Austria-Hungary's skilled labor force, its scientific and technological know-how, and its economic and military power guaranteed it an influential role, especially in southeastern Europe.

After military defeats had led to its expulsion from the Italian peninsula (1859, 1866) and from what became the German Empire (1866), Austria-Hungary refocused its Imperial ambitions on southeastern Europe, where the Ottoman Empire was in decline. Developments in this region over the second half of the nineteenth century made it a natural target for Austro-Hungarian efforts to expand its economic, cultural, and military influence. The declining administrative power of the Ottoman Empire and the rise of aggressive Russian policies in the region also forced the Empire to try to stabilize the deteriorating political situation there, especially from 1878 to 1914. In 1800, the Ottoman Empire had fully controlled the entire Balkan Peninsula and bordered the Austrian Empire directly to the south and east. Since the early nineteenth century, however, a series of successful regional rebellions had chipped away at Ottoman control. By the middle of the century, Russia also bid openly to achieve greater influence in the region, often by supporting those regional rebellions. Ultimately, Russian policy aimed to win control over Istanbul and the Dardanelle straits that controlled passage from the Black Sea to the Mediterranean. Britain and France, meanwhile, sought to contain Russia's expansion.

At first, local rebellions against the Ottomans produced political entities like Serbia (1804), Greece (1830), the provinces of Wallachia and Moldavia (later Romania), and Bulgaria that gained limited political autonomy *within* the Ottoman Empire. Eventually, however, their elites asserted full independence

---

[12] Except for a small concession Austria-Hungary gained in the Chinese port city of Tianjin in 1902—after sending fewer than 100 troops to help quell the Chinese Boxer Rebellion—the state did not rule directly over colonies outside of Europe.

from Ottoman rule, again with the explicit support of Russia. Russia justified its support for the creation of these autonomous regions that later became independent states by claiming a right to protect the region's Orthodox Christian peoples against an allegedly alien Muslim Ottoman rule. However, in the nineteenth century—even more than today—southeastern Europe included substantial populations that considered themselves neither Orthodox Christian in religion nor Slavic in language or culture. Many were Muslims, some of whom also used Slavic languages (like today's Bosnian, Bulgarian, or Greek Muslims). Others were Ottoman Turks whose ancestors had settled in the Balkans four centuries before. Still others were Albanian speakers (who might be Muslim or Orthodox Christians) or Jews or Roma, who were certainly not claimed by any of the region's nationalists. There were also Slavic peoples who called themselves Macedonians, and whose national allegiance was vigorously disputed among Bulgaria, Greece, and Serbia.

Although the map of southeast Europe today contains states named for many of these groups, it would be misleading to presume that in the nineteenth century their elite Orthodox religious and nationalist political leaders spoke for the desires of mass populations. Moreover, these elite local actors often used the conflicts between the Orthodox religious and nationalist leaders on the one hand and the Ottoman Empire on the other hand in highly opportunistic ways, shifting their allegiances depending on circumstances, using the conflicts to assert their own local interests. Peasant populations, for example, often followed rebel leaders who promised them relief from overbearing landlords or tax collectors, not national independence.

By 1900, a series of independent sovereign states had replaced Ottoman rule over most of the region. The new states jostled their neighbors for the opportunity to absorb the final pieces of Ottoman territory that remained in southeastern Europe, and each new state claimed territory claimed or held by one or two of the others. Greece, Bulgaria, and Serbia for example, each coveted the remaining Ottoman territory called Macedonia (including Kosovo), and each sponsored paramilitary organizations that used violence to disrupt Ottoman rule there. Greece and Serbia also claimed Ottoman regions inhabited by Albanian speakers, and Serb nationalists had their eyes on the neighboring Ottoman provinces of Bosnia and Herzegovina. Austria-Hungary also took an active role in these conflicts.

Bosnia and Herzegovina

In 1878, in response to an 1875 rural rebellion against the Ottomans, Austria-Hungary occupied the provinces of Bosnia and Herzegovina. In doing so, the Empire committed itself to an active policy in the Balkans backed up by military action. This action largely shaped the difficult situation in which Austria-Hungary would find itself in 1914, that situation that its military leaders believed could only be solved by a war against Serbia.

Austria-Hungary had originally invaded the two Ottoman provinces ostensibly to restore stability and order. With the eventual agreement of the other great powers, however, Austria-Hungary assumed responsibility for formally administering the territories. According to the Treaty of Berlin (1878), the Habsburg occupation of Bosnia-Herzegovina was to last thirty years. Many Austro-Hungarians expected that after this period their Empire would simply annex the provinces outright. Unlike the situation in 1914, however, when an absence of debate marked the declaration of war, in 1878 the question of military occupation was the subject of lively debate among politicians in both Austria and Hungary. In Austria, for example, a government led by the German liberal parties collapsed precisely over its unwillingness to bear the costs of the occupation.[13] Most German liberal deputies in parliament opposed the occupation because of the enormous expense it involved. The liberal cabinet, however, supported an occupation because the emperor desired it. After fruitless negotiations over reconstituting a liberal cabinet, and thanks to liberal intransigence over the very question of occupation, Francis Joseph replaced it with a more conservative government that supported the occupation policy. In Hungary too, many politicians expressed concern about occupying the provinces, warning against the addition of more Slavic-speaking populations to the Empire. Because the architect of the occupation, Foreign Minister Count Julius Andrássy (1823–90) was an influential Hungarian politician, however, his support for the policy prevailed over the concerns of the Hungarian opposition.

But Austria-Hungary was not the only state in the region interested in occupying these two Ottoman provinces. Given Bosnia's substantial Orthodox Christian population—close to 40 percent—many nationalist state builders in neighboring Serbia had long viewed the two provinces as key to their strategy to build a "greater Serbia." With Bosnia and Herzegovina, Serbia would also gain an outlet to the Adriatic Sea, another of its principle strategic aims, and one implicitly supported by Russia, with an eye to winning a reliably friendly port in the Adriatic. Serbia and Russia were not the only other interested parties. In the early twentieth century, the so-called "Young Turk" movement that promoted Ottoman renewal in the region also plotted to regain the occupied provinces for a reformed Ottoman Empire.

From the start of its occupation regime, Austro-Hungarian propaganda depicted its activities in Bosnia and Herzegovina in terms of a benevolent civilizational mission. The occupation would not only bring stability to a semi-oriental neighboring territory, it was argued, but a vigorous program of economic

---

[13] Pieter M. Judson, *Exclusive Revolutionaries: Liberal Politics, Social Experience, and National Identity in the Austrian Empire, 1848–1914* (Ann Arbor, MI: University of Michigan Press, 1996), 184–7.

development, improved infrastructure, and educational reform for both sexes would change its very character. Austria-Hungary's regional influence already extended well beyond Bosnia and Herzegovina thanks to its strong economic position in Balkan markets for textiles, processed food products, and machinery, including weapons. The occupiers would build roads, railroads, and schools, extend their state tobacco monopoly into Bosnia, and encourage Austrian and Hungarian businesses to relocate to Bosnia-Herzegovina. They would also relocate hundreds of low-level male and female civil servants and teachers (often Croat or Serb nationalists) from across the Monarchy. Success would create loyalty that would among other things, insulate the population from the blandishments of neighboring Serbia. The occupiers regularly sought to advertise Austria-Hungary's alleged cultural triumphs in Bosnia Herzegovina to international audiences such as those who attended the Paris Exhibition of 1900. There, for example, visitors experienced a special Bosnian pavilion with art nouveau decorations depicting Bosnian scenes by Bohemian artist Alphons Mucha.[14] Success on the ground, however, was another matter.

One problem was that all these hopes came at a very high cost. Who, in fact, would pay for the ambitious renovations of Bosnia Herzegovina? Austria-Hungary had nowhere near the necessary financial resources to transform the occupied provinces in the ambitious image it advertised to the world. Francis Joseph had assigned the joint Ministry of Finance to govern the provinces, and that Ministry had to pay the costs of administration. Given this financial constraint it was easier—and cheaper—to leave many Ottoman social structures in place, particularly the traditional organization of agriculture that gave unpopular Muslim large landlords a monopoly on land. This may have had the advantage of making Bosnian Muslim elites co-responsible for maintaining social stability and order in the provinces. However, it also meant that the new rulers never addressed the social conditions in rural society that had caused the peasant rebellions against the Ottomans in the first place. In 1881-2, for example, Herzergovina was racked by another series of rebellions, stoked by the extension of three-year military conscription to all men reaching the age of 20. In fact, this rebellion was equally a product of the fact that Austria-Hungary had made no serious changes to the land tenure system that had sparked the earlier rebellion against the Ottomans.[15]

The arrangement for rule over the occupied territories also required the Joint Minister of Finance to find creative ways to fund his ambitious economic, infrastructural, and educational goals for the provinces. He had to attract companies and capital investment from the Dual Monarchy and abroad to build business

---

[14] Edin Hajdarpasic, *Whose Bosnia? Nationalism and Political Imagination in the Balkans, 1840-1914* (Ithaca: Cornell University Press, 2015), 193-4.

[15] Charles Jelavich, "The Revolt in Bosnia-Hercegovina, 1881-2," *The Slavonic and East European Review* 31, no. 77 (1953): 420-36.

and industry which he could then tax. Joint Finance Minister from 1882–1902, the Hungarian Benjamin Kállay (1839–1903) was particularly ambitious and determined in this regard. He also sought to forge a pro-Habsburg "Bosnian cultural identity" in the provinces separate from competing Croatian and Serb forms of national identification.[16]

If in 1878 Austria-Hungary had the backing of the other great powers to face down a weakened Ottoman Empire and an aggressive Russia, by 1908 the situation had changed dramatically. Now, at least five self-styled nation-states sought to dominate the region, often with strong Russian support: Serbia, Montenegro, Romania, Greece, and Bulgaria (not to mention a revived Ottoman Empire). Along with political independence, these states increasingly pursued their own national interests, attracting capital and trade from beyond the Balkans, often seeking to escape Austria-Hungary's economic dominance in the region.

As to the other great powers, Britain remained committed to maintaining a status quo in the region, but France increasingly aligned with Russian interests. Austria-Hungary's one major ally Germany was not fully reliable when it came to Balkan issues. Austro-Hungarian policymakers feared what they viewed as an increasingly dangerous situation in neighboring southeastern Europe for two reasons. First, because states like Serbia and Montenegro harbored territorial ambitions that clashed with Austria-Hungary's. In particular, Serbia's ongoing ambition to obtain an outlet to the Adriatic Sea guaranteed future conflict with Austria-Hungary. Dangerous secondly, because elite Austro-Hungarian policymakers believed—with some justification—that extreme nationalists in Serbia or Romania were trying to attract Serb- or Romanian-speakers in the Dual Monarchy to the irredentist cause of a "greater Serbia" or a "greater Romania."

In the summer of 1908 Austria-Hungary's Joint Foreign Minister, Alois Count Lexa von Aehrenthal (1854–1912) tried to settle the issue of Bosnia Herzegovina's future status permanently by having the dual Monarchy annex the two provinces. Why annexation, and why specifically in 1908? Ever since his appointment as Joint Foreign Minister in 1906, Aehrenthal had sought to revive Austria-Hungary's global profile, both to influence domestic politics positively, and to reestablish Austria-Hungary's importance on the world stage. Bosnia offered him the perfect opportunity. Earlier in 1908, the Young Turk rebellion in Macedonia had forced Sultan Abdulhamid II to restore the Ottoman constitution of 1876, which required electing a parliament for that Empire. The Young Turks, it was feared, would challenge the Austro-Hungarian occupation by making the residents of Bosnia and Herzegovina eligible to vote for the Ottoman parliament. Annexation, however, would forestall that potential crisis. Additionally, annexation would conveniently deny Serbia's expansionist ambitions. As a territorial enlargement of the

---

[16] Robin Okey, *Taming Balkan Nationalism: The Habsburg "Civilizing Mission" in Bosnia 1878–1914* (Oxford: Oxford University Press, 2007).

Habsburg Empire, annexation would also promote the government's popularity and increase patriotic unity among its citizens. Russia, it was believed, would have no choice but to agree, however unwillingly, to annexation. Its debilitating defeat by Japan coupled with a revolution at home (1904–5) left Russia in no position to fight a European war in support of its Serb client.

In September 1908, Aehrenthal negotiated directly and in secret with his Russian counterpart, Foreign Minister Alexander Izvolsky (1856–1919) at the a castle in Moravia, far from newspaper reporters and far from the other great powers that had signed the original treaty of Berlin in 1878. Izvolsky agreed to a future annexation of the two provinces in return for Austria-Hungary's promised support to open the Ottoman Dardanelles straits to Russian ships, so that they could pass from the Black Sea to the Mediterranean. Once this basic formula was agreed however, Aehrenthal went ahead without warning and surprised the Russians with an immediate annexation on October 6. The Russians saw this as a catastrophic betrayal. They had not yet prepared their client Serbia for the possibility of annexation, and they believed—correctly—that the time was hardly right for Russia to demand the opening of the Straits, to which Britain, the strongest sea power in the Mediterranean, would object. In a reference to Aehrenthal's rumored Jewish ancestry, Izvolsky raged to the German Chancellor von Bülow that "the dirty Jew has deceived me!"[17]

The annexation pleased some inside the Monarchy, but not for the reasons that Aehrenthal had predicted. In Slovene- and Croatian-speaking regions, for example, nationalist activists hailed it as a first step toward the creation of a Habsburg South-Slav ("Yugoslav") state that could become the basis for a trialism to replace dualism. The provincial diet of Carniola, for example, adopted a resolution supported by both the normally warring Catholic and Liberal Slovene parties. It expressed their hope "that this was the first step toward the unification of all South Slavs of our Monarchy into a constitutionally independent organism under the scepter of the Habsburg dynasty."[18]

Outside the Monarchy, however, the annexation quickly caused an international crisis. For some time, it was not immediately clear whether Serbia and Russia might in fact declare war on Austria-Hungary, while the other signatory powers to the original Berlin Treaty complained that they had not been consulted. Nor did Ottoman society take this fait accompli lying down. Protests erupted across the Ottoman Empire from Anatolia to the Middle East, to North Africa, setting in motion a popular and highly effective boycott of Austro-Hungarian products, including the ubiquitous red fez caps made in Austria. Faced with dire

---

[17] James Joll and Gordon Martel, *The Origins of the First World War* (London: Pearson/Longman, 2007), 69.
[18] Quoted in Peter Štih, Vasko Simoniti, and Peter Vodopivec, *Slowenische Geschichte: Gesellschaft—Politik—Kultur* (Graz: Leykam, 2008).

economic consequences, Austria-Hungary quickly settled that matter in February 1909 by making a 2.2 million Ottoman Lira payment to the Sultan for the cost of the public lands in Bosnia Herzegovina.

Meanwhile, the very day after Aehrenthal's annexation announcement, Serbia mobilized its armed forces and demanded territorial compensation in return for accepting the annexation. When the Serb threat did not die down, Austria-Hungary had to engage in a very expensive partial military mobilization in March 1909. At this point, several officers on the General Staff actively hoped to wage a war that would finally give them the chance to crush what they saw as a growing Serb threat both to Austria-Hungary's southeastern borders and to its domestic politics.

While the annexation crisis allowed the military elite to argue for a preventive war against Serbia, the Foreign Office under Aehrenthal counseled peace and prevailed against them. Without Russian support, Serbia eventually backed down and recognized the legitimacy of Austria-Hungary's egregious act. Russia, meanwhile, could do little to protest, because among other things, Aehrenthal threatened to make public the secret negotiations in which Izvolsky had willingly agreed to annexation.[19] A precarious new status quo held, even as all the players prepared for the possibility of a coming war. Aehrenthal himself died of Leukemia in February 1912, but not before counseling a "watchful, and at the same time exploratory policy" to preserve the peace.[20] As Günther Kronenbitter points out, Austria-Hungary—like many other European states at the time—had not yet institutionalized some form of security politics (*Sicherheitspolitik*) that might have coordinated foreign policy and military strategy. Instead, the Foreign Ministry and the Military High Command functioned separately, often clashed, and only communicated in moments of crisis.[21]

War

When war in the region did break out in October of 1912, it did not at first involve Austria-Hungary directly. Serbia, Montenegro, and Bulgaria joined with Greece to form a "Balkan League." With tacit Russian backing the League attacked the Ottoman Empire, hoping to seize its remaining territory in southeastern Europe. The moment seemed ripe because the Ottomans were engaged in fighting off Italian efforts to conquer their territory in North Africa (today's Libya). The Balkan League

---

[19] In fact, Aehrenthal eventually made public documents showing that back in 1876–7 Russia had agreed to Austria-Hungary's free hand in Bosnia Herzegovina and to an eventual annexation. Rauchensteiner, *First World War*, 20.
[20] Quoted in József Galántai, *Hungary in the First World War*, trans. Éva Grusz and Judit Pokoly, rev. Mark Goodman (Budapest: Akadémiai Kiadó, 1989), 12.
[21] Kronenbitter, "Die Akteure der Macht," 93.

was remarkably successful, quickly driving Ottoman forces from the Adriatic coast, from Macedonia, and from Thrace, and even threatening Constantinople. Austria-Hungary's military and diplomatic leaders watched anxiously as Russia, too, mobilized along the Galician border to prevent Austro-Hungarian intervention against the Balkan League.[22]

In December 1912, in an ominous sign for the future, Emperor King Francis Joseph decided to reinstate Conrad von Hötzendorf as Chief of the Austro-Hungarian General Staff, as mentioned above. Conrad's had long been the strongest military voice in ruling circles to demand war against Serbia when he had first served as Chief of Staff from 1906–1911. Recalling Conrad now, however, appeared to give official validation to his aggressive views. During this dangerous period, it was now the heir to the throne, Archduke Francis Ferdinand, who argued most vociferously for staying out of the war and maintaining peace. Francis Ferdinand agreed with Conrad about the goal of containing Serbia, but he feared that if the Empire declared war, Russia would enter the war to support Serbia. "A war with Russia means the end for us," he allegedly told his adjutant Carl von Bardolff in 1913.[23] Hungary's Prime Minister Tizsa also argued against war, believing—correctly, as it turned out—that Hungary's eastern border with Romania was relatively defenseless in case of attack. Romania was secretly a party to Austria-Hungary's Triple Alliance with Germany and Italy, but Tisza—and others—did not doubt that given the opportunity to make territorial gains, Romania might easily switch sides.

As a precaution, during the fall and winter of 1912–13, and in answer to Russian mobilization near Galicia, Austria-Hungary once again mobilized its military. And once again this precaution cost the budget a staggering amount of money. By now Austro-Hungarian policy was vacillating precariously between bellicose demands that, for example, Serbia and Montenegro evacuate their troops from formerly Ottoman coastal territories, while nevertheless retreating from declaring war outright. Russian policy also vacillated. For some months Russia threatened Galicia with a military buildup across the border, partly intended to keep Austria-Hungary out of the Balkan War. Eventually, however, the Russians removed their military threat to Galicia and this diffused much of the tension.

At the same time, representatives of the great powers met regularly in London to negotiate an acceptable end to the Balkan hostilities. A peace treaty signed in London in May 1913 adjudicated new borders in the region and ended what later became known as the "first Balkan War." The ink was hardly dry on this treaty, however, when on June 29, a new conflict broke out in the Balkans over the

---

[22] On Galicia's strategic significance as border region with the Romanov Empire, see Hans-Christian Maner, *Galizien: eine Grenzregion im Kalkül der Donaumonarchie im 18. und 19. Jahrhundert* (Munich: IKGS-Verl, 2007).

[23] Carl von Bardolff, *Soldat Im Alten Österreich: Erinnerungen Aus Meinem Leben* (Jena: Diederich, 1938), 177.

division of the territorial spoils of war. This "second Balkan War" pitted Bulgaria against its erstwhile allies Serbia and Greece over territories taken from the Ottomans in Macedonia and Thrace. Formerly neutral Romania now entered this conflict as well, hoping to gain territorial compensation from Bulgaria. The Ottoman Empire too, took the opportunity to attack a weakened Bulgaria to regain some of the lands it had lost in the previous war. Russia abandoned its erstwhile ally Bulgaria and tacitly supported Serbia and Romania. Within a month Bulgaria was defeated, and treaties in Bucharest (August), Constantinople (September), and Athens (November) settled the new borders.

One reason that the Bulgarians had broken their alliance with Serbia in 1913 was the two states' conflicting claims over the Ottoman region of Macedonia. Before the first Balkan War, they had agreed that Macedonia would go to Bulgaria, while Serbia would take the Ottoman coastal territory that is today Albania. In the spring of 1912, however, great power pressure from Austria-Hungary and Italy prevented Serbia from taking Ottoman coastal territory to achieve its longed-for outlet to the Adriatic Sea. Instead, the great powers at London—with Russia's reluctant agreement—created a brand-new state out of Ottoman territory on the Adriatic coast: Albania. This act frustrated Greek designs in the south and Serbian designs in the north of the coastal territory, and the Serbs decided instead to take the Macedonian territory that Bulgaria coveted.

The creation of Albania was no coincidence of the moment. It was in large part a product of twenty years of informal Austro-Hungarian consular engagement in the region, building networks of support for Austria-Hungary among local leaders.[24] It also resulted from recurring Habsburg fears, shared with the Italians, that a Serb port on the Adriatic would essentially serve Russia's interests in the region. But Serbia did not give up so easily, and throughout 1913 Serb military units occupied strategic regions of the new Albanian state. Austria-Hungary's repeated warnings to Serbia failed to have any noticeable effect until, on October 17, 1913, it presented Serbia with a final ultimatum: evacuate Albanian territory or face war. Two days later Serbia backed down. As Christopher Clark notes in his study of the outbreak of the First World War, the success of this ultimatum caused Austria-Hungary's leadership to believe in the effectiveness of the ultimatum as a general strategy. And it also made Austria-Hungary appear strong after having vacillated for so long. This experience in 1913 would offer Austria-Hungary's military leaders a deceptive solution only a few months later in July 1914.[25]

The two Balkan Wars ended some older alliances and further radicalized the anxious military elites in the two neighboring great powers, Austria-Hungary,

---

[24] Krisztián Csaplár-Degovics, "Austro-Hungarian Colonial Ventures: The Case of Albania," *The Hungarian Historical Review* 11, no. 2 (2022): 267–304; Krisztián Csaplár-Degovics, "Die Internationale Kontrollkommission Albaniens und die albanischen Machtzentren (1913/1914). Beitrag zur Geschichte der Staatsbildung Albaniens," *Südost-Forschungen* 2014, no. 73 (2016): 231–67.

[25] Clark, *The Sleepwalkers*, 287.

and Russia. The wars also had devastating effects on the populations of the region. The Balkan Wars prefigured many of the so-called "horrors" of the First World War in the ways they were fought and especially in the ways they impacted civilians. The combatant states in the first Balkan War had mobilized their societies in a war effort that targeted civilians as much as soldiers. The combatant states often relied on the efforts of unofficial paramilitary units to terrorize local populations and enforce violent ethnic cleansing in the territories they occupied. Tens of thousands of Muslim Europeans fled the region to find refuge in the Ottoman Empire. Bulgarian, Greek, and Serb paramilitary units worked swiftly to establish their own ethnic populations in conquered regions and to force others to flee. These actions often followed no real logic, partly because it was often impractical to differentiate nationally among local Orthodox populations. Were they in fact Bulgarians? Serbs? Greeks? Nationalists made all kinds of claims about the identifications of local populations, especially in Macedonia, but no one could say for certain, for example, how or with whom, Macedonians themselves identified.

The horrific violence directed against civilians was carefully documented by the Carnegie Foundation. This brutality reinforced myths in the West that considered the region to be fundamentally unstable, thanks to the alleged murderous antagonism of its many linguistic and religious groups. This antagonism had supposedly dominated the region for centuries, even though, as many historians have shown, the region was traditionally peaceful, and much ethnic conflict had largely been introduced by the new nation-states and their secretly funded paramilitary units.[26]

Officials in both the Romanov and Austro-Hungarian Empires also feared that their own influence in the region and their foreign policy options had severely diminished. Russia's role was no longer so prominent among the Orthodox populations, having backed Serbia in the Second Balkan War and alienated its traditional ally Bulgaria. At the same time, Russia was even more committed to backing Serbia in whatever policy that state might choose to pursue. Austria-Hungary, meanwhile, faced a Serbia doubled in size, more economically influential

---

[26] Mark Mazower, *The Balkans: From the End of Byzantium to the Present Day* (London: Weidenfeld and Nicolson, 2000); Larry Wolff, "The Western Representation of Eastern Europe on the Eve of World War I: Mediated Encounters and Intellectual Expertise in Dalmatia, Albania, and Macedonia," *The Journal of Modern History* 86, no. 2 (2014): 381–407 (pp. 397–401); Mariia Nikolaeva Todorova, *Imagining the Balkans* (New York: Oxford University Press, 1997). On the Imperial context of Austro-Hungarian Balkan ethnography (including Arthur Haberlandt, who took part in a wartime expedition to the region in 1916), see Christian Marchetti, *Balkanexpedition: Die Kriegserfahrung Der Österreichischen Volkskunde—Eine Historisch-Ethnographische Erkundung* (Tübingen: Tübinger Vereinigung für Volkskunde e.V, 2013); Christian Marchetti, "Austro-Hungarian Volkskunde at War: Scientists on Ethnographic Mission in World War I," in *Doing Anthropology in Wartime and War Zones: World War I and the Cultural Sciences in Europe*, ed. Reinhard Johler, Christian Marchetti, and Monique Scheer (New Brunswick, NJ: Transaction Publishers, 2010), 207–30. On Habsburg "albanology" as an Imperial project, see Kurt Gostentschnigg, *Wissenschaft Im Spannungsfeld von Politik und Militär: Die Österreichisch-Ungarische Albanologie 1867–1918* (Wiesbaden: Springer VS, 2018).

in the region, and backed to the hilt by a Romanov Empire that had apparently recovered militarily from its disastrous 1904–5 war against Japan far more swiftly than expected. If Austro-Hungarian military elites had for some time wanted to deal Serbia a death blow to "solve the Serbia problem" for good, they now faced the terrifying possibility that dealing Serbia that death blow would mean fighting a war with Russia as well. This possibility provoked equal levels of anxiety among Hungarian politicians, among whom the prospect of war with Russia, Serbia, and maybe Romania raised fears of invasions of Transylvania in the east and the Banat to the south. On the other hand, Serbia faced the challenge of integrating vast new territories, and its rulers recognized that it was hardly positioned to fight yet another war.

The effect of the Balkan Wars also reinforced the already mentioned and mistaken convictions held by the Habsburg military elite, that whole national groups of Austro-Hungarian citizens would not do their patriotic duty in case of war. It wasn't simply that the elite believed domestic political conflicts—especially nationalist ones—undermined the integrating power of the Empire. They were more than ever convinced that most Serb-speakers in Austria-Hungary wanted to join Serbia, that Romanian-speakers in Transylvania wanted to join with neighboring Romania, and that Italian-speakers wanted their territories to be joined to Italy. They also harbored suspicions about the reliability of Ukrainian citizens in Eastern Galicia whom they baselessly believed would support a Russian invasion. Against almost all evidence to the contrary, they presumed that in the case of war they would have to fight a rearguard action against their own citizens. The fact that voluntary charitable organizations in Austria-Hungary like the Red Cross had collected funds for Serb relief efforts in the Balkan Wars—especially among Croatian, Czech, Slovak, Slovene, and Serb nationalists—only increased questions about the patriotism of these parts of the population.[27]

The Military's Domestic Ambitions

Many in the General Staff and its circles regularly spoke as if entire language groups within the Monarchy (especially Serb speakers, but also Romanian-, Italian-, and Ukrainian- speakers) constituted networks of traitorous fifth columns working to destabilize the Dual Monarchy from within. This fundamental mistrust of its own

---

[27] Eric Becker Weaver, "Yugoslavism in Hungary during the Balkan Wars," in *War in the Balkans: Conflict and Diplomacy before World War I*, ed. James Pettifer and Tom Buchanan (London: I.B. Tauris, 2016), 47–75. Weaver argues that the extent of loyalty to, indifference to, or outright hostility to Habsburg Hungary among its south Slav populations is impossible to determine, but that there is clear evidence for South Slav or Yugoslav enthusiasm among non-elite Hungarian Slavs during the Balkan Wars and that this boded ill for the Monarchy. At the same time, Weaver also shows that the Hungarian regime itself was highly paranoid on this issue and was ready to see examples of treason and disloyalty everywhere.

citizens was one reason that the Military High Command sought to fight a war that would, in its members' view, solve both foreign and domestic challenges at once. In the years before 1914, the same officers hoped to use war not only to establish Austro-Hungarian dominance in the Balkans, but also to transform Austria-Hungary's internal political system as well.

One frighteningly real example of how the prejudices of the High Command and fears surrounding the Bosnian annexation could influence the domestic rule of law, was a notorious treason trial of fifty-two alleged Serb traitors held in Zagreb during and after the Bosnian annexation crisis. Using fabricated evidence and arguments that strained credulity, and with strong support from the Hungarian government, prosecutors argued that Serb politicians in Croatia were secretly working for the Serb government to detach Croatia, Bosnia, and Herzegovina from the Empire. Accusations as petty as that the accused used the perfectly legal Cyrillic alphabet, or that they performed their commitment to Serb nationalism in their daily lives by flying Serb colors or owned portraits of the Serb King Petar I, were all cited to prove their treasonous intent. As Mark Cornwall has argued, the trial inadvertently cast doubt on the idea that patriotism and nationalism could coexist. Could a Serb nationalist also be a Habsburg patriot? The prosecution argued no. Critics of the trial—and there were many—argued that the defendants were being charged with acts and behaviors that would otherwise be tolerated among Hungarian-, Italian-, or Polish- speaking citizens, but not by Serb speakers. In the end, after thirty-one of the defendants were found guilty of treason, revelations swiftly came to light to prove that the evidence had been forged and the charges trumped up.[28] The rule of law had somehow prevailed, although the failed ability of the prosecutors to manipulate the evidence suggested that there were powerful forces in the Monarchy that would undermine the rule of law to achieve their goals, if given the chance.

War, it turned out almost immediately, did not only mean war against Austria-Hungary's external enemies. Their anxious suspicion about significant groups of the Monarchy's own citizens among many of its powerful military elites was partly responsible for secret efforts to craft emergency legislation that essentially gave the military free reign over Austrian society in the case of war. Since 1867, the military elite had increasingly chafed at the increasing power that political and administrative institutions assumed in society, apparently at their expense. By the end of the nineteenth century, as John Deak and Jonathan Gumz have pointed out, the military openly competed with the civil administration for budgetary funds. Given the increasing power of political parties and their voters in both halves of the Monarchy, civilian administration almost always won out because

---

[28] Mark Cornwall, "Loyalty and Treason in Late Habsburg Croatia: A Violent Political Discourse Before the First World War," in *Exploring Loyalty*, ed. Jana Osterkamp and Martin Schulze Wessel (Göttingen: Vandenhoeck & Ruprecht, 2017).

its increased funding showed tangible results in the everyday lives of the Monarchy's citizens. As the Habsburg administrators extended their reach into ever increasing areas from public health (hospitals, medical staff) to urban infrastructure (water, gas, electricity), political parties saw potential benefits in their expansion, benefits with which the military, with its own enormous budget demands, could not compete. This often meant that military leaders blamed the administration for doing the bidding of political parties, even as they blamed the bickering political parties for having destroyed Austria-Hungary's great power status. It was not simply political conflict that bothered these leaders. A great power, so they believed, required a kind of social unity that increased democratization made impossible. They dreamed of returning Austria-Hungary to an imagined golden age characterized by a hierarchically organized society ruled over by an authoritarian state that enforced unity and projected power. War might give them the chance to impose their vision and turn back the clock to this imagined golden age.[29]

All the European states that fought the First World War imposed some form of emergency legislation on their societies, including strict censorship, harsh regulation of labor, and internal spying. But who executed this authority? In Austria, secret emergency war legislation agreed to by Parliament in 1906 and amended in 1909 and 1912 gave extraordinary powers to the military outside the power of the Austrian parliament to restrain them. This independence helps to explain parallel actions undertaken by military leaders in the years following the 1908 annexation, actions that would decisively damage the popular legitimacy of the state during the First World War. The same military men who thirsted for a preventive war to crush Serbia, and who doubted the loyalty of Slav and Italian citizens, used the excuse of wartime emergency to realize their own radical domestic political ambitions.

Already in 1906 the Minister of War sought to develop a coherent set of emergency decrees that would apply to the entire Monarchy in the case of war. As Tamara Scheer explains, the goal was to transform a little-known paragraph of the Austrian constitution that allowed for a temporary emergency suspension of civil rights into a broad policy adapted to the entire Monarchy, including Bosnia and Herzegovina.[30] After the annexation crisis of 1908 and again during the Balkan Wars of 1912–13, members of the Military High Command [*Armeeoberkommando* or AOK] continued to elaborate this secret set of far-reaching domestic emergency decrees. In case of a war, these decrees enabled them to take over the governing

---

[29] Deak and Gumz, "How to Break a State"; John Deak, *Forging a Multinational State: State Making in Imperial Austria from the Enlightenment to the First World War*, Stanford Studies on Central and Eastern Europe (Stanford: Stanford University Press, 2015), chap. 6.

[30] Tamara Sheer, *Die Ringstrassenfront: Österreich-Ungarn, Das Kriegsüberwachungsamt und der Ausnahmezustand Während des Ersten Weltkrieges* (Vienna: Heeresgeschichtliches Museum, 2010), chap. 9.

institutions of civil society by suspending constitutional rule and most civil rights, replacing civilian administration with military institutions, suspending trial by jury and imposing a system of severe military justice [*Standrecht*] on the population, imposing strict censorship, monitoring telephone and telegraph communications, and generally reshaping domestic social policy. In regions near the front, the planned laws gave the military the right to replace civilian administrators with its own appointees. In essence, the military would replace the state.[31] Eventually, the authors of the plan decided that the planned area of military competence had become so broad that they needed to lay the basis for a vast new surveillance institution, and this became the *Kriegsüberwachungsamt* [KÜA] that we will encounter in chapter 2. The General Staff had the right to appoint the head of the KÜA from its own ranks.

The legislation did not apply to Hungary, although starting in 1906, the War Ministry and High Command did its best to extend these exceptional laws to Hungary. But when the Joint Minister for Defense suggested this possibility in the fall of 1906, Julius Andrássy, Hungarian Minister of the Interior, argued that "in our country special power should be entrusted not to the army, but to civil authority, i.e. the responsible government." Andrássy especially opposed the extension of the KÜA's power of surveillance to Hungary. It would, in the words of Hungary's Minister of Justice, ensure that "the other country's [Austria's] legal institutions which are opposite to ours, would come into effect." Even the legislature in Bosnia Herzegovina, a province which, after annexation remained in a kind of constitutional limbo outside of both Austrian and Hungarian constitutional authority, had in 1910 legislated an emergency powers law similar to Austria's. These powers would be exercised with even greater strictness than in Austria, if such a thing could be imagined. The Hungarian politicians asserted their constitutional independence, however, and refused to consider adopting a similar law. Finally, during the Balkan War crisis the Hungarian government passed its own law on emergency war measures in November 1912.[32] That law made it clear that in the case of war, the joint military would not assume functions from the civil administration in Hungary, nor could it, for example, engage in requisitioning. Only in the most extreme cases might the military even go to local village administrators for this purpose. Most of the extreme wartime dictatorial powers, which did not differ in quality from Austria's as far as the experience of everyday Hungarians went, were nevertheless assigned to the civil government.

As mentioned above, this domestic legislation for wartime was hardly exceptional in Europe. In 1914, every belligerent state had legislation on the books that gave the military emergency powers in the case of war, but in few states did the military enjoy such strikingly unrestrained power as in the Habsburg Monarchy,

---

[31] For an analysis of the legislation and its analysis, see Sheer, *Die Ringstrassenfront*.
[32] For the quotations, Galántai, *Hungary*, 75–6. For an analysis of the Hungarian law, Galántai, 76–9.

and especially in Austria and Bosnia Herzegovina. It is for this reason that the Austro-Hungarian experience turned out to be extreme even by general European wartime standards. Small circles of the military and political elite elaborated the implementation of the emergency decrees to create a vast military dictatorship in Austria, and Hungary followed suit, even if ultimate power there lay with the cabinet. The military conceived a complete restructuring of Austria's domestic administration and politics, one they planned should last well beyond the war's end, and one that would terminate the influence of what they saw as "squabbling political parties" in Austria's elected institutions. In other words, they sought to reverse decades of liberal administrative and politically democratizing trends and practices.

That a small group of men could exert this extraordinary degree of political influence in case of war was a long-term byproduct of the Austro-Hungarian system that placed the military under the sole jurisdiction of the emperor king, outside any responsibility to civil authorities. It was also something that most people in 1914—even those in the administration and judiciary—would not have expected or known much about. The broad scope of this secret dictatorial project was especially unexpected, precisely because political developments before 1914 generally pointed to the development of broader and more consensual forms of government in both Austria and Hungary—albeit in fits and starts. The rule of law [*Rechsstaat*] was a cornerstone of the administrative, judicial, and bureaucratic systems in Austria-Hungary going back to the late eighteenth century.

For men like Conrad von Hötzendorf, war became an opportunity to re-establish Austria-Hungary's great power status. In domestic terms, this meant transforming Austria's and eventually Hungary's political systems in ways that would have been impossible in peacetime. War, they believed, gave them their last best chance to shape domestic political life at the expense of both the hated civilian administrators and the elected politicians. Seeing political debate as political weakness, these leaders saw Austria-Hungary's trajectory only in terms of decline and possible ruin. For them, political conflict tore at the state's very legitimacy and undermined its ability to maintain international respect.

Political conflict in society could also be understood as a sign of vitality. As more people participated in decision-making debates at every level of politics, from village councils to the parliament, they became more invested in the state. Still, Austria-Hungary's military leaders willfully ignored the many signs that proved the popularity of the dynasty, just as they later ignored the patriotic responses to the outbreak of war. They were determined to replace the constitutional parliamentary regime and its civil administration with a unified dictatorship that was allegedly "above politics." In July of 1914, Austria-Hungary swiftly went from being a state governed by long-term constitutional practice and administrative efficiency to a highly inefficient military dictatorship ruled by the paranoid and pessimist visions of small military and governmental cliques. This would prove to be one of the most disastrous results of the war.

July 1914

The Military High Command wanted war with Serbia, and during the Balkan Wars Conrad had repeatedly lobbied the emperor king and the cabinet to take a more bellicose stance. The Foreign Ministry, however, while sharing the military's attitude to Serbia, wanted to change the balance of power in the Balkans through diplomatic means if possible. From a different perspective, during the crisis of 1912–13, Hungary's Prime Minister Tisza had also refused to consider war. He argued that an annexation of Serbia, Conrad's goal, would add millions of Slavs to the Empire's population. This, in turn, would de facto create a trialist Monarchy, that is, a settlement that produced an Austria-Hungary-South Slav state. Dualism (and decisive Hungarian influence within it), would be finished.

The June 1914 assassination of Archduke Franz Ferdinand took the joint cabinet and the military back to its debates from late 1913, only this time, the arguments for taking military action succeeded, especially once Austria-Hungary's German ally agreed to support a declaration of war against Serbia. Unlike the situation in 1912–13, when Germany had shown little interest in supporting an Austro-Hungarian war in the Balkans, now Berlin expressed its readiness to support action against Serbia. By the end of the first week of July, Francis Joseph, Foreign Minister Leopold Berchtold, and Austrian Prime Minister Karl Count Stürgkh all endorsed a war. They agreed to the idea of presenting Serbia with an ultimatum whose conditions could not realistically be fulfilled. Only Tisza held out to oppose war.

As in the case of the recent Balkan Wars, Tisza again rejected any plan whose goal was annexation that would substantially increase the Slav population of the Empire. And in July 1914 most war proponents saw precisely such an annexation as their favored outcome. In the July 7 meeting of the joint cabinet, Tisza agreed to support a strong—but not impossible to comply with—ultimatum to Serbia, but he also repeated his strong opposition to the annexation plans of his colleagues. "[T]he territory of Serbia should be reduced, but, if only with regard to Russia, she must not be completely annihilated." More importantly, Tisza reiterated that "As Hungarian prime minister he would never allow the Monarchy to annex part of Serbia."[33]

Secondly, and more immediately, Tisza sought assurances that war against Serbia would not bring Romania into the war on the side of Serbia and Russia.[34] He sought some guarantees that Germany would work to keep Romania in the Triple Alliance, and that both Austria-Hungary and Germany would work to

---

[33] Quoted in Galántai, *Hungary*, 34.
[34] Tisza had recently held talks with leading Romanian nationalist politicians a few months earlier that had produced no results, and Tisza feared the possibility of a Romanian revolt in Transylvania, should the Romanian state invade. Galántai, *Hungary*, 29–30.

develop an alliance with Bulgaria that would act as a potential threat against Romania joining the war. He also sought promises that the military would devote some resources to building up credible lines of defense in Transylvania. "We would not be able to put up serious resistance to the Romanian army" and he predicted darkly that "the Romanian army will enter Transylvania, there will be insurrections in the regions inhabited by Romanians, and our Army fighting against Serbia will be attacked on the flank in the rear."[35]

By the end of the second week in July, Tisza had received assurances from the Germans that they would contact the Romanians and agree to bringing Bulgaria into the Triple Alliance. The joint cabinet, too, now spoke rather of partitioning Serbia among its neighbors (after making some border adjustments and demanding an indemnity) and no longer of annexation. These conditions now made it possible for Tisza to support the harsh ultimatum whose rejection would require a declaration of war.

Clearly, the alleged support given by the Serb government to the conspirators who assassinated Archduke Francis Ferdinand and his wife Sophie was only one of many reasons that impelled Austria-Hungary to declare war on Serbia.[36] This fact is made all the more clear by the initial Austro-Hungarian investigation in Sarajevo that reported in a confidential telegram on July 13 that "Nothing proves, nor even suggests, that the Serb government was aware of the preparations for the attempt, or of the acquisition of arms." This report makes it all the clearer that the highest authorities in the Monarchy, including the emperor king, were determined to go to war, no matter what the facts of the case turned out to be. For this reason, their ultimatum to Serbia had to be as harsh as possible to avoid the possibility of Serb agreement to its terms. As the Foreign Ministry's Chief of Staff, Count Hoyos (1876–1937) described it, "The claims are such that it is impossible for any state which has the least amount of self-respect and dignity to accept them."[37] This was important because, in fact, at this particular moment Serbia was in no position to risk war with its powerful neighbor. Under these conditions it is possible that the Serb government might well have agreed to many of Austria-Hungary's less extreme demands.

There is another critical issue to address as we document Austria-Hungary's headlong rush to war. In every one of the crises we have mentioned so far, from the annexation of Bosnia Herzegovina to the Balkan Wars, to the assassination of the Archduke and his wife, the hawks in the Military High Command who argued

---

[35] Memorandum quoted in Galántai, *Hungary*, 35.

[36] Dragutin Dimitrijević (nicknamed Apis) (1876–1917), chief of the military intelligence section of the Serb General Staff but also a prominent member of the secret military society called "Black Hand" responsible for the murder of Serbia's previous King Alexandar and Queen Draga in 1903, was believed to have provided the Bosnian conspirators with weapons and training in Belgrade before the assassination. In 1917 the Serb government in exile executed him for treasonous activities unrelated to the 1914 assassination. See Clark, *The Sleepwalkers*, 11–13, 46–9.

[37] From a conversation with the German *chargé d'affaires* in Vienna, quoted in Galántai, *Hungary*, 41.

for a war always envisioned it as somehow limited to Serbia. They did recognize openly that such a war might possibly provoke Russia to declare war on the Monarchy, as had seemed dangerously likely in 1912, but they treated this possibility either as remote or as somehow manageable with the help of their German ally. One reason Conrad's view had not prevailed during the Balkan War crises was the fact that Germany remained unwilling to support a war in the Balkans and Austria-Hungary could not go it alone. Now Germany supported war, and in fact began to push for a quick start to the war so that it could gain an advantage on the other powers that might also enter. Yet as we will see in the next chapter, Conrad and his colleagues maintained the extraordinary belief throughout the crisis that Russia would not enter the war, and for this reason, they pursued a mobilization plan that envisioned a localized war against Serbia and Montenegro.

Why or how did they delude themselves into this way of thinking? It is quite clear from any analysis of events in the first half of July that Austria-Hungary's leaders wanted war, that they, not their German ally, were responsible for the war that broke out. But a world war? Without their almost unanimous determination to crush Serbia, Germany would never have had the opportunity to put its own war plans against France and Russia in motion. Was it simply that these men existed in an information bubble of their own making, and that they only heard what they wanted or needed to hear from those on the ground?

So it was that even after the Serb government surprisingly agreed to many but not all the demands in the ultimatum, on July 28, 1914, Austria-Hungary declared war on Serbia.

The Great War and the Transformation of Habsburg Central Europe. Pieter M. Judson & Tara Zahra,
Oxford University Press. © Pieter M. Judson & Tara Zahra 2025. DOI: 10.1093/9780191842306.003.0002

2
Mobilizations

When Austria-Hungary declared war on Serbia (July 28) and on Russia nine days later (August 6), military deployment was only a small part of the mobilizations that swiftly transformed every aspect of the Monarchy's society. Wartime mobilization meant far more than simply calling up hundreds of thousands of recruits. First and foremost, it meant transporting them to the northern and southern fronts to wage war against Russia and Serbia. It also meant supplying these troops (and their animals) with sufficient resources to live and fight. The state soon learned that fighting a longer war than expected also required organizing industrial and agricultural production and distribution to serve the war effort more effectively. It meant controlling access to certain resources, replacing unavailable supplies with substitutes wherever possible, and coordinating the rhythms of daily life with the demands of total war. There was no blueprint for this kind of massive shift in social and economic organization, and certainly no prior experience that could show the way.

Within the space of a few months the unanticipated length of the war, the British blockade of the continent, and drastic military defeats all produced a cascade of previously unimaginable demands on Austro-Hungarian society. In response to these demands, different social groups from industrialists to workers to peasants to civil administrators to women drafted into industry, each struggled to exert some agency over the very bleak circumstances they confronted. For some, the crisis presented unexpected opportunities for expansion. Existing factories, for example, could not keep pace with the military's insatiable demand, not only for weapons and munitions, but also for uniforms, boots, and other requirements to equip the soldiers. In response to shortages, the state gave several war industries access to increasingly rare resources in order to increase production of military goods. In doing so, it shifted resources away from civilian manufactures, and this soon resulted in shortages of many consumer goods. This in turn produced an ongoing inflation of prices.

Putting the Austrian and Hungarian economies on a more dedicated war footing also required shifting sectors of the remaining domestic population, including eventually thousands of women, into war-related production efforts, measures that the conservative military had originally hoped to avoid. Workers in these new factories found themselves subjected not only to long hours and harsh military discipline, but also, as we will see, to dangerous conditions and terrifying industrial accidents. Yet another unanticipated crisis that required a drastic reorganization

Figure 2.1 Hungarian reservists march to their barracks through the streets of Budapest after being issued their rifles upon mobilization.

Source: Alamy: https://www.alamy.com/reservists-march-through-budapest-1914-image68845341.html?imageid=EE554A36-EF2E-40E3-8331-DC27F1AF8AC1&p=291611&pn=4&searchId=29ffeeea737ce4e415a3cc559e1d6572&searchtype=0

of production and distribution resulted from the rapidly dwindling food supplies available both to domestic consumers and to men at the front. The loss of most of agricultural Galicia to the Russians in the very first weeks of the war, the effects of the blockade, and the inability of the Austrian and Hungarian governments to coordinate policy effectively with each other, required the local rationing of foodstuffs, fuels, and other resources by the spring of 1915.

Given its antipathy to popular politics and its expectations for a short war, the High Command had not developed plans to mobilize domestic society for war. It certainly did not want to give civilian administrators and politicians any voice in organizing wartime civilian life. The High Command showed some willingness to promote a kind of general civilian sacrifice for the sake of a larger war effort, but certainly not to activate society for that purpose. The unexpected demands of fighting a brutally long war, however, soon changed all that.

If at first the military elite and the government had hoped to limit the effect of war on the domestic population, and thereby limit the people's political influence, Austria-Hungary's citizens soon made their own demands on the state. It was not long before government propaganda reluctantly conceded that the concept of "sacrifice" applied not only to the acts of soldiers at the front, but also to the population that remained at home. In fact, in recognition of people's daily sacrifices, but also of its growing importance to the war effort, the "home" gradually became known as the "home front," an area equally subjected to mobilization, control, government planning, military discipline, and martyrdom.

There is an important paradox in the ways that the Austria-Hungary's military rulers sought—often haphazardly and reluctantly—to mobilize society for the war effort. As we saw in the last chapter, before Austria-Hungary had even begun to mobilize its troops for war, its military and civil leaders had swiftly imposed largely unfamiliar emergency laws on both halves of the dual monarchy. These laws sought to demobilize citizen activism by drastically limiting civil rights and curtailing legal, political, and constitutional norms. Yet while the military severely reduced individuals' rights of movement, their access to information, their rights to free expression, and, worse, their rights to civilian justice, the same military eventually had to mobilize the people to support the war effort more actively. As new dictatorial laws tightened a noose around society, its military rulers conceded that they must build popular enthusiasm for the war to engage women, children, and those men who could not serve at the front more fully in the broader war effort. This effort demanded an unimaginable level of physical, psychological, and emotional sacrifice from them all.

All these forms of mobilization were highly experimental and utterly unplanned for. Both the unfamiliar controls placed on society coupled with the regular incitements to certain kinds of sacrificial action could produce unforeseen and highly dangerous consequences both for society and for Austria-Hungary's military rulers. This apparent paradox of control coupled with incitement helps us to understand both the regime's military failures as well as Austria-Hungary's remarkable ability to remain in the war for more than four long years.

Economies

By itself, military mobilization produced an endless series of related crises of demand and supply that no one had anticipated. War plans that focused on strategy did not include realistic assessments of the ability of Austria-Hungary's transport and communication systems to accommodate the rapid movement and supply of hundreds of thousands of men to the Balkan or Russian fronts. The demands of military mobilization alone caused immediate chaos to the transportation infrastructure in early August, especially because the military suddenly reversed its own mobilization plans within barely a week's time.

On July 26, Austria-Hungary began to mobilize for a Balkan War, sending military units south to invade Serbia. On July 31, however, the High Command suddenly reversed this plan completely and replaced it with a plan for war against both Russia in the northeast and against Serbia in the south. Now trains suddenly had to be found to transport the majority of troops—many of whom were already on their way south, back north, and east to the Galician front. As it turned out, there were not enough locomotives available to transport troops simultaneously to both destinations, so the general mobilization could not even start until August 4. The war plan against Russia had always relied on the presumption that Austro-Hungarian troops would arrive at the front long before the Russians could mobilize, thus making an advance into Russia possible. The lost time in mobilization now gave the Russians time to mobilize far more troops than had been expected to the Galician front. By the time the Austro-Hungarians arrived there, the Russians already outnumbered them. This was only the first of what turned out to be countless blunders subsequently perpetrated by the High Command, which often seemed to depend more on wishful thinking than on facts. Confronted with this new situation, for example, Chief of Staff Franz Conrad von Hötzendorf wavered irresolutely between holding to the original plan for a robust invasion of Russia after the defeat of Serbia, or placing more late-arriving troops in a defensive position in Galicia.[1]

Strategic blunders at the front were accompanied by poor planning in the factories. As in other combatant societies, the swift mobilization of recruits frequently removed the highly skilled workers who produced war-related materiel from the factories, creating slowdowns and bottlenecks in supply chains. The unprecedented scale of this mobilization also demanded the frenzied efforts of administrators whose expertise and specialized knowledge, for example, could keep critical communications, transport, and production systems functioning smoothly. Many of these men too had been called up, and had to be located, called back, or simply replaced.

In a general sense, how prepared was Austria-Hungary for war in 1914? How did its preparations compare to those of other states? Did its economy and technological know-how give it any advantages over its enemies? In terms of population numbers alone, the Entente powers had an enormous advantage over the Central Powers. During the war, thanks in part to their ability to mobilize colonial troops, the Entente allies mobilized 41.6 million soldiers, as opposed to the 23.5 million mobilized by the Central Powers. In terms of preparations, we have already seen that Austria-Hungary's military had long suffered from declining budgets. Steps had only been initiated in 1912 to remedy perceived comparative weaknesses in the military, especially regarding equipment and weaponry. Still, according to economic historian Herbert Matis, Austria-Hungary was indeed competitive with its enemies when it came to the production of certain weapons, especially heavy artillery (the Škoda works in Bohemia, for example) and machinery.[2] During the war, Austria-Hungary also managed to increase its

---

[1] Watson, *Ring of Steel*, 137–40.
[2] In terms of population, the Central Powers were outnumbered by a factor of five to one, and in terms of gross domestic product (GDP) they were outnumbered by a factor of 2.9 to one. Herbert Matis,

production of weapons in areas where it lagged significantly behind the other great powers (machine guns) at least through 1917.

Over time, however, a lack of sufficient energy sources such as coal would eventually cripple production and rail transport in the Monarchy. Although the Empire had developed an oil industry as well as water-powered sources of electricity, the Russian occupations of Galicia—where oil was located—frequently crippled access to that resource, as did a lack of refineries and pipelines.[3] The mobilization of able-bodied men to the front seriously interrupted coal mining as well.

In terms of new military technologies, Austria was a leader in some areas (artillery, tank design, torpedoes, wireless communication) but highly underdeveloped in others (airplanes). And according to most historians, Austria-Hungary had wasted precious resources on efforts to construct a modern navy whose ships—like those of its German ally to the north—spent most of the war hidden away in Adriatic ports. The deciding factor regarding technology, however, was not so much its availability but rather the ability or failure of the military leadership to use it creatively, based on the experience of battle. In this regard, Austria-Hungary's leadership learned very little, similar to the failed military leadership in all the combatant states.

In the first years of the war, the state rarely stepped in to exert direct control over the economy. This may seem surprising, given the relatively free hand the 1912 war production legislation had assigned to the military state. Moreover, in 1914 the parliament was shut down, the unions generally expressed support for the war, and emergency legislation and censorship had quelled any potential public opposition to government intervention. Yet most of the military and civil leadership believed that a free-market policy remained the most efficient strategy. The state only intervened where absolutely necessary with regard to the production and distribution of war-related products and materials. In the first months of the war, the state published countless regulations (prepared in advance) to control the import and export of certain vital resources. Even this approach, however, sought to make the regulated goods more available to those companies that produced war-related goods, rather than to control them directly. This approach also had harsh and unexpected consequences for nonwar-related industries.[4]

"Wirtschaft, Technik Und Rüstung Als Kriegsentscheidende Faktoren," in *Wirtschaft, Technik und das Militär, 1914–1918: Österreich-Ungarn Im Ersten Weltkrieg*, ed. Herbert Matis, Juliane Mikoletzky, and Wolfgang Reiter, Austria: Forschung Und Wissenschaft. Geschichte, Band 11 (Vienna: Lit Verlag, 2014), 11–50.

[3] Alison Fleig Frank, *Oil Empire: Visions of Prosperity in Austrian Galicia*, Harvard Historical Studies (Cambridge, MA: Harvard University Press, 2005).

[4] Tamara Scheer, "Die Kriegswirtschaft am Übergang von der liberal-privaten zur staatlich-regulierten Arbeitswelt," in *Die Habsburgermonarchie 1848–1918*, vol. 11/1/1, 437–84 (pp. 443–4); Máté Rigó, *Capitalism in Chaos: How the Business Elites of Europe Prospered in the Era of the Great War* (Ithaca, NY: Cornell University Press, 2022), 65–6. On the nonwar-related industries that either fail or switch to war-related production, see Rauchensteiner, *The First World War*, 413.

Eventually, this relative hands-off approach proved disastrous, when in the early months of the war the military faced serious supply problems and general shortages of munitions. These resulted not simply from economic challenges, but even more from the fragmented character of the military leadership, divided as it was between Austria and Hungary, and from the overall decline of military budgets in past decades. As mentioned above, the 1912 legislation had sought to address this decline by planning rearmament over the coming decade. The same legislation had also given the Minister of War the right to take over and run directly whole factories and to place their workers under military discipline.

The war produced unforeseen economic crises around food provision as well, and not simply because farmers were called up to serve in the military at the very moment of the autumn harvest in 1914. In the very first month of the war, after some minor forays into Russian territory, the military suffered repeated and catastrophic defeats at the hands of the advancing Russians. The Galician capital Lemberg/L'viv/Lwów fell on September 2. By late September, most of Galicia, Austria's most important grain-producing region, had fallen to a brutal and destructive Russian occupation. Only the massive Galician fortress town of Przemyśl managed to hold out against a Russian siege until it too finally fell in March 1915, with a humiliating surrender of 117,000 Austro-Hungarian troops.[5] Altogether, in only four months, by the end of 1914 on the Galician and Serb fronts, Austria-Hungary had lost 1,250,000 men out of 3,350,000 originally mobilized: 189,000 killed, another 491,200 wounded, 291,800 sick, and 278,000 taken prisoner.[6]

Meanwhile, a British naval blockade of the Central Powers added to the economic crisis by preventing Austria-Hungary and its German ally from importing much-needed foodstuffs, fuel, and resources necessary to the production of war materiel. The Austrian half of the Dual Monarchy suffered as well from being cut off from imports of Hungarian agricultural products, which now went directly to feed the military or Hungarian cities. Having given no special advance thought to society's potential food needs, the military faced several insoluble domestic crises involving that very society for whose interests it apparently cared so little and whose elected representatives it had chosen to ignore. Even military victories over and subsequent occupations of agrarian Romania and Russia in 1917, not to mention Serbia and Poland in 1916, did nothing to mitigate the shortages, despite the hopes they raised among the urban population.

---

[5] On the siege, see Alexander Watson's unfortunately titled book, *The Fortress: The Siege of Przemyśl and the Making of Europe's Bloodlands* (New York: Basic Books, 2020).

[6] Edmund Glaise-Horstenau, ed., *Österreich-Ungarns letzter Krieg, 1914–1918: Das Kriegsjahr 1916*, vol. 4 (Vienna: Verlag der Militärwissenschaftlichen Mitteilungen, 1933), Beilage 4, Tabelle 2, quoted in Ke-Chin Hsia, *Victims' State: War and Welfare in Austria, 1868–1925* (New York: Oxford University Press, 2022), 47; Holger H. Herwig, *The First World War: Germany and Austria-Hungary, 1914–1918*, Modern Wars (London: Arnold, 1998), 91–4.

These may have been the most obvious and critical crises produced by military mobilization. Very quickly, however, mobilization caused other dangerous and unanticipated developments that created new and informal forms of popular mobilization. Beginning in September 1914, for example, the Russian occupation of Eastern Galicia and Bukovina sent tens of thousands of refugees fleeing westward, seeking safety, refuge, and sustenance in Austria's and Hungary's cities. No one had foreseen the possibility of such a disruptive movement of people, and, as we will see in the next chapter, the government struggled to find ways to house and support these refugees. At the same time, harsh censorship of all forms of media gave rise to a different kind of mobilization: a growing culture of rumor and denunciation that often dissolved social relations of trust in urban neighborhoods and diminished popular confidence in the regime.

Rumors from Above and from Below

On August 4, 1914, Vienna's *Neue Freie Presse* newspaper published a brief notice from Austria's Telegraph Correspondence Bureau titled "Preventing and Combatting Dangerous Attacks Inside the Monarchy." According to the report, reliable sources indicated that quite a few subversive elements were on the loose in the Monarchy and they might imperil the safety of both the public and state. The text invited—one might say incited—patriotic Austrians to be on the lookout for any such dangerous elements. "Serious reports," the article concluded, "should be forwarded to the KÜA, housed in Vienna's War Ministry."[7] Although novelist Stefan Zweig immediately wrote to the KÜA to suggest that the public required a more precise definition of "subversive elements" (as well as offering his services as a writer to the War Ministry), the regime left all possibilities open. Consequently, the KÜA found itself deluged in the first months of the war with all kinds of reports from Austrians alleging subversion on the part of their neighbors. From cloistered French nuns who supposedly refused to pray for Austria-Hungary's victory to mysterious cars allegedly carrying supplies of gold destined for the enemy, citizens saw subversion and treachery everywhere.[8] In Sarajevo, for example, local authorities even decided that to avoid the danger of espionage, veiled Muslim women would not be allowed to travel alone. They would have to be accompanied by a man, in whose documents their identities should be entered (although without a photograph, since their religion forbade it).[9]

Wartime conditions and early military defeats, along with the sudden appearance of refugees, fears about potential spies, and the catastrophic failures of the

---

[7] *Neue Freie Presse*, August 3, 1914. [8] Scheer, *Die Ringstrassenfront*, 75–7.
[9] Scheer reproduces this document in *Die Ringstrassenfront*, 78.

urban food provision system all became subjects for endless popular speculation.[10] The military aggravated this speculation through its own behavior. From the moment war was declared, misguided military prejudice presumed that some of Austria-Hungary's linguistic groups—at first Ruthenes and Serbs, later Italians, Czechs, and Romanians—would for some reason betray their country to the enemy. As we have seen, these accusations built on prewar military presumptions that nationalist political conflict reflected defeatism, irredentism, and even treachery by entire linguistic communities. These same attitudes also offered the military leadership convenient explanations for its own stunning failures on both the Serb and Russian fronts.

The military and the media constantly invoked the subversive actions of alleged Ruthene or Ukrainian Russophile spies to explain its defeats at the hands of the Russians early in the war. In September, Vienna's *Neue Freie Presse* reported, for example, that traitorous Ruthene peasants frequently drove herds of cattle to the front lines to signal the position of Austro-Hungarian troops to Russian artillery. ("Artillery shells always seem to follow the appearance of Ukrainian herds…"). That same week the writer—now reporter—Alexander Roda related from the Galician front that Ruthene spies used mirrors to signal the Russians, including in one egregious case, a mirror painted with an icon carried in an apparently innocent religious procession.[11] Later on, a study commissioned by the High Command even asserted that the Russians had recruited Ruthene orphans and child prostitutes to serve as spies.[12] These examples may seem laughable to us in retrospect, but Austria's emergency legislation allowed the military to court-martial civilians charged with political crimes in war zones like Galicia. The court-martial procedure relieved the military of having to investigate cases and rendered any defense against the accusation close to impossible. When found guilty, the court-martial also required that the accused civilian be immediately executed with no option for appeal.[13] In the first months of the war when the

---

[10] Generally on urban rumor, anger at speculation, and anti-Semitism, Healy, *Vienna*, 122–59; Morelon, *Streetscapes*, 31–42; Rigó, *Capitalism in Chaos*, 112–13.

[11] Examples reported from the front by Alexander Roda Roda quoted in Elisabeth Haid, *Im Blickfeld zweier Imperien: Galizien in der österreichischen und russischen Presseberichterstattung während des Ersten Weltkriegs (1914–1917)*, Studien zur Ostmitteleuropaforschung 43 (Marburg: Verlag Herder-Institut, 2019), 181–2.

[12] Bernhard Bachinger, Wolfram Dornik, and Schmitz, eds., "Tapfer, zäh und schlecht geführt: Kriegserfahrungen österreichisch-ungarischer Offiziere mit den russischen Gegnern 1914–1917," in *Jenseits des Schützengrabens: der Erste Weltkrieg im Osten: Erfahrung—Wahrnehmung—Kontext*, Veröffentlichungen des Ludwig-Boltzmann-Instituts für Kriegsfolgen-Forschung, Graz-Wien-Klagenfurt 14 (Innsbruck: Studienverlag, 2013), 59. Also quoted in Andreas Agocs, "The Emperor's Broken Bust: Representations of the Habsburg 'Shatterzone' in World War I," in *World War I in Central and Eastern Europe: Politics, Conflict and Military Experience*, ed. Judith Devlin, John Paul Newman, and Maria Falina (London: I.B. Taurus & Co, 2018), 187.

[13] Anton Holzer, *Das Lächeln der Henker: der unbekannte Krieg gegen die Zivilbevölkerung 1914–1918* (Darmstadt: Primus, 2008), 56–65.

military failed on both Russian and Serb fronts, thousands of civilians wrongly accused of treachery paid for these military fiascos with their lives.[14]

Military leaders repeatedly and unsuccessfully pressured Austrian Prime Minister Count Stürgkh to extend their court-martialing powers to nonwar-zone regions like Bohemia, where the military wrongly claimed that thousands of domestic Slav (Czech nationalist) traitors lurked.[15] Looking for the smallest signs of treason, the military also encouraged civilian administrators, local police, and provincial gendarmes (who were now under military command) to report and aggressively punish potentially suspicious civilian behavior in nonwar zones. Taking their cue from the military leadership, different nationalist groups frequently and baselessly accused their local nationalist opponents of fomenting treachery on the home front. In some linguistically mixed regions of the Monarchy, neighbors turned on each other, reporting the most bizarre rumors about each other to local authorities. In Southern Styria, whose population was both Slovene- and German-speaking, denunciations against alleged Serb sympathizers cascaded into a mass hysteria. In less than a month, these unsubstantiated accusations led to the unjustified incarceration of over 900 people. Those accused were usually loyal patriots who often lost their livelihoods, and as a parliamentary inquiry in 1917 determined, also lost their confidence in the state as an impartial arbiter of justice. The hysteria only died down in September when both Stürgkh and Governor Clary of Styria called for an official reassessment of the situation. They now insisted that local gendarmes should only make arrests in cases where clear evidence warranted it.[16]

In Austria and Hungary, meanwhile, the Serb gymnastics society "Sokol" served as a lightning rod for both government and popular action even before the official start of mobilization. In Dalmatia on July 26, the regional government dissolved thirty-eight Croatian and Serb nationalist associations, including all local branches of the Sokol.[17] Already on July 15, however, Austria-Hungary's Minister of Defense Alexander Krobatkin had expressed the opinion to Hungarian Prime Minister István Tizsa that local branches of the Serb Sokol or gymnastics association in Croatia-Slavonia had long sheltered activists for an alleged "Serb revolutionary movement." Tizsa hardly required an excuse to act, since well before the outbreak of war he had explicitly directed the attention of his

---

[14] Mark Cornwall, "Traitors and the Meaning of Treason in Austria-Hungary's Great War," *Transactions of the Royal Historical Society* 25 (2015): 113–34 (pp. 119–22).

[15] Mark Lewis, *The Failed Quest for Total Surveillance: The Internal Security Service in Austria-Hungary During World War I*, ed. Judith Devlin, John Paul Newman, and Maria Falina (London: I.B. Taurus & Co, 2018), 28.

[16] On this wave of denunciation and its later reverberations, see the excellent work by Martin Moll, *Kein Burgfrieden: Der Deutsch-Slowenische Nationalitätenkonflikt in der Steiermark 1900-1918* (Innsbruck: Studien, 2007).

[17] Johannes Kalwoda, *Parteien, Politik und Staatsgewalt in Dalmatien (1900–1918): Zur Wechselwirkung zwischen staatlicher Verwaltung und parlamentarischer Vertretung* (Wien: Verlag der österreichischen Akademie der Wissenschaften, 2023), 456.

own county administrators to "demonstrate strength" against the non-Hungarian population (specifically Serb, Romanian, and Ruthene speakers). After war was declared, police in Southern Hungary immediately arrested several local Sokol leaders and members. At the same time, popular anti-Serb riots broke out in linguistically and religiously mixed regions of Croatia, often fueled by local anti-Serb political parties. Austro-Hungarian military officials used the disorder as an excuse to clamp down on a range of Serb national organizations in Hungary, and in one town even took Serb-speaking hostages as a guarantee against further disorder.[18]

On the other hand, Tisza protested vigorously against such Austro-Hungarian military excesses in Hungary, as when, for example, a retired Romanian-speaking major general of the Austro-Hungarian army, Nickolaus Cena, was placed under arrest at the outbreak of the war for no apparent reason other than his Romanian background. Irina Marin's analysis of this case demonstrates the general lack of clarity and the overwhelming paranoid fears within the military about how to treat putative nationalists—even when it came to high military officials—and at a time when the Monarchy was not even at war with Romania.[19] At the same time however, when Tisza and other Hungarian officials protested to Vienna against such actions, it was because they infringed on Hungary's constitutional rights rather than out of concern for the rights of their Serb- or Romanian-speaking fellow citizens. As historian József Galántai argued, "the characteristic structure of the exceptional measures in Hungary during the time of crisis impeded the practice of military dictatorship but facilitated the fact that the government itself could adopt such a dictatorship."[20]

Similar paranoic suspicions elsewhere in the Monarchy extended beyond military officers to include a range of bureaucratic officials whose only crime was their putative nationality or nationalist sympathies. In September 1914, for example, commander of the Balkan forces and governor of Bosnia Herzegovina, Oskar Potiorek, demanded that the governor of Dalmatia remove Vladimir Budisavljević as District Captain of Cattaro/Kotor. Budisavljević was a loyal and popular civil servant, frequently honored by the emperor for his service and who had most recently received the title of *Hofrat* only a year before. Nevertheless, Potiorek accused the district captain falsely of harboring Serb sympathies, suggesting that as administrator, Budisavljević would betray this Austrian coastal town and naval base that bordered Montenegro to Serbia. Dalmatia's governor Count Attems who valued Budisavljević's service, especially his past efforts to control Serb nationalism, protested to the military. In the end, however, Attems reluctantly pensioned off Budisavljević, writing that in wartime, the wishes of the military had to be

---

[18] Galántai, *Hungary*, 97–8.
[19] Irina Marin, "World War I and Internal Repression: The Case of Major General Nikolaus Cena," *Austrian History Yearbook* 44 (April 2013): 195–208.
[20] Galántai, *Hungary*, 75.

decisive.[21] Almost immediately, however, Attems regretted having capitulated to the military demands, and attempted without success to rehabilitate Budisavljević. By 1915, Attems was writing to the Interior Ministry recommending that it apply the state-of-exception laws less harshly, and as Johannes Kalwoda points out, even criticizing the government for "state-police reprisals" [*staatspolizeilichen Represalien*].[22]

By late September 1914, even Emperor King Francis Joseph worried that unjustified arrests could turn the most loyal citizens against the state. He called on the military to act with greater restraint against civilians and only to prosecute them in cases of the most serious suspicions.[23] And in the spring of 1915 when Italy entered the war against Austria-Hungary, the Ministry of the Interior instructed administrators in Austria's Italian-speaking regions to avoid agitating the population and especially the "loyal elements." "[L]oyal supporters of the [Austro-Hungarian] State of Italian nationality," it ordered "should be protected from unjustified attacks and denunciation."[24] This warning may have restricted the actions of local gendarmes and civil administrators from encouraging popular denunciations, but it could not diminish the profound nationalist prejudices that circulated among Austria-Hungary's military elite.

In her work on wartime Prague, Claire Morelon details similar efforts by the military authorities in Bohemia to ban the Czech nationalist branches of the same gymnastics society "Sokol" in 1914 based on their alleged pan-Slavic and therefore pro-Russia and pro-Serbia character. In typical fashion, one military commander wrote that, although he could cite no concrete evidence of Sokol treachery, he nevertheless asserted that, "they are a hotbed of pan-Slavists." Military leaders debated these charges even as newspapers and independent military observers praised Czech Sokol members for their patriotic wartime service.[25]

This was only the beginning of several eventually successful efforts by the military to outlaw specifically Czech nationalist organizations during the war and eventually to prosecute leading Czech nationalist politicians Karel Kramář and Alois Rašín on trumped up charges of treason.[26] After high numbers of Czech-speaking infantrymen from Regiment 28 allegedly defected to the Russians at a

---

[21] This case (and many others regarding Serb- and Italian-speaking officials) is recounted and analyzed by Johannes Kalwoda, *Dalmatien*, 467–72 who points out that Attems immediately regretted his actions and attempted to rehabilitate Budisavljević by arranging a different position for him after a "medical leave," but the latter refused.
[22] Kalwoda, *Dalmatien*, 463.   [23] Scheer, *Die Ringstrassenfront*, 77.
[24] Moll, *Kein Burgfrieden*, 446; Francesco Frizzera, *Cittadini Dimezzati: I Profughi Trentini in Austria-Ungheria e in Italia (1914–1919)*, Annali Dell'Istituto Storico Italo-Germanico in Trento. Quaderni 101 (Bologna: Società editrice Il mulino, 2018). See also Alessandro Livio, "The Wartime Treatment of the Italian-Speaking Population in Austria-Hungary," *European Review of History: Revue Européenne d'histoire* 24, no. 2 (March 4, 2017): 185–99.
[25] Morelon, *Streetscapes*, 66.
[26] Mark Cornwall, "Treason in an Era of Regime Change: The Case of the Habsburg Monarchy," *Austrian History Yearbook* 50 (April 2019): 124–49 (pp. 134–41); Cornwall, "Traitors"; Morelon, *Streetscapes*, 66.

battle in April 1915, for example, the military reacted by dissolving the regiment and blaming Czech-speaking units for the defeat. When investigations proved that the accusations had no basis in truth, the Ministry of War nevertheless refused to pursue those responsible for spreading manifestly false rumors about Czech-speaking troops, most probably because of their high military rank. Ironically, this false accusation later became the basis for one of the heroic founding myths of the first Czechoslovak Republic. Both Czech and German nationalists—for very different reasons—were only too happy to repeat this apocryphal story about Czech nationalist subversion during the war. As historian Richard Lein has definitively shown, the story of mass Czech defections to the Russians was a myth propagated by the military elite in order once again to shift blame for defeat away from its own incompetence.[27] Nevertheless, at the time, many Czech nationalist leaders and elected officials sent manifestos of loyalty to the government that rejected the treasonous behavior of the alleged deserters.

Clearly, warnings from the Emperor/King, to say nothing of the Prime Ministers, Provincial Governors, or Minister of the Interior could not effectively brake the larger phenomenon of rumor, whose influence became more corrosive as the war dragged on. The confusion that resulted from military coercion and censorship only encouraged desperate people to develop new forms of agency by selective use of denunciation and the spread of rumor. The more the military sought to control information through heavy censorship, the more it incited the spread of rumors about every possible topic. As historian Maureen Healy argued for wartime Vienna, when faced with an economy of rationed information, ordinary people reacted to censorship and propaganda by spreading rumors or denouncing neighbors in an effort to maintain what they believed were standards of fairness and legality.[28]

Food

Nowhere were these twin mobilizing phenomena of censorship and rumor more apparent than with the provision and consumption of food.[29] We have already seen that the conscription of peasants, the loss of draft animals, and the Russian occupation of Galicia had created immediate and unanticipated food shortages, especially in Austria-Hungary's cities. The monopolization of Hungarian agricultural produce for the military made it worse. Whereas Austria had traditionally

---

[27] Richard Lein, *Pflichterfüllung oder Hochverrat? die tschechischen Soldaten Österreich-Ungarns im Ersten Weltkrieg* (Wien Berlin: LIT, 2011); Morelon, *Streetscapes*, 66.
[28] Healy, *Vienna*, 122–59.
[29] The classic work on this subject for the Central Powers (focused on Germany and Berlin) is Belinda J. Davis, *Home Fires Burning: Food, Politics, and Everyday Life in World War I Berlin* (Chapel Hill, NC: University of North Carolina Press, 2000). See also Healy, *Vienna* and Morelon, *Streetscapes* for specifically Austrian examples.

relied on annual imports of 2.1 million tons of Hungarian grain prior to the war, by 1916 the Hungarians could barely spare 100,000 tons for their Austrian neighbors. In response to their desperate pleas Hungarian officials regularly reminded Austrian administrators and politicians that Hungary was also responsible for feeding over 3 million enlisted men and animals in the Austro-Hungarian army, not to mention its own population.[30]

Given these circumstances, the Austrian harvest for 1915 (wheat and rye) constituted less than half of the already dismal harvest of 1914. The 1916 and 1917 harvests fell even further to 40 percent of 1914 levels. The militarized regime had not anticipated this kind of crisis, in part because no one had a plan for a war that would last more than a few months. As early as October 31, 1914 the Austrian government decreed a reduction of wheat and rye flour in commercially produced bread. Thirty percent of these flours had to be replaced by an ersatz (barley, corn, potato), a number that was quickly raised to 50 percent in January 1915.[31] In December 1914, the Austrian government tried to combat inflated food prices by introducing maximum prices for some consumer items.[32] Only a few months later, in February 1915, the crisis worsened, and the Austrian government created a War Grain Control Agency to oversee the general distribution of flour and bread. Two months later, some municipal governments introduced ration cards for flour and bread, quickly followed by sugar, milk, coffee, and fats. The cards gave individuals the right to purchase only a limited amount of a particular product in a town's local markets.[33] In November 1915, the government also forbade the sale of cream, which from now on could only be used to produce butter.[34] At the same time, regional and urban governments also began to contract with private firms to create local cartels to obtain foodstuffs and fuel and to oversee their rationing. However, the ongoing problem that could never be solved was how to ensure that local markets had a large enough supply of those rationed products to satisfy the needs of all those who presented ration cards. Simply showing a ration card that entitled the bearer to a certain amount of bread, meat, fats, or milk, did not guarantee the availability of those items. This stark reality led to the practice

---

[30] Roman Sandgruber, *Ökonomie und Politik: Österreichische Wirtschaftsgeschichte vom Mittelalter bis zur Gegenwart*, Österreichische Geschichte (Wien: Ueberreuter, 1995), 324–5; Helmut Rumpler and Anatol Schmied-Kowarzik, eds., *Die Habsburgermonarchie 1848–1918*, vol. 11/2, *Weltkriegsstatistik Österreich-Ungarn 1914–1918 Bevölkerungsbewegung, Kriegstote, Kriegswirtschaft* (Wien: Verlag der Österreichischen Akademie der Wissenschaften, 2014); Galántai, *Hungary*, 80–1.

[31] Franz Vojir, "Ersatzlebensmittel Im Ersten Weltkrieg in Österreich," in *Wirtschaft, Technik und das Militär, 1914–1918: Österreich-Ungarn Im Ersten Weltkrieg*, ed. Herbert Matis, Juliane Mikoletzky, and Wolfgang Reiter (Wien: Lit, 2014), 255. In January 1915 the government also outlawed the use of the small amounts of flour used to separate bread from the baking form.

[32] Morelon, *Streetscapes*, 158.

[33] Healy, *Vienna*, 43–4. In response to the worsening crisis, the Austrian government organized a Food Office for all of Austria in November 1916. See Ottokar Landwehr von Pragenau, *Hunger: die Erschöpfungsjahre der Mittelmächte 1917/1918* (Zürich: Amalthea, 1931), 6.

[34] Milk and cream could no longer be used by businesses to produce sweets or ice cream. Vojir, "Ersatzlebensmittel," 255.

of consumers "lining up" for hours—often overnight—before a shop opened, to ensure that they could in fact obtain the desired items. Women whose work hours prevented them from lining up often sent their children to hold a place in line. Healy cites a Viennese journalist who observed that anyone lining up after 3:00 a.m. would probably miss out on obtaining food the next morning when the market opened.[35]

The situation was little better in Hungary, even though Hungarian farms produced far more grain per person than did Austrian farms during the war. Hungarian emergency legislation gave the civilian government broad powers to fix prices for consumer goods. Given the shortages that resulted thanks to military requisitions and supply problems in regions near the Serb or Russian fronts, the government introduced food coupons in Budapest in March 1915 and by December of that year the authorities had begun to ration bread.[36] Rationing and access to food, however, were not the only problems that faced Austrian and Hungarian consumers. Consumers not only faced shortages of necessary food products, but a marked decline in the nutritional content of those few products that were available. As the war ground on, and as local governments found it necessary to cut the rations for bread, local producers increasingly mixed lower quality ingredients with wheat or rye—eventually even using sawdust—in bread.[37] The governments were also well aware that ruthless entrepreneurs repeatedly introduced products to the market that claimed to serve as legitimate and acceptable substitutes for rationed products. Many of these were nutritionally completely worthless and often detrimental to public health.

Unable to solve the problem of supply, the governments tried to shape demand by controlling consumption. In May 1915, all Austrian businesses that fed their employees were obligated to observe two meatless days per week. Meat was defined as beef, veal, pork, boar, lamb, goat, horse, rabbit, poultry, meat conserves, smoked meats, ham, and sausage, but not fish or sausage made of blood or offal. In July 1916, this meatless rule was extended to private households as well. By September of 1916, the number of required meatless days was raised to three per week, although after March 1917 with permission it could be lowered to two days per week. Along with the strictures limiting meat, the authorities also limited the consumption of fats, especially fried foods, and fried desserts on Saturdays.[38] A 1917 law forbade restaurants to use sugar to sweeten drinks or to provide sugar on tables, although customers were allowed to bring and use their own sugar. Local officials also tried to control consumption and remedy hunger by instituting public dining halls or public kitchens where civilians could obtain simple meals at a relatively cheap price. Yet these institutions did little to quell the agitated public mood, especially given the poor quality of the food they offered.

---

[35] Healy, *Vienna*, 73–8.   [36] Galántai, *Hungary*, 80–4.
[37] Morelon, *Streetscapes*, 172; Healy, *Vienna*, 49, 53.   [38] Vojir, "Ersatzlebensmittel," 256.

For four long years, anxieties about food and its procurement dominated daily life across the Monarchy, creating powerful forms of neighborhood mobilization. At first, hunger became the subject of popular grumbling, then, when officials appeared incapable of solving the problem, it became the subject of rumors to explain the shortages. Eventually, the failure of the regime to provide a consistent solution to the food crisis—despite new bureaucracies devoted solely to the management of food—produced popular demonstrations and marches that could turn violent and that further weakened the state's very legitimacy in the eyes of the people.

Urban rumors abounded about people who profited illegally from the misery of their fellow citizens, new millionaires who profited directly from supplying the military, anti-Semitic accusations against alleged Jewish middlemen, about the vile actions of unscrupulous hoarders, and about the selfish peasants who allegedly profited at the expense of starving townspeople. Why was it, after all, that despite their constant assurances that things would soon improve, the local and Imperial authorities could never effectively control the system and make it function fairly? The flow of "information" from below that sought to make sense of these conundrums also produced demonstrations and marches largely by women seeking help for their families. One Prague policeman quoted by Morelon worried that lining up overnight for food created extra security concerns, and that the crowds "could, with the smallest provocation, get violently agitated."[39] When markets ran out of necessities, crowds of women often marched to other markets where rumor had it that food was available. When this proved untrue, they often marched to the town hall demanding food and punishment for hoarders. Crowd frustration could frequently and swiftly lead to more pointedly political demonstrations, labor strikes, and to violence.[40]

The powerful internal logic underlying popular mobilization was not simply about satisfying hunger, but about restoring fairness and justice to what seemed to be a lawless and disorganized system that consistently privileged criminal opportunists and the wealthy. Denouncing alleged hoarders and black marketeers to the authorities, for example, gave people a strategy to impose integrity and order from below on a fundamentally unfair situation. It also focused people's anger specifically on those perceived to be outsiders to the neighborhood, especially refugees and specifically Jewish refugees, who often served as convenient scapegoats for the crisis. Denunciation also served to restore people's sense of individual agency and control in a profoundly unpredictable situation. Finally, denunciations served as constant reminders to the authorities of the debt they

---

[39] Morelon, *Streetscapes*, 229. For Hungarian press accusations against war profiteers, new millionaires, and "Jewish middlemen," see Rigó, *Capitalism in Chaos*, 112–13.

[40] Peter Heumos, "'Kartoffeln her oder es gibt eine Revolution': Hungerkrawalle, Streiks und Massenproteste in den böhmischen Ländern, 1914–1918," in *Der Erste Weltkrieg und die Beziehungen zwischen Tschechen, Slowaken und Deutschen*, ed. Hans Mommsen et al. (Essen: Klartext, 2001), 255–86.

owed to the citizens, those ordinary people who made thousands of daily sacrifices for the sake of the war and of the men at the front.

Local town officials and administrators well understood how dangerous the food situation was to the successful prosecution of the war. As the frontline representatives of the state, these administrators not only recognized the dangers, they also often sympathized with and shared in the plight of their constituents. They too complained frequently to the Imperial government that their towns and cities did not receive promised amounts of necessary provisions. When in 1917 the governor of Trieste protested that instead of the promised 2,400 wagons of potatoes, the city had only received 1,680, he warned that, "The mood of the population, which so far has born the manifest hardships of war in exemplary fashion, cannot be subjected to further burdens." He pointed out that malnutrition was also causing a rise in deadly epidemics such as tuberculosis, a dangerous development that officials in many other Austrian cities noted as well.[41] Local politicians and administrators, however sympathetic they might be, were completely unprepared for the kinds of popular demands they now faced. They tended to respond in legalistic fashion by passing new ordinances against hoarding, against black market activities, or against watering down food, promising to enforce their prosecution more strictly. This only resulted in broken promises that further diminished the public's trust in the ability of the state to provide for people's basic necessities.

Work

The exhaustion and disease suffered by so many of the women and men who remained in what was called the "home front" was not merely a product of their hunger. It also resulted from the state's voracious need for labor in war-related industries. Wartime demands for specific industrial products at first produced a rapid (and haphazard) expansion of certain businesses and factories, as well as to an expansion of working hours and harsh labor discipline within their walls.[42] Men who had been released from frontline service to work in war-related industries thanks to their particular skills, were usually subject to harsh military discipline in the factory. The War Production Law of 1912 had in fact given the War Ministry the right to take over whole factories, to employ specific workers there, and to place them under military law.[43] But military discipline and repeated threats

---

[41] Quoted in Judson, *The Habsburg Empire*, 141. On disease in Prague and Vienna, see Morelon, *Streetscapes*, 141; Healy, *Vienna*, 8, 42, 146, 307.

[42] On the rapid expansion of some businesses, see examples in Rigó, *Capitalism in Chaos*, chap. 3.

[43] Matis, "Wirtschaft, Technik und Rüstung als kriegsentscheidende Faktoren," in *Wirtschaft, Technik und das Militär 1914–1918*, 41.

of being sent back to the front were not enough to prevent waves of industrial strikes in 1917 and particularly early in 1918 against intolerable working and living conditions, as we will see in chapter 5.

At the outset of the war, the influential Austrian Socialist Party had expressed patriotic support for what it called a "defensive war" against reactionary Russia, partly as a way to increase its potential political and social influence under a future postwar settlement. Wartime cooperation with the regime also gave the socialists some ability to influence working conditions in war-related industries, as well as positions on important government advisory boards that dealt with a range of social and economic wartime issues including food distribution. In return, however, the socialist leadership was at least tacitly expected to maintain discipline, order, and predictability among the workers. As the war went on, however, and demands on civilian labor increased, the Socialist Party increasingly failed to prevent strikes. With an ongoing lack of sufficient workers, the state demanded ever more overtime from war workers. The Škoda munitions factories in Pilsen/Plzeň, for example, demanded an extreme of 110 hours weekly from its workers.[44]

The state's need for labor also resulted in an unprecedented mobilization of women into positions previously occupied by male workers. This phenomenon was perhaps most noticeable in the public service sector where women took over unaccustomed and highly visible positions. By 1915, for example, the cities of Budapest, Graz, Pressburg/Pozsony, and Vienna now hired women to serve as conductors on city trams, an employment that required shifts of up to fourteen hours at a time.[45] Even the military was not immune to this development, when it finally hired women to replace the men who had formerly occupied secretarial and even some administrative positions. By 1917, as Scheer points out, even the KÜA ordered that "those men only half fit for front line duty must be called up...Wherever possible male teams must be replaced with female temporary assistants." Special service regulations were drawn up to govern the workplace labor, behavior, and rights of women assistants. As Healy has shown, the military even created a special uniform for women working in its offices, one designed to embody the contradictory demands of both maintaining women's traditional femininity while discretely emphasizing their newly found competence and authority in male positions.[46]

Less visible but perhaps more pervasive, by 1916 women constituted 40 percent of the war industry workforce in the Austrian half of the Dual Monarchy.

---

[44] Robert J. Wegs, *Die österreichische Kriegswirtschaft*, 112.
[45] Rauchensteiner, *The First World War*, 424; Sigrid Augeneder, *Arbeiterinnen im Ersten Weltkrieg: Lebens- und Arbeitsbedingungen proletarischer Frauen in Österreich* (Wien: Europaverl, 1987).
[46] Scheer, *Ringstrassenfront*, 63; Maureen Healy, "Becoming Austrian: Women, the State, and Citizenship in World War I," *Central European History* 35, no. 1 (March 2002): 1–35.

Although the government had immediately sought to make women's employment easier for employers by lifting restrictions on women's night work in October 1914, some industries were slow to hire women. Even though they could pay women at well below the rates they paid male workers, many industries such as iron and steel nevertheless lagged behind their counterparts in France and Germany in employment of women.[47] This was not true in the industrial region around Pilsen/Plzeň, Bohemia, where employment of women in steel and machinery factories jumped from 2 percent before the war to 20 percent in 1915 and 1916 (at the Škoda works, for example, they were entrusted with servicing heavy cranes).[48] One branch that was quick to hire women, however, was the burgeoning munitions industry. At one munitions factory in Budapest women quickly came to constitute 50 percent of the labor force. In the Prague suburb of Žižkov, women constituted more than half of the labor force at the newly expanded munitions plant. In general, so many women joined the munitions industries that by December 1915 the War Ministry referred to them approvingly as "soldiers of the hinterland."[49] In his analysis of wartime working-class gender relations, historian Rudolf Kučera noted that the influx of women was so extraordinary that in January 1917 the government actually removed gender from the categories that determined workers' right to various health insurance benefits.[50]

Women working long hours in certain kinds of munitions factories faced considerable danger from industrial accidents owing to constant pressures to raise production rates and the outrageously lax safety measures that enabled these demands to be met. The privately owned Wöllersdorf factory in Lower Austria, for example, had long produced explosives and ammunition well before the outbreak of war. In 1914, the company employed 3,500 workers who daily produced 100,000 pieces of infantry ammunition and 560 artillery shells. Once war broke out, the factory expanded significantly, thanks to government contracts and access to rationed resources. In 1916, it now employed up to 40,000 workers, at least half of them women. On September 18, 1918, at 11:45 a.m., a terrible explosion rocked one of the Wöllersdorf factory buildings where a mostly female labor force filled shell casings with dynamite, nitrocellulose, and nitroglycerin. The effects of the explosion were made catastrophic by the fact that the doors to the factory had been locked beforehand to prevent the women from starting their lunch break too early. With no windows, and all doors locked except one, the desperate women trapped inside could not escape the inferno that consumed their workplace. The owners reported 277 deaths, itself a horrific statistic. Witnesses, however, declared that of the 500 workers inside the affected building, only twenty had managed to escape. In their official report, the owners added,

---

[47] Rauchensteiner, *The First World War*, 424.
[49] Rauchensteiner, *The First World War*, 424.
[48] Kučera, *Rationed Life*, 113.
[50] Kučera, *Rationed Life*, 114.

nevertheless, that, "the operation of the factory was not disturbed by the event and continues in good order."[51]

The mobilization of women into formerly male occupations in factories and white-collar professions created a range of unaccustomed social challenges that—along with other crises—threatened the survival of many families. Women in the factories worked long hours, leaving them little time to carry out the family responsibilities with which they had been left: to shop, prepare meals, or care for their children. At the same time, schools often closed when male teachers and administrators were sent to the front. Mothers who now worked in factories had to send their children to stand in line for them—often overnight—at the markets. As we will see in chapter 5, among other effects of these practices, observers in many cities and towns fretted about an apparent rise of juvenile delinquency.

Figure 2.2 Der Wehrman at the Přerov/Prerau train station. Wehrman statues appeared throughout Austria-Hungary beginning in 1915 and became focal points for patriotic demonstrations.
Source: Herder-Institut: https://www.herder-institut.de/bildkatalog/iv/257529

---

[51] Hubert Weitensfelder, "Metalle, Sprengstoff, Pflanzenfasern: Kriegsbedingte Ersatzmittel Und Ersatzverfahren," in *Wirtschaft, Technik Und Das Militär, 1914–1918: Österreich-Ungarn Im Ersten Weltkrieg*, ed. Herbert Matis, Juliane Mikoletzky, and Wolfgang Reiter (Wien: Lit, 2014); *WoMen at War* (Heeresgeschichtliches Museum, 2013).

Von der österreichisch-ungarischen Munitionsindustrie. Die Skodawerke.
Zünderwerkstätte. (Revision.)

Figure 2.3 Women making munitions during World War I in the Bohemian Škoda arms factory.

Source: Alamy: https://www.alamy.com/women-making-munitions-during-world-war-i-in-an-arms-factory-in-austria-hungary-automated-translation-image446963121.html?imageid=6FE56375-C114-452F-95F3-08CEBDD3AD67&p=1760052&pn=1&searchId=4bd20e541ccedf238662732b8a1aa03a&searchtype=0

Positive Incitements

Although it may have seemed so, Austria-Hungary's military and wartime governments did not simply demand a never-ending program of sacrifice from the people. Departing from the Military High Command's early rejection of the need mobilize popular support for war, several ministries and eventually also military institutions in Austria and Hungary initiated relatively modest civilian and military propaganda projects. In thinking about these efforts, it is important to note Mark Cornwall's contention that, for much of the war, positive war propaganda in Austria-Hungary had no particular or considered aim but was rather a growing byproduct of diverse efforts to promote war bonds or charitable donations.[52] As they developed, however, these efforts sought to solidify diverse forms of

---

[52] On war propaganda in both Hungary and Austria generally, see the superb chapter by Mark Cornwall, "Das Ringen um die Moral des Hinterlandes," in *Die Habsburgermonarchie 1848–1918*, vol. 11/1/1, 393–436 (p. 415).

patriotism by encouraging people's active participation in ventures at the level of the neighborhood. In the first years of the war, public campaigns mobilized women and children to collect metal, rags, precious metals etc. for the war effort.[53] The popular "Ich gab Gold für Eisen" ["I gave gold for iron"] campaigns encouraged wives to trade their gold wedding rings for iron bands. Schools quickly adopted a wartime pedagogy that incorporated the war into children's games and toys. In Hungary, a teacher at an elementary school reported on this popular game:

> The boys divided into two camps consisting of a group of Hungarians and one of Russians. Hungarians attacked and fired away, and some of the Russians fell on the ground, while the others began to run away…Next, stretcher bearers gathered together the fallen; treating them as wounded, they carried them off and laid them on little benches. Then the doctor came to examine them. The light casualties were entrusted to the care of nurses, while the seriously wounded were taken to hospital, and the little girls stroked the patients, giving them drinks, laying them down, and dressing their wounds with the most amazing tenderness.[54]

Regular War Bond campaigns used a range of artistic imagery of war and home fronts to persuade middle-class Austrians and Hungarians to contribute their savings to fund the war effort. After victory was achieved the bond holders would receive their money along with a large interest payment. This, not surprisingly, was the preferred way of funding the war in Austria-Hungary and Germany, rather than raising new taxes. In the first years of the war, wooden statues of medieval knights standing with large shields were also erected in town squares in Austria, Hungary, and Bosnia-Herzegovina. Inhabitants, local associations, and school groups who donated to the widows' and orphans' funds could hammer an iron, silver, or gold nail into the statue's shield. These so-called *Wehrmann* statues proved a popular symbol for consumers, at least in the early years of the war, spawning related sales of postcard images, jewelry, and small models of the statues. His figure was even occasionally adapted to the specifics of local symbolism: in maritime Trieste and Pula/Pola, the statues depicted a sailor and a lighthouse.[55]

---

[53] Tara Zahra, *Kidnapped Souls: National Indifference and the Battle for Children in the Bohemian Lands, 1900–1948* (Ithaca, NY: Cornell University Press, 2008), 82–8; Healy, *Vienna*, 105; Morelon, *Streetscapes*, 97–103.

[54] Boldizsár Vörös, "Children's War Games and Toys in Hungary, 1914–1918," *Historical Studies on Central Europe* 3, no. 1 (July 31, 2023): 144–62.

[55] In 1914–15, some 350 such statues were erected, and in the first year they earned 358,000 crowns. After 1916, however, their popularity declined markedly. On the practice of the Wehrmann in all regions of the Empire, Kathryn E. Densford, "The Wehrmann in Eisen: Nailed Statues as Barometers of Habsburg Social Order during the First World War," *European Review of History: Revue Européenne d'histoire* 24, no. 2 (March 4, 2017): 305–24. On the *Wehrmann* in Prague, Morelon, *Streetscapes*, 89–90; on the Vienna *Wehrmann*, Healy, *Vienna*, 1–3, 24.

Figure 2.4 A 1917 war bond poster in Hungarian. To the left, a group of civilians throw gold coins onto the ground. To the right, a group of Austro-Hungarian infantrymen aim their rifles. The text reads "The homeland is defended by our civilians at home, [and] our soldiers at the front. Subscribe to the war loan at the Hungarian Discount and Exchange Bank."
Source: Imperial War Museum: https://www.iwm.org.uk/collections/item/object/2340

It took the military some time before it too reluctantly admitted the potential use of propaganda, popular mobilization, and a greater—if controlled—flow of information. At the start, unlike their counterparts in Germany who played up reports of even the smallest victories, the Austro-Hungarian military reported very little even about the few successes at the front. Civilian leaders like Prime Ministers Tisza and Stürgkh, along with the Joint Ministers of Foreign Affairs and Finance, argued that the press should be able to report news from the fronts, even in cases of failure. Stürgkh, for example, suggested profiling the details of individual accomplishments at the front, since "The purpose is to maintain the positive attitude of the people, and thus to maintain the positive mood."[56] Conrad, however, strongly opposed any effort to give the press access to the front.[57]

Nevertheless, over time, the military found it necessary to modify—only somewhat—its tight control of information and to consider the potential benefits

---

[56] Rauchensteiner, *The First World War*, 241.
[57] In his memoir, Conrad reluctantly admitted his mistake about the potential and effectiveness propaganda. Cornwall, "Das Ringen," 81.

to the war effort of a targeted and controlled propaganda campaign. As part of the effort to control the flow and content of information about the war, as well as to mobilize popular support for War Bonds, the military reluctantly gave greater opportunities to the Austrian War Ministry's War Press Bureau [*Kriegspressequartier*] and reporters.[58] In 1915, the Bureau, initiated in July 1914 as part of the 1909 emergency legislation in Austria, began to publish books and pamphlets about the war. These incorporated carefully chosen illustrations by well-known artists and photographers of well-known figures, of life at the different fronts. These artists and some well-known writers were gradually given greater access to the frontlines, or rather to the frontline regions, although they remained subjected to severe censorship. A War Archive established in Vienna collected the illustrations, censored them, and sent them on traveling exhibitions to the major cities of the Monarchy. The first such exhibition in October 1915 presented some 500 pictures by forty artists in Vienna's *Künstlerhaus*, before traveling to Budapest. In subsequent years, mobile exhibitions visited Graz, Zagreb, Salzburg, Innsbruck, and Prague. The purpose of these exhibits, in the words of the organizer at a Prague opening, was "to nurture an intimate feeling for everything that happens [far] away, this interaction between the hinterlands and the front."[59]

The civilian Austrian Ministry of the Interior, meanwhile, established a *Kriegshilfsbüro* that mass produced products from black-yellow cockades to postcards to commemorative coins, patriotic publications, and even ladies' perfume. Later more diverse forms of media and activities sought to bring the war home to civilians, to explain its significance, and to do so in more popular venues.[60] The Austrian War Ministry raised money through its *Kriegsfürsorgeamt* that, together with the Red Cross, produced and sold millions of postcards for circulation between the trenches and the home front.[61] In May 1916, a War Exhibition opened in Vienna's Prater Park. The Exhibition combined information (experience a trench!) with consumption possibilities and indeed entertainment. In the first two months alone, 500,000 people visited. A year later, the number had grown to a million.[62] Vienna was not the only city to exhibit aspects of the war. In Wenceslas square, Prague held its own exhibition organized by four Czech war relief associations and the recently disbanded *Sokol* that ran from late 1915 until mid-1916. Focused on aid efforts to the troops and their families, the exhibition of photographs, drawings, and two dioramas attracted 60,000 people, a full tenth of the Prague population. As Morelon's analysis of these efforts demonstrates, the dis-

---

[58] On the war press bureau and its efforts, Cornwall, "Das Ringen," 393–435.
[59] Cornwall, "Das Ringen," 417.   [60] See also examples in Morelon, *Streetscapes*.
[61] Morelon, *Streetscapes*, 16; Joachim Bürgschwentner, "War Relief, Patriotism, and Art: the State-Run Production of Picture Postcards in Austria 1914–1918," *Austrian Studies* 21 (2013): 99–120.
[62] Maureen Healy, "Exhibiting a War in Progress: Entertainment and Propaganda in Vienna, 1914–1918," *Austrian History Yearbook* 31 (2000): 57–85. The Vienna Exhibition was the largest of such war-related exhibitions in Europe.

banded *Sokol*, often treated as a subversive organization that supported the Czech Legions and the allied war efforts, in fact proved a staunch supporter of the war. In Prague, with the blessings of the High Command, two officers also organized the so-called "Prague Trench" in the fall of 1915. Here, for a minimal price, civilians could allegedly experience the war more effectively than from reading illustrated depictions in the newspapers. Like Vienna's War Exhibition, a visit to the Prague Trench proved highly popular excursion, and within two months 40,000 Praguers had made the trip.[63]

The Vienna Exhibition, as Maureen Healy's critical analysis tells us, "boasted forty display halls and theme rooms, several outdoor plazas, a theater, a cinema, two restaurants, two coffee houses, several souvenir stands, a naval pavilion, a panorama of a mountain battle site, and an overhead observation skydeck." Outside, visitors "could tour an 'authentic' recreation of a network of battle trenches." In Healy's reading, the Exhibition revealed "the complex mutually dependent relationship of propaganda and entertainment during World War I." This is particularly important when we consider that public entertainments from nightclubs to wine cellars—and any venues where women might be present—drew disapproving attitudes and often police intervention. All citizens were called to make extreme sacrifices during the war, and women who could not fight at the front should, could in Healy's words "perform a kind of second order sacrifice by foregoing amusement." And yet all of those same citizens craved some diversion to deal with the daily demands of sacrifice and tragedy they faced. The Exhibition, like the wartime cinema as we will see below, successfully squared this circle. As Healy argues, "Whereas many Viennese felt initially that war precluded entertainment, they gradually accepted the notion that war could provide entertainment."[64]

Film was another media that presented the war to ordinary citizens in all parts of the Monarchy, combining elements of propaganda and entertainment. Almost every city and town had some kind of cinema in 1914. Vienna and Budapest alone boasted over 150 in 1915, while smaller cities like Cluj/Kolozsvári, Zagreb, or Pressburg/Pozsony (Bratislava today) counted at least six. In 1915, communities in Hungary boasted 270 cinema houses.[65] Already in 1914, Maximilian von Hoen, who led the Press bureau, obtained permission from the High Command to establish ten filming sites in the war zones. Much wartime film initiative, however, also came from private film companies and directors who sought to use film less for explicitly propagandistic purposes than to keep up general morale on the home front.[66] As a source of entertainment, and perhaps also of information, both newsreels and dramas remained highly popular throughout the war. One of the most successful Austrian films, "The Dream of an Austrian Reservist," was

---

[63] Morelon, *Streetscapes*, 20.   [64] Healy, "Exhibiting a War," 58, 64, 66.

[65] Healy emphasizes, however, the wide range of establishments that counted as cinemas, from private basements to large glamorous movie houses. Healy, "Exhibiting a War," 66–7.

[66] On film generally, Cornwall, "Das Ringen," 418–23.

shown repeatedly by popular demand to sold out audiences in Prague. Wartime newsreels were also popular, such as the one that documented the recapture of Lemberg/Lwów/Lviv in 1915, which Prague's *Národní listy* called "the most interesting war film so far."[67] The newsreels could also provoke public outbursts from a cynical audience, however, as both Healy and Morelon document in Vienna (a case of *lesé majesté*) and in Prague (boos when Kaiser Wilhelm appeared).[68] Clearly, one could neither predict nor control public reactions to the films, especially those that dealt directly with war news.

Conclusion

Austria-Hungary's military regime had hoped to use war to impose its visions of a nonpolitical, unified, and disciplined public culture on a docile and patriotic society. In its place, however, the military unwittingly provoked a range of social mobilizations around rumor, food provision, work conditions, and general questions of sacrifice among Austria-Hungary's population. Instead of strict discipline, the military incited social chaos, disorganization, and impossible expectations for victory and for food. Young unaccompanied children running wild on the streets, schools closed, mothers working long hours in unregulated factories, severe food shortages, market demonstrations, invasions of the countryside by city folk, wildcat labor strikes, all of these were the unexpected byproducts of the various forms of suppression and mobilization undertaken by Austria-Hungary's wartime regime. Yet, in many smaller ways, the war also created opportunities to instigate significant social changes. Soon, as we will see in chapter 5, wartime crises led to the creation of new welfare schemes both by social reformers and the state governments. Civilians on the home front increasingly and aggressively equated their own suffering and sacrifice with those of the soldiers at the front and demanded tangible rewards for their sacrifice.

These various planned and unplanned mobilizations also created hopes among Austrians and Hungarians about what they might achieve politically for themselves at the end of the war. As we will see, many organizations, from labor unions to socialist parties to nationalist associations, all saw in these unprecedented mobilizations possibilities for achieving their own visionary goals in a postwar world. The fact that the contours of a postwar world remained imprecise and unclear rendered them ripe for utopian projections by all kinds of ideological groups and movements in the Empire.

The Great War and the Transformation of Habsburg Central Europe. Pieter M. Judson & Tara Zahra,
Oxford University Press. © Pieter M. Judson & Tara Zahra 2025. DOI: 10.1093/9780191842306.003.0003

---

[67] Morelon, *Streetscapes*, 85.   [68] Healy, "Exhibition," 69; Morelon, *Streetscapes*, 85.

3

The Fortunes of War

Occupation Regimes

Having confronted (with varying degrees of cooperation and success) the challenge of mobilizing the people and resources of their own vast Empire, Austrian military officials soon faced an even more vexing dilemma: how to rule over and mobilize the vast swathes of foreign people and territory that it occupied. Austria's wartime holdings eventually stretched all along its frontiers. They included Serbia and Montenegro from 1915 to 1918, parts of Albania and Romania from 1916 to 1918 (including Bucharest), and Southeastern Congress Poland from 1915 onward. Later, after the November 1917 victory at Caporetto/Kobarid, the Austro-Hungarian military also held former Italian territories until October 1918, and after the treaty of Brest-Litovsk in March 1918, parts of Ukraine. By 1918, the Empire had controlled (at least for a time) 400,000 square kilometers of new territory with 20 million additional inhabitants. Since the total population of the Empire in 1910 was just over 51,000,000, this amounted to a massive expansion of people and territory to govern, at a time when resources were already stretched thin.[1]

A short account of the larger military campaigns follows, to provide a chronology that places the different occupation regimes in the broader context of war. In the first year of the war, Austria-Hungary occupied almost no territory and suffered catastrophic losses. As we saw in chapter 2, Austria-Hungary originally sought to overwhelm Serbia swiftly using the bulk of its numerically vastly superior forces, and then to move a large contingent of the same troops from the Balkan front to the Russian front in Galicia and Bukovina. Those regions would, in the meantime, be held by a much smaller force because it was presumed that Russia would mobilize its full complement of force at a significantly slower pace than Austria-Hungary. Conrad, and even the Emperor King Francis Joseph, justified this presumption thanks in part to the catastrophe suffered by Russia only ten years earlier at the hands of Japan, and because of Russia's ultimate unwillingness to risk war in the Balkan crises of 1909 and 1912. When, however, it became clear that these predictions might be far off the mark, Conrad had been forced to shift most of his Balkan forces to Galicia to meet a Russian invasion that arrived

---

[1] For a comprehensive overview of Austro-Hungarian occupations, see Scheer, *Zwischen Front und Heimat*.

Figure 3.1 Ski troops cross a beam bridge.
Source: Imperial War Museum: https://www.iwm.org.uk/collections/item/object/205081847

much sooner than predicted. The Austro-Hungarians, not the Russians, had suffered considerable disarray in mobilizing first for one plan and then for another. This, along with the lack of an organized plan to defend Galicia, had produced the swift series of Russian victories and the Russian occupation of most of Galicia and Bukovina. It also had meant that Austria-Hungary failed to defeat Serbia.

By the end of 1914, despite a two-week occupation of Belgrade in December, the failed Austro-Hungarian Balkan campaign had suffered 28,276 dead, more than four times as many wounded, and 47,000 lost to cholera and dysentery epidemic.[2] The casualty numbers on the Galician front were even more catastrophic: over 160,000 dead, 368,000 wounded, and 210,000 missing or taken prisoner. In sum, over a million men in just four months of fighting. In Rauchensteiner's words, "Everyone was...to be merely part of what was described as a 'well-oiled' war machine. Now this machine had shuddered to a halt."[3]

---

[2] Rudolf Jeřábek, "Militärisches Potential und Kriegsverlauf 1918," in *Die Habsburgermonarchie 1848–1918*, vol. 11/1/1, 228. Rauchensteiner points out that commanders of the Imperial and Royal 4th corps, fighting in the East, recommended inoculation of their troops. The Commander of the 2nd army rejected the request because the aftereffects of inoculation might have incapacitated the troops for up to two weeks. Rauchensteiner, *The First World War*, 250.

[3] To these horrific numbers Rauchensteiner adds the unexpected psychological toll on the troops. "Officers and soldiers suffered the shock of realization in discovering that they were not simply entering a war against an enemy who would be beaten after just one battle. Not even the effect of the weaponry alone had become the key element of the war, but aspects that no one had considered before. There was the infernal noise generated by the guns and exploding shells. Thousands of people were shouting, the wounded were screaming, and injured and dying horses were bellowing. Soldiers who were brought to the front marched into this cacophony, aware that they could be hit at any

Figure 3.2 Austro-Hungarian troops in a trench.
Source: Imperial War Museum: https://www.iwm.org.uk/collections/item/object/205268360

Nevertheless, despite high casualties, Conrad stubbornly pursued offensive action in the Carpathian Mountains in the winter of 1915 that in turn produced more shocking defeats and more horrendous casualties, many from the severe winter weather conditions. By this point, as historian István Deák noted, because Austria-Hungary had already lost over 22,000 career and reservist officers who had to be replaced by hastily-trained "civilians in uniform," its forces had become, for all intents and purposes more a type of "militia" than a professional military force.[4]

In the spring of 1915, the Germans diverted several of their own divisions from the Western Front to Galicia to undertake what quickly became a successful mutual offensive against Russia in May 1915. By late June the combined attack had liberated Lemberg/Lviv/Lwów and most of Galicia, while taking a quarter of a million Russians prisoner. To the north, a German-led offensive progressed deep into Russian territory, capturing Warsaw, Kaunas/Kovno, Vilnius, and Brest Litovsk in August 1915.

---

moment and join the choir of sufferers. At some point, the noise of war died down, and there was quiet, which played no less a part in testing the psychological resilience of every individual to its limits." Rauchensteiner, *The First World War*, 280–1.

[4] István Deák, *Beyond Nationalism*, 192–5.

Figure 3.3 The recapture of Lviv/Lwów/Lemberg, June 22, 1915, with a double portrait of Germany's Kaiser Wilhelm II and Austria-Hungary's Emperor-King Franz Josef I.
Source: Herder-Institut: https://www.herder-institut.de/bildkatalog/index/pic?id=a13755110ea9f4be466e6122d3c75d9c

Bulgaria had meanwhile joined the war on the side of the Central Powers in September 1915, partly thanks to Germany's commitment to aiding Austria-Hungary's efforts against Serbia. The Bulgarians were only too happy to agree to German leadership of the Balkan campaign, clearly signaling Austria-Hungary's declining reputation in the region, since by itself, it had failed utterly in its efforts to defeat Serbia.[5] By mid-October of 1915, Austria-Hungary—again with German and Bulgarian aid—finally overcame Serbia, thanks to their massive military superiority that overwhelmed determined resistance in Belgrade.

So it was only at the end of 1915, and thanks to the assistance of its allies, that Austria-Hungary became a serious occupying power in the war. The Empire now occupied north and central Serbia and Montenegro, while Bulgaria took the southeast (Macedonia). Along with thousands of civilian refugees, the Serb army retreated across Albania during the winter of 1915–16. Upon reaching the Adriatic coast, those who had managed to survive disease, hunger, enemy attack, and generally horrendous conditions, were ferried to Greek islands and eventually to Salonica by Italian convoy in February 1916. In their wake came the Austro-Hungarian military that occupied most of Albania as a "friendly occupied state" [*bestetztes Freundesland*].

---

[5] Jerábek, "Militärisches Potential und Kriegsverlauf," 242–3.

Figure 3.4 Austro-Hungarian troops in front of a burning village in Poland, 1916.
Source: Herder-Institut: https://www.herder-institut.de/bildkatalog/index/pic?id=0b7e43eef0c29579317ccbaabfeb71f8

For Austria-Hungary, the relief of Galicia in 1915 and the long-awaited victory against Serbia had to be balanced against Italy's entrance into the war on the side of Britain, France, and Russia. Italy had technically been Austria-Hungary's ally (albeit only if Austria-Hungary were attacked), but in the secret Treaty of London of April 1915, the British and French had promised Italy massive territorial gains on the Adriatic at Austria-Hungary's expense (not to mention the Tyrol). And although there was in fact much popular ambivalence in Italy about joining the war, Italy declared war against Austria-Hungary on April 26, 1915. This new southwest front forced Austria-Hungary to send men from the east across the entire Monarchy to defend its largely mountainous borders with Italy. Here in the Alps and along the Karst region (today's Slovenia), a murderous campaign opened in which neither side gained a significant advantage until late 1917. Both sides suffered immense casualties as part of the challenge of fighting an alpine campaign. In June of the following year, however, the transfer of men to the Italian front created an opening in Galicia for a successful Russian counteroffensive under General Aleksei Brusilov, who reoccupied parts of Galicia in the summer of 1916.

During that same summer of 1916 the worst fears of many Hungarians, including Prime Minister Tisza, also came to pass. Romania, seeing the apparent successes of the Brusilov offensive, and negotiating its own territorial demands with the allies, decided to enter the war against Austria-Hungary.[6] Tisza had already

---

[6] As with Italy, the allies agreed (August 17, 1916) to give Romania Austro-Hungarian territories well beyond those where their fellow Romanian-speakers lived, including all of Transylvania, Bukovina, and parts of Banat. Galántai, *Hungary*, 186–7.

warned Francis Joseph and the joint cabinet repeatedly in July about the potential for a Romanian invasion, given the recent Russian victories. He demanded that troops be removed from the Russian front to add to the small force of 34,000 that defended Transylvania and suggested that Bulgaria should pressure the Romanians from the south. By the time 500,000 Romanian troops invaded Transylvania on August 27, Hungary had prepared for this contingency by evacuating civilian industries and cities in the path of the Romanian invasion.

Transylvania was not only a valuable industrial center, it was also a linguistically mixed region that was intensely contested by Hungarian and Romanian nationalists, and this gave it outsized symbolic importance to both sides.[7] The successful invasion contributed to the eventual downfall of Tisza, as well as that of Erich von Falkenhayn, head of the German General Staff. In the short time it held on to Transylvanian territory, the Romanian government indicated that it had big plans for the Romanization of the region. This included everything from immediately changing street and shop signs into Romanian, to liquidating the assets of Hungarian firms to preparations for a land reform to benefit Romanian speaking peasants at the expense of Hungarian speaking landowners.[8]

In September 1916, Germany sent more troops to reinforce all three Austro-Hungarian fronts, the Italian, Romanian, and Russian, and in each case the combined forces successfully drove back the enemies' advances. Invading from Bulgaria to the south, the Germans swiftly occupied most of Romania and its capital Bucharest by the end of 1916. Nevertheless, Romania's brief occupation of Hungary's largest coal reserves in the Jiu valley of Transylvania had badly affected Austro-Hungarian transport and heating.[9]

Even as Germany and Austria-Hungary divided up occupied Romanian territory—with Germany acquiring the greater share—they immediately began to compete with one another for influence and oil. Both parties had ambitious plans for Imperial expansion into Europe's east. As Rigó points out, Hungarian businessmen often complained that Germany was marginalizing their legitimate interests by preventing them from claiming compensation for damages during the brief Romanian occupation, and even denying them visa applications when they sought to reclaim their assets in occupied Romania.[10]

On the whole, Austria-Hungary had only just managed to survive another severe military threat to its very existence, but in consequence, the Monarchy was forced to confirm openly and in practice that Germany held the upper hand within the alliance. In September, before invading Romania, Germany had forced a takeover of the unified command of the Central Powers, now with the agreement of its Austro-Hungarian, Bulgarian, and Turkish allies.

---

[7] See Holly Case, *Between States: The Transylvanian Question and the European Idea during World War II* (Stanford: Stanford University Press, 2009).
[8] Rigó, *Capitalism in Chaos*, 113–16.   [9] Rigó, *Capitalism in Chaos*, 113.
[10] Rigó, *Capitalism in Chaos*, 116–17.

Up until this point, Conrad and other military leaders had asserted their independence from or equality to the Germans in terms of strategic planning and command. This new agreement in September, however, articulated openly what was already the case in practice. It stated that "his majesty the Emperor of Germany takes over the supreme command of all operations in which the Central Powers and their allies engage."[11] Francis Joseph, who had spent a lifetime jealously guarding his control of the military, agreed that, given Austria-Hungary's weaknesses, Germany should have the upper hand in the relationship. It was also at this key moment, as we will see later on, that Germany gained the upper hand in determining common foreign policy issues such as the future location and character of an independent Poland. Thus, Germany cemented its growing economic dominance within the alliance through the imposition of the *Mitteleuropa* concept that placed it at the center of a vast new economic empire that included its allies, their territories, and the occupied territories. By 1917, Austria-Hungary had at least stabilized its territorial position. Its troops occupied Montenegro, most of Serbia and Albania, as well as significant parts of Russian Poland. By the end of 1917, with its crucial victory against the Italians at Caporetto/Kobarid, it would obtain a slice of Italy as well.

The conquest, occupation, and expropriation of foreign lands was nothing new in the First World War. During this war, Europe's great powers drew on techniques, like hostage-taking, internment, and forced labor, that had already been tested out in colonial contexts and the Balkan Wars. European observers nonetheless often expressed shock to see these tactics applied to white European populations. All warring powers accused their enemies of violating fundamental laws of war and "civilization," in what became a propaganda war that played out alongside the actual war.

As the Habsburg Empire created its own occupation regimes in Russian Poland, Serbia, Montenegro, Albania, and Romania, it faced some serious issues. How to incorporate occupied territories and populations into the Empire's already complex structure of political checks and balances? How to extract resources effectively for the war effort without inciting revolt? How to compete for influence with other potential occupiers and allies, especially Germany? As the military government negotiated these challenges, it was hampered by ongoing conflicts with the Austrian bureaucracy, between Austria and Hungary, and between Austria and its allies.

Military authorities viewed occupied territories primarily as treasure chests: a source of resources that could make the difference between defeat and victory. But they also served as laboratories for social and political experimentation, as authorities struggled to determine how best to extract resources, competed over

---

[11] Galántai, *Hungary*, 188–9.

the future of contested territories, and tried to develop systems of rule that they could usefully apply to a future postwar era in Austria and Hungary. In this regard the occupation regimes of all the First World War combatant states were often shaped by fantasies about the war's final settlement, as each European power hoped to emerge from war richer in land, resources, and people. While these were relatively benign occupations compared to those of the Second World War, they nevertheless left profound marks on both the material and political culture of Central Europe and on the psyches and bodies of the civilian populations that survived them.

In each occupied territory, the High Command (*AOK*) held absolute authority, with military governors assigned to rule occupied Poland, Serbia, and Montenegro and command corps taking charge in smaller territories like Albania. But if the militarization of government and society was ubiquitous, this did not translate into uniform policies or experiences. The fate of occupied populations varied greatly according to international calculations, available resources, and the army's own view of the population's loyalty. Occupations also differed based on the quirks of individual military commanders, who interpreted and enforced military laws in diverse ways, as Tamara Scheer has demonstrated. These differences could often determine matters of life and death: some local commanders in Serbia made frequent use of the death penalty for minor infractions, for example, while others did not, even with the same laws on the books.[12]

The administration of occupied territories was also complicated on the ground by severe conflicts over the basic goals of these regimes.[13] Military leaders generally wanted to pacify the local population and maximally exploit the territory's resources for the army's own use. As in Austria-Hungary itself, they were allergic to any kind of politics. They were also often at odds with Austrian bureaucrats, whose own priorities included provisioning civilians at home and winning the loyalties of local populations. Until late 1917, the military's priorities generally trumped all others, but ultimately, local military rulers often depended more than they liked on the expertise and experience of civilian administrators and judges. Moreover, after the death of Francis Joseph and with the reforms of his successor Charles (chapter 6), and as the Empire began to crumble under the weight of

---

[12] Tamara Scheer, "Mikrokosmos und Persönlichkeitsprinzip: Österreich-Ungarns Besatzungsregime in Serbien und Montenegro im Ersten Weltkrieg (1915–1918)," in *Die Mittelmächte und der Erste Weltkrieg*, ed. Hans Hubertus Mack and M. Christian Ortner (Vienna: Verlag Militaria, 2016), 279–91. This was equally true of the Western Front. See Alex Dowdall, *Communities under Fire: Urban Life at the Western Front, 1914–1918* (Oxford: Oxford University Press, 2020).

[13] For a general overview and background on each occupation, see Watson, *Ring of Steel*; Jonathan Gumz, *Habsburg Serbia*; Ristović, "Occupation"; Blumi, "Albania"; Stephan Lehnstaedt, "Occupation During and After the War (East Central Europe)," *1914–1918, Online International Encyclopedia of the First World War*, 2014, https://doi.org/10.15463/IE1418.10395.

provisioning crises and social unrest in late 1917, civilian leaders regained the upper hand.[14]

Austrian and Hungarian officials were meanwhile at war with one another as they plotted the fate of newly acquired territories. While everyone hoped that the territories would enrich the Habsburg lands, there was less agreement about the precise nature of their attachment to the Empire. Directly annexing Serbia or Congress Poland would have vastly expanded the Empire's Slavic population, threatening to upset the fragile Dualist compromise between Austria and Hungary. Many Hungarian leaders feared that increasing the number of Poles or South Slavs might buttress calls for a trialist or federalist reorganization of the Empire, decreasing Hungary's relative standing.[15]

Finally, throughout the war Austria-Hungary found itself in constant competition with, and increasingly subordinate to and dependent on, its own German ally. The German Empire had its own ambitious goals to enhance its power and prestige through vast territorial gains in the East. Particularly in Congress Poland and Romania, the two Central European empires competed for influence and for the loyalty of local elites. This competition could work to the advantage of locals, protecting them from the worst abuses of occupation regimes.[16]

When Austro-Hungarian troops marched into foreign territory, they came armed with blueprints shaped by the Empire's earlier colonial-style missions. In October 1915, for example, one Austro-Hungarian officer, Lothar Ritter von Pachmann, claimed that the Austro-Hungarian administration in Bosnia, which began in 1878, had actually represented "the first large European military occupation." From this experience, he insisted, Imperial authorities had learned that foreign civilians in occupied territories had both "rights and duties." These included the right to earn a living, to property, and to exercise their religion, along with the "duty" to obey military orders and to accept Austrian currency and exchange rates.[17]

Pachmann's treatise reflected a broader effort to represent Austria-Hungary as a civilized and civilizing occupier, far more benevolent than its German counterpart. The poet and dramatist Hugo von Hofmannsthal, who spent the war writing

---

[14] On tensions between the military and bureaucracy, see especially Gumz, *Habsburg Serbia*; Deak and Gumz, "How to Break a State."

[15] Galántai, *Hungary*, 150–63.

[16] For a comparison of German and Austrian occupations in Poland, see Joachim Bürgschwentner et al., eds., "Two Kinds of Occupation? German and Austro-Hungarian Economic Policy in Congress Poland, 1915–1918," in *Other Fronts, Other Wars? First World War Studies on the Eve of the Centennial* (Leiden: Brill, 2014), 197–217; on German occupation in Poland, see Jesse Kauffman, *Elusive Alliance: The German Occupation of Poland in World War I* (Cambridge, MA: Harvard University Press, 2015); Vejas Liulevicius, *War Land on the Eastern Front: Culture, National Identity, and German Occupation in World War I* (Cambridge: Cambridge University Press, 2005).

[17] Oberleutnant Lothar Ritter von Pachmann bei den Windischgratz-Dragonern, "Rechte und Pflichten eines fremden Staatsangehörigen in besetzten Gebieten," *Österreichische Zeitschrift für Verwaltung* 28 (October 1915): 173–4.

propaganda for Austria-Hungary, reinforced this idea of fundamental differences between Austria and Germany in a 1915 essay in the *Neue Freie Presse*.

> There's something else, a certain generosity of heart and that which can scarcely be defined, that which weighs so heavily in the coexistence of nations: tact. It is given to us, more than to the Germans, to be able to dwell with strangers: as neighbors, as masters, as temporary administrators, as friends...among peasants, nobles, townsmen, industrialists, and Jews, the organs of our administration, our officers and soldiers, move with effortless tact.[18]

Other Habsburg officials made the same point by comparing Austria's wartime occupations with earlier "civilizing" missions. Hugo Kerchnawe, Chief of the General Staff of the Military Government in Serbia from July 1916 to November 1918 (and the first historian of the occupations), later claimed that from the very beginning of the war, "military government" had a higher purpose in Austria. He compared the goals and achievements of the military occupation in Serbia to those of eighteenth-century colonists in Austrian Galicia, who had, he claimed, "transformed land composed of completely wild, infertile steppes, marshes, and swamps into rich and fertile land, the granary of Central Europe."[19]

Of course, not everyone agreed that the Austrian occupation was effortlessly tactful. Traveling through Galicia in 1915, writer Stefan Zweig, who also occasionally wrote war propaganda, expressed a rather different opinion. Writing about the state of hospital trains there, he observed "how little they resembled the well-lit, white, carefully cleaned ambulance trains in which the archduchesses and the fashionable ladies of Viennese society had their pictures taken as nurses at the beginning of the war!"[20]

Just as in earlier colonial missions, Austria-Hungary legitimated its occupations by evoking its multinational character, its experience governing diverse populations. And in fact, the Habsburg military did sometimes enjoy a better reputation among civilians than did rival armies (including those of Russia and Germany in Congress Poland and Romania, Italy in Albania, and Bulgaria in Serbia). In principle, the military extended Austro-Hungarian laws guaranteeing equal rights to all national and confessional groups in all the territories it occupied. In some cases, minority groups acquired new rights for the first time. In Poland, for example, the Austro-Hungarian military government overturned

---

[18] Hugo von Hofmannsthal, "Unsere Militärverwaltung in Polen," *Neue Freie Presse*, August 8, 1915, quoted in Larry Wolff, *The Shadow of the Empress: Fairy-Tale Opera and the End of the Habsburg Monarchy* (Stanford: Stanford University Press, 2023), 151–2.
[19] Hugo Kerchnawe, *Die Militärverwaltung in den von den österreich-ungarischen Truppen besetzen Gebieten* (Vienna: Hölder Pichler Tempsky, 1928), 2.
[20] Stefan Zweig, *The World of Yesterday* (1943; repr., Lincoln: University of Nebraska Press, 1964), 247–9, quoted in Wolff, *The Shadow of the Empress*, 152.

Russian laws that excluded Jews from public offices as well as the *numerus clausus* in schools and universities that limited the possibility of Jews to attend those institutions. Many children in Poland received primary school instruction in their native language for the first time. In Montenegro, the military supported the construction of churches and mosques for Catholic and Muslim inhabitants, on the grounds that these two groups had previously been disadvantaged by the Orthodox regime. Even in Serbia, local governments and courts could choose their languages of operation. In some cases, this respect for religious beliefs even provoked accusations of unfair privileges. In Albania, the military refrained from housing troops in Muslim homes or conscripting Muslim women into labor battalions out of respect for religious traditions, a dispensation that generated resentment among some non-Muslims.[21]

On the other hand, respect for national and minority rights depended heavily on political calculations, such as whether the army actually sought the favor of locals. And goodwill was easy to squander when the primary goal was to extract resources and impose military order. This was true on the home front as well, where as we have seen, the militarization of society resulted in the erosion of the rule of law, including of laws that had formerly protected linguistic and national rights.

Austria-Hungary enjoyed another significant advantage thanks to its multinational army. Unlike their German counterparts, most of the military governors and many personnel in occupied territories could actually speak local languages and had some knowledge of the land and culture. General Consul Felix Sobotka, stationed in Romania, boasted that the "entire administration is bringing positive results, in particular the Austro-Hungarian officers, civil servants, and soldiers were often familiar with the land and the language, most come from neighboring regions, and could quickly orient themselves to the basic conditions." Of course, familiarity could just as well breed distrust and paranoia. Military leaders feared that Polish-speaking or Romanian-speaking officers stationed in occupied Poland or Romania might have a bit too much sympathy for the occupied population, or even be disloyal to the Empire's interests.[22] And as the war dragged on, it became more and more difficult to find soldiers who spoke local languages, compromising the efficiency and reputation of occupation regimes.[23]

Even on Austrian territory, moreover, communication between locals and soldiers was sometimes challenging. The writer Manès Sperber was 10 years old in 1915 when his hometown of Zablotow in Eastern Galicia was repeatedly invaded and liberated by Russian and Austro-Hungarian troops. He recalled years later

---

[21] Scheer, *Zwischen Front und Heimat*, 189–95.
[22] Scheer, *Zwischen Front und Heimat*, 74–85, quotation, 80.
[23] Jonathan E. Gumz, *The Resurrection and Collapse of Empire in Habsburg Serbia, 1914–1918* (Cambridge: Cambridge University Press, 2009), 94.

that Habsburg troops in retreat from the front sometimes set up camp in the shtetl for days or weeks.

> The babel of tongues in the Austro-Hungarian army made communicating with the soldiers difficult, sometimes dangerous. The biggest problem was with the Hungarians, whose language none of us understood...A miserable barter flourished: the soldiers had no money, so they paid with their food rations, pieces of their uniforms, shoes, tobacco and the like. In dark back streets, they met Jewish and Christian girls, as well as young war widows, buying their favors with food or a few crowns. Everything was done standing...The shtetl, usually so strict, refused to condemn them; people looked the other way.[24]

Neither Austria-Hungary's claim to have "liberated" Poland from the yoke of Russian oppression, nor its insistence that it was extending a "civilizing mission" to occupied lands such as Albania or Serbia ultimately protected civilians from internment, severe military justice, plunder, forced labor, rape, or hunger.

The Austrian occupation of Serbia began in a storm of violence and repression that lasted several years. The assassination of Francis Ferdinand in Sarajevo had confirmed the suspicions of Austro-Hungarian military leaders that Serbs were the bitter enemies of Austria-Hungary. The military marched into Serbia convinced that severe measures would be required to stave off rebellion. But as Jonathan Gumz has argued, this violence was not an artifact of a new mode of "Total War" that indiscriminately targeted civilians. Rather, the Austrian High Command was engaged in a headstrong struggle to defend a nineteenth-century principles of warfare, to stave off what they believed to be the corrosive effects of mass politics, particularly nationalist politics.[25]

Gumz asserts that the military High Command was particularly committed to maintaining a strict and hierarchical division between soldiers and civilians—if needed by force. Terrorist guerillas, called *Komitadjis*, had allegedly infected the population with anti-state propaganda, blurring traditional lines between civilians and combatants. Not all Serb soldiers had uniforms. In the eyes of the Austro-Hungarian High Command, these guerillas violated the fundamental laws of warfare. In a world in which women and children might be agents of surprise attacks, in which Serbs were rumored to poison water wells or slice off the ears and noses and penises of captured soldiers, in which combatants might dress as civilians, any Serb had to be considered a potential combatant.

The army thereby justified violence against Serbian civilians as a form of self-defense. During the invasion of Serbia, the Austro-Hungarian military took thousands of hostages, executed suspected guerillas or spies without trial, and

---

[24] Manès Sperber, *God's Water Carriers* (New York: Holmes & Meier, 1987), 92.
[25] Gumz, *Habsburg Serbia*, 21–62, 58 for numbers.

ultimately killed around 3500 civilians in three short weeks in August 1914, many in mass shootings. This treatment of civilians was similar to the treatment of native populations in in European colonies, where civilians were interned in concentration camps in the name of defense against guerilla warfare.[26]

As with allied accusations against its German enemy on the Western Front, the Austrian military's actions in Serbia became fodder for an international propaganda battle over war atrocities.[27] Rudolph Archibald Reiss, a Swiss German forensic scientist and the founder of the Institute for Forensic Science at the University of Lausanne, was well known before the war for his use of photography in criminal forensics. Even before the Austro-Hungarian military set up its occupation regime in Serbia, the Serbian government commissioned him to document atrocities committed by the former in its early—and failed—efforts to conquer that country. In 1914 he traveled through Serbia to interview both Habsburg and Serb soldiers as well as local Serbs. Reiss used criminal forensic techniques he had developed to investigate robberies and murders to produce his 1916 *Report upon the atrocities committed by the Austro-Hungarian during the first invasion of Serbia*. The 192-page exposé, published in English, included first-person testimonies as well as graphic atrocity photos, including photographs of dead and mutilated bodies. In a preface, Voyslav M. Yovanovitch of the Serbian War Press Bureau declared that the evidence assembled by a "distinguished man of science (who is furthermore a neutral)" decisively proved that the "charming Austrian people and the proud and gallant Magyar race' have had the doubtful honor of surpassing, if possible, their Prussian friends in bestiality."[28]

Reiss was hardly neutral in his loyalties. In 1915 he joined the Serbian army and fought with Serb troops until the war's bitter end. After the armistice, Reiss remained in Yugoslavia and even represented Serbia at the Paris Peace Conference. When he died, his body was buried in the Topčider cemetery and his heart on the Kajmakčalan hill, the site of a September 1916 battle between Serbian and Bulgarian troops in which Serbs had been victorious.[29] Austria-Hungary published a rebuttal to Reiss's report in English and French, aimed squarely at an

---

[26] On colonial concentration camps, see Jonathan Hyslop, "The Invention of the Concentration Camp: Cuba, South Africa, and the Philippines," *Southern Africa Historical Journal* 63 (2011), 251–76.

[27] On the German occupation on the Western Front, see Alex Dowdall, *Communities Under Fire: Urban Life at the Western Front* (Oxford: Oxford University Press, 2020). On war atrocities during the First World War more broadly, see John Horne and Alan Kramer, *German Atrocities, 1914: A History of Denial* (New Haven: Yale University Press, 2001); Isabel V. Hull, *A Scrap of Paper: Breaking and Making International Law During the Great War* (Ithaca: Cornell University Press, 2013).

[28] Rudolph Archibald Reiss, *Report Upon the Atrocities Committed by the Austro-Hungarian Army During the First Invasion of Serbia*, trans. F.S. Copeland (London: Simpkin, Marchall, Hamilton, Kent & Co, 1916), preface.

[29] Nicolas Quinche, "Reiss et la Serbie: des scènes de crime aux champs de bataille, l'enquête continue," in *Le théâtre du crime: Rodolphe A. Reiss (1875–1929)* (Lausanne: Presses polytechniques et universitaires romandes, 2009), 289–306; Matteo Scianna, "Reporting Atrocities: Archibald Reiss in Serbia, 1914–1918," *The Journal of Slavic Military Studies* 25, no. 4 (2012): 596–617.

international public (*The Lies about Austro-Hungarian Warfare in Servia*). The reply insisted that Reiss had manipulated his photographs and that the mutilated bodies he depicted had in fact been ravaged by wild boars and not Austrian soldiers. However, many examples of atrocities cited by Reiss were also corroborated by internal Austrian sources.[30]

This propaganda battle over war crimes had a profound legacy. It transformed the nature in which such crimes were investigated, documented, and politicized. Reiss's report, as well as the propaganda surrounding German war atrocities in Northern France and Belgium, reflected the crystallization of an understanding of a wartime atrocity as a violent crime committed against civilians, and the strategic publicization of such atrocities to win an international battle for public opinion. As such it constituted a critical moment in the history of ideas about human rights.[31]

Repression in Serbia hardly ended with the establishment of a formal military government in January 1916. It now became the instrument of coercive social policy designed to depoliticize and manage the Serb population. Austro-Hungarian authorities imagined that at the end of the war, Serbia would become a part of the Dual Monarchy, and began to prepare for that future by attempting to repress Serb nationalism. Plans were made to erect a giant statue of Franz-Joseph on a Montenegrin mountain peak. The remains of the former Montenegrin ruler Petar II Petrović Njegoš were even moved to make space for the monument to the emperor on Mount Lovćen.

Teachers were meanwhile purged from schools and replaced with soldiers, who were assigned to instill loyalty in young Serbs. The Cyrillic alphabet was banned. As in Galicia or southern Hungary with Austrian Ruthenes or Hungarian Serbs, the army relied on spies and flimsy denunciations to identify potential subversives. By the end of 1916, the military had interned at least 70,000 Serbian civilians, of whom 5,000 died in internment.[32]

For individuals—including Habsburg citizens—whom Austria-Hungary deemed unfriendly to the militarized Habsburg state, deportation and internment elsewhere in the Monarchy was another new reality. The first targets of these policies had been Ukrainian- (Ruthene-) speaking citizens in Galicia who were suspected, like Serbs, of being sympathetic to the Russians. From the outset the military treated them with genocidal brutality. Many were not even deported but simply executed on the spot. "We fight on our own territory as in hostile land," Chief of Staff Conrad von Hötzendorf lamented. "Everywhere Ruthenes are being executed under martial law." Up to 30,000 Galician Ruthenes—citizens

---

[30] Gumz, *Habsburg Serbia*, 54–8.
[31] On the use of forensics in human rights investigations, see Peggy O'Donnell, "Bones of Contention: Forensic Science and Human Rights Violations, from the Katyn Forest to The Hague," (PhD diss., University of California, Berkeley, 2016).
[32] Gumz, *Habsburg Serbia*, 98.

of the Empire—were probably executed without trial thanks to the militarization of civilian justice in that war zone.[33]

In September 1914, the first internment camp for allegedly disloyal Ruthenes was created near Graz. By November more than 7,000 Ruthenes were interned there. Sanitary conditions were atrocious, and many died of disease, malnutrition, or exposure in the months that followed. Officials in the Interior Ministry conceded that there was no legal basis for these internments, but insisted nonetheless, "these measures must be taken from a national security and warfare point of view, even though the applicable laws for these dispositions have no legal basis."[34] Once Italy declared war against Austria-Hungary in May 1915, Italian-speakers were accorded similar treatment. Sometimes they were interned simply because they belonged to Italian associations, or because they had associated with deserters or Italian nationalists. Others claimed to have no idea at all why they had been interned. Jacob Linossi, who was born in Italy but had lived in Salzburg for thirty years, where he had the right to domicile, appealed to the mayor of Salzburg for his release. "I am in every respect innocent, the father of three German-educated children and a good Austrian patriot," he protested. Angela Polso, interned in St. Pölten, was simply confused. "I cannot imagine on what grounds I am interned here. I, who has always been a good Austrian, loyal to my state, and an enemy of the neighboring Kingdom!" And Giuseppina Gottardi, interned in Linz, wrote to her family at home that, "because of a mistake we are together with Italian internees."[35] Italian-speaking Austrians living in territories that were occupied by the Italian army did not fare much better, as they were just as mistrusted by Italian authorities. After occupying a border town, one Italian general warned local Austrian Italian-speakers, "My soldiers are convinced that they are conducting a war of liberation, not occupation and woe betide you, if they learn that you are not content to be liberated from Austria."[36]

Internment was not the worst fate of such deportees, however. As part of the emergency decrees, the AOK also extended military law to civilians in militarized zones. They were now subject to the death penalty for thirty-four offenses, including robbery or disloyal speech. Residents of Serbia (along with citizens of many Austrian crownlands and other occupied "enemy territories") were also subject to summary justice (*Standesrecht*). This meant that the accused potentially faced summary judgments and death sentences without any possibility for appeal (at the discretion of local commanders).[37]

---

[33] Cited in Watson, *Ring of Steel*, 154.
[34] Alessandro Livio, "The Wartime Treatment," 190; Watson, *Ring of Steel*, 154–5.
[35] Bericht, Italienische Zensurgruppe, July 7, 1915, KA, AOK, GZNB, Karton 3728. See also Alessandro Livio, "The Wartime Treatment," 185–99. Frizzera, *Cittadini dimezzati*.
[36] Quoted in Laurence Cole, *Military Culture and Popular Patriotism in Late Imperial Austria* (Oxford: Oxford University Press, 2014), 320.
[37] On mass internment and military justice, see Gumz, *Habsburg Serbia*, chaps. 2–3; On forced labor, see Hugo Kerchnawe, "Die k.u.k. Militärverwaltung in Serbien," in *Die Militärverwaltung in*

All these measures undermined the legitimacy of the Empire, but the goal of the High Command was never really to achieve popular legitimacy. It was to impose its own vision of Imperial society. In this vision, both Austrians and occupied peoples would become docile, depoliticized, and denationalized subjects, and both society and the bureaucracy would defer to the military.[38] Ironically, in the name of safeguarding the distinction between civilians and combatants, the Austro-Hungarian military flagrantly violated that very distinction. Even if it was not the architect of a policy of "Total War," Austria-Hungary's military helped transform civilian populations into targets and victims of wartime violence.

The occupation in Congress Poland was milder than that which the regime imposed on Serbia but still plagued by conflicts over strategy and resources. The Central Powers and Russia pushed each other back and forth across the Eastern Front throughout the summer of 1914, but by mid-1915 Austria-Hungary and Germany had regained lost territory, swept into Russia, and occupied Congress Poland. Germany seized control of 62,000 sq km and a population of 6 million people, while Austria-Hungary occupied the more agrarian southeast, including the cities of Radom, Kielce, and Lublin. The AOK based its occupation of Poland in Kielce in August 1915 and then moved to Lublin after October of that year.[39]

Unlike Serbs, the military officially defined Polish civilians as "liberated" people rather than subversive enemies. This was not because they were beyond suspicion, but because Austria-Hungary was competing with Germany for future control of Congress Poland. To win over the population, both regimes granted more civil rights than had existed under Russian rule and promised to invest in roads, railways, and schools. In September 1915, the first Habsburg Governor General of the occupied Polish territory, Erich Baron Diller, declared in Kielce that if the Central Powers won the war, "You and your homeland will enter a new era of free national development and progress on all sides."[40]

Both Austria-Hungary and Germany represented their regimes as benevolent missions to liberate Russian subjects from autocracy. Austria-Hungary again had an edge in this regard, since Polish, Ruthene, and Jewish nationalist movements had flourished for decades under Habsburg rule in Austrian Galicia, while they were severely repressed in both Prussia and Russia. An Austrian official traveling through Austrian-occupied Poland in June 1915 declared that the occupation was "true to the principle that we must win the hearts of the Polish population through good treatment and respect of their national claims and sensitivities in daily life, but not through inappropriate promises and introduction of

---

den von den österreichisch-ungarischen Truppen besetzten Gebieten, ed. Hugo Kerchnawe (Vienna: Hölder-Pichler-Tempsky A.G., 1928), 101.

[38] See Gumz, Habsburg Serbia, 10–21 for a concise articulation of this argument.
[39] Scheer, Zwischen Front und Heimat, 19–22; Lehnstaedt, "Two Kinds of Occupation?" 197–208.
[40] Aufruf des Generalgouverneurs Freiherrn v. Diller, Kielce, September 1915, Carton 918, Liasse Krieg 11a, PA I, MdA, HHstA.

self-government." He compared the behavior of Austrian troops positively to that of German soldiers, who allegedly plundered castles, stripped private apartments of furniture, and sent all the loot back to Germany.[41]

On the other hand, Austria also had an easier task than Germany, since its zone of occupation was mostly rural, and peasants could feed themselves. Germany faced the unenviable task of feeding large cities like Warsaw and Łódź. The occupation was compromised on both sides, however, by a lack of clarity about its end goals. Germany and Austria never came to an agreement about how to settle the so-called "Polish question" in the event of victory. Powerful constituencies in both states feared that direct annexation would upset their ethnic balance sheets. If Poland became an Austrian crownland, Polish nationalists would lobby for equal status with Hungary, which Hungary opposed. If Congress Poland were annexed to the German Reich, it would undermine efforts to "Germanize" Prussia. Alternatively, the Central Powers could attempt to transform Poland into a nominally independent state under German and/or Austrian influence, but what would be the fate of the large Polish-speaking populations in Galicia and Prussia?[42] Late in the war Austria-Hungary proposed creating a Polish Kingdom under a Habsburg ruler that would enjoy either close relations with or a kind of federal status within the Austrian half of the dual Monarchy. This proposal too created more domestic political conflict because, as we will see, the government also sought to establish a Ukrainian federal unit within the Monarchy. Both nationalist groups claimed Eastern Galicia and the city of L'viv/Lwów/Lemberg for their future federal or independent units.

Complications on the ground, meanwhile, undermined Austria's reputation as a liberator, beginning with the army's rapacious approach to Polish resources. As in Serbia, conflicts fired up between bureaucrats in Vienna and military authorities over the use of these resources. In response to complaints about the total destruction of Polish forests, for example, the AOK replied that concerns about the "aesthetics of forests" seemed "curious" in the "midst of an ongoing bloody and sacrifice-laden war for survival." The Austro-Hungarian Foreign Ministry frequently urged the AOK to increase provisions for the native population in the occupied territories. But the AOK refused, insisting, "All other considerations must be secondary to the needs of the war effort."[43] So the AOK requisitioned the Polish harvest of 1915, and seized control of food distribution. In response, some peasants committed acts of sabotage, destroying their crops. The results were predictable. As early as March 1915, a Professor of Agriculture from the Jagellonian University in Cracow, Kasimir von Rogozski, traveled through the Austrian occu-

---

[41] Reise nach Miechów, Dabrowa, und Jasna Góra, June 23, 1915, Carton 918, Liasse Krieg 11a, PA I, MdA, HHstA.
[42] Lehnstaedt, "Two Kinds of Occupation?," 199–203.
[43] Wirtschaftliche Ausbeutung des Okkupationsgebietes, January 1, 1916, Carton 919, Liasse Krieg, PA I, MdA, HHstA.

pation zone. In Olkusz, he encountered "large crowds of wandering people carrying sacks on their shoulders...All of these people were driven by hunger to set out in the world in search of bread and potatoes, in spite of their fear of the prohibition against crossing the borders of the district."[44]

Policies of expropriation and exploitation extended to all the occupied provinces, right down to bedding and furniture. In Italy after Caporetto, occupied territories included the provinces of Udine and Belluno, as well as parts of Venezia, Treviso, and Vicenza, with a peacetime population of around 1 million people. Several hundred thousand Italians, including most industrialists, doctors, engineers, shopkeepers, and civil servants, fled the occupied territory before the Austro-Hungarians arrived. Habsburg troops wasted no time looting empty apartments and homes, even seizing cars and bicycles for the army's use.[45]

The "benevolent" Habsburg administration won even fewer hearts or minds when it introduced conscription for forced labor. In Serbia, workers were dragged out of cafes and off the streets to be conscripted into labor battalions. In occupied Poland, the AOK mobilized 81,000 workers by the end of 1915. While many unemployed Poles volunteered, many others panicked and fled into the woods. The military responded with repressive and counterproductive tactics. In Lublin on New Year's Day 1916, military authorities attempted to round up laborers from churches, synagogues, theaters, and streets. If a man was not found at home, soldiers confiscated his cow or bedding. Rumors circulated that the Austrian rulers had sold the peasants back into serfdom; many feared that they would be conscripted into the military and sent to the Italian front. Wives of conscripted laborers rioted, and in Iłża, there was a bloody confrontation between peasants and Austrian soldiers. A military decree on January 2, 1916 guaranteed that no one would be drafted into the military and that workers would remain close to home, but labor conscription remained unpopular. By July 1916, the AOK had given up on the practice.[46]

Albania, like Poland, was considered a "friendly occupied territory" when it was occupied in 1916. Once again, Austro-Hungarian authorities claimed to be liberators, this time from Serbian and Italian domination. The AOK retained local administrators, and promised national autonomy, Albanian schools, economic development, and protection. This was partly a matter of necessity,

---

[44] Kasimir Ritter von Rogozski, Professor der Acker und Pflanzenbaulehre an der kk Jaglllonischen Universität in Krakau, Bericht über die wirtschaftliche Lage der 5 südlichen Kreise Polens, Reise, March 19–26, 1915, Carton 918, Liasse Krieg 11a, PA I, MdA, HHstA.

[45] Hermann Leidl, "Die Verwaltung des besetzten Gebietes Italiens," in Kerchnawe, "Die Militärverwaltung," 317, 324–6; Scheer, *Zwischen Front und Heimat*, 45–9.

[46] Gefahr von Bauernunruhen in Öster-ung. Okkupationsgebiet, January 1916; Vertreter des k.u.k. Ministeriums des Äussern beim AOK, February 3, 2016, Carton 919, Liasse Krieg, PA I, MdA, HHstA; see also Stephan Lehnstaedt, "Das Militärgeneralgouvernement Lublin: Die 'Nutzbarmachung' Polens durch Österreich-Ungarn im Ersten Weltkrieg," *Zeitschrift für Ostmitteleuropa-Forschung*, January 22, 2012, 1–26 Seiten; Lehnstaedt, "Occupation During and After the War (East Central Europe)."

because in contrast to other occupied territories, there were very few Austro-Hungarian officers or soldiers who had any familiarity with Albanian language or culture. In the end, however, the military's economic needs triumphed over its political promises, and the population grew increasingly disillusioned.[47]

By the time they occupied their share of Romania, the military of the Dual Monarchy should also have learned its lesson in Poland: coercive policies did not pay off. Yet Hungarian interests still pursued a retaliatory "small war" against Romanians in Transylvania, aggressively seeking to reduce Romanian influence and land-ownership and launching an unsuccessful campaign against Romanian banks.[48] Meanwhile, economic and social conditions deteriorated quickly as German and Austrian troops drained reserves of food and oil.[49] In March 1917, Austrian authorities reported from Bucharest that while provisions in the city had been adequate two months earlier, there were now critical shortages due to overcultivation, transport difficulties, and the army's requisitioning policies. Romanian women began to demonstrate against food shortages and inflation.[50] Many Romanians blamed Jews and foreigners for the shortages, equating the two with Austria-Hungary's occupation. By April 1918, Habsburg authorities warned that the lives of Jews and Habsburg citizens alike would be at risk after the withdrawal of Austro-Hungarian troops. "The Romanians are not hiding the fact that after our troops withdraw they will slaughter Jews on the open streets."[51]

Many Poles also blamed Jews for the hardships of wartime occupation, and associated Jews with the occupiers. And while the military government in Poland did overturn Russia's anti-Jewish legislation, Austro-Hungarian commanders did not want to be seen as overly sympathetic to Jews, for fear of alienating local Poles and Ruthenes. Jewish newspapers were banned in November 1916, and Jewish leaders complained that many Jews were denied food aid by local authorities. Austrian military authorities did little to curb what the Viennese Zionist Office called a "historically unprecedented" wave of anti-Jewish agitation in Poland. In Poland and Romania alike, Jews were blamed for black marketeering and for shortages that were actually the fault of the military occupiers. The conditions were ripe by the end of the war for the pogroms that would sweep Central Europe in 1918–19.[52]

---

[47] Scheer, *Zwischen Front und Heimat*, 38–42, 81–2.   [48] Rigó, *Capitalism in Chaos*, 113–16.

[49] Ristović, "Occupation During and After the War (South East Europe)." See also Lisa Mayerhofer, *Zwischen Freund und Feind: deutsche Besatzung in Rumänien 1916–1918* (Munich: M. Meidenbauer, 2010).

[50] Demonstration rümanischer Frauen, March 23, 1917; Bukarest, March 14, 1917, Carton 1044, Liasse Krieg, PA I, HHstA.

[51] Stimmung in Braila, April 3, 1918, Carton 1044, Liasse Krieg, PA I, HHstA.

[52] Vertraulich! February 17, 1916, Carton 919, Liasse Krieg, PA I, MdA, HHstA. See also Jan Rybak, *Everyday Zionism in East-Central Europe: Nation-Building in War and Revolution, 1914–1920* (Oxford: Oxford University Press, 2021).

Across the board, the Habsburg Empire's approach to occupation did change in the war's final year, as civilian bureaucrats slowly regained control of the government. As we will see in chapter 6, following the death of Franz Joseph in November 1916, his successor Charles I sought a return to the rule of law and to diminish the military's power. A flurry of reform efforts began to address the massive crisis of legitimacy that now threatened the entire Empire, including its occupied territories. In Poland, for example, this translated into new promises of independence. On November 5, 1916, the governors of the two occupation zones proclaimed their support for an independent Polish state after the war. The declaration was intended to be a public relations coup and to generate fresh Polish recruits for the armies of the Central Powers. It fell fall short of that goal, however, perhaps because many Poles sniffed out the blatantly instrumental nature of the promise. Only 3,200 men had volunteered as of February 1917.[53] On the other hand, the proclamation did signal a shift in the tone of the occupation, toward cooptation and partnership rather than force.[54]

A similar change of tone took place in Serbia in 1917. In particular, the desperate need for food inspired a gentler approach to occupied territories, now increasingly valued as a last-ditch source of provisions. Serbian farmers could not be expected to deliver crops under a regime of militarized terror. The army's view of Serbs changed accordingly. No longer a nation of terrorists, they were now depicted as apolitical victims of intimidation by a small minority of militant nationalist guerillas. The return of the rule of law did not diminish conflicts over the spoils of occupation, however. Competition for resources between civilian and military authorities, between Austria and Hungary, and between Germany and Austria-Hungary remained fierce as food supplies dwindled and urban Austrians and Hungarians starved at home. Civilian officials including the mayors of Vienna and Budapest directly lobbied the AOK for a greater share of foodstuffs from the occupied territories. The army was not easily persuaded, insisting that feeding soldiers should be everyone's first priority. Officers were even allowed to send care packages home.[55]

Yet the occupation of southeastern Europe did provide new economic opportunities for some Habsburg industrialists, as Máté Rigó has shown. The Allied naval blockade had convinced Central European leaders of the need to expand their continental empires to guarantee critical supplies; lands to the east and south of Germany and Austria were imagined as future sources of critical natural resources and markets for finished products. The drive for greater economic self-sufficiency—and conflict between the two halves of the Dual Monarchy—meanwhile reshaped

---

[53] Watson, *Ring of Steel*, 413–14.
[54] Rudolf Mitzka, "Der k.u.k. Militärverwaltung in Russisch-Polen," in Kerchnawe, *Die Militärverwaltung*, 17.
[55] Gumz, *Habsburg Serbia*, chaps. 4 and 5.

trade between Austria and Hungary. Hungarian leaders had been keen to support local industries against Austrian imports since the late nineteenth century. Although Austria and Hungary were supposed to have an integrated economy, Hungarian leaders pushed for more economic independence from Austria during the war, a development that was almost certainly counterproductive to the war effort.

Instead of exporting food products, grain, cattle, and other resources to Austria, Hungarian firms often sold their goods to the German Reich, which was willing to pay more. Austria, in turn, slapped high import tariffs on several Hungarian goods and banned exporting products such as finished leather to Hungary. Meanwhile, the demands of the Austro-Hungarian army meant that Hungarian factories massively ramped up production. Under these circumstances, as Máté Rigó recounts, Transylvanian leather tanneries fared well. Their products, substituted for banned Austrian imports, kept the massive army shod in leather boots, and met demands for leather products in occupied territories to the southeast. One such tanner, Mózes Farkas, increased his profits from 27,000 crowns in 1914 to 1 million crowns in 1918. Bankers and industrialists in Hungary attracted additional investment by representing themselves as architects of a future economic empire in southeastern Europe, an Imperial project that they framed as a civilizing mission. Many of their more ambitious plans for postwar Imperial expansion remained hypothetical at best, but the ravenous demand of the army provided more immediate opportunities for enrichment. Hungarian industrialists also profited from low corporate tax rates, shady bookkeeping, the inability of the state to regulate or tax wartime profit, and the assumption that Hungary's influence in southeastern Europe would only continue grow after the armistice.[56]

In spite of the abuses, failures, and conflicts that besmirched Austria-Hungary's occupation regimes, military leaders held fast to the myth of the occupation (and of the Empire itself) as a civilizing force. Ten years after the war ended and the Empire had been dissolved, the Carnegie Foundation published the first historical account of Austria's military occupations. Rudolf Mitzka, a former Referent for Poland in the AOK insisted, "An objective evaluation of the accomplishments of the military occupation must recognize that...we accomplished very significant cultural work," installing an administration "animated by the spirit of humanity." Interwar Poland was the major beneficiary, he claimed, as the new Polish state "took over a well-organized administrative apparatus and continued to rebuild upon this foundation." Hugo Kerchnawe, Serbia's former Military Governor, was even more self-congratulatory in his account of the Albanian occupation:

---

[56] Rigó, *Capitalism in Chaos*, chap. 3.

Albanians today still speak wistfully of the time when the Austro-Hungarian soldiers were in their land, building streets, railways, churches, and schools, clearing forests and reclaiming infertile land…that they accomplished all this, what all of the Pashas and warriors from Istanbul could not accomplish in 500 years…that is what impressed the wild mountain people the most about our soldiers.[57]

While Austria-Hungary did not survive the war, these former military officials sought to redeem the Empire in its afterlife.

The Great War and the Transformation of Habsburg Central Europe. Pieter M. Judson & Tara Zahra,
Oxford University Press. © Pieter M. Judson & Tara Zahra 2025. DOI: 10.1093/9780191842306.003.0004

---

[57] Mitzka, "Der k.u.k. Militärverwaltung," 52; Kerchnawe, "Die Militärverwaltung in Serbien," 266–9, 304.

4

The Empire in Camps

Refugees & POWS

Max Schapp was 10 years old when in August 1914 the Russians occupied his home town of Vizhnitsa in the Carpathian Mountains of Bukovina. The first thing he heard was canons on cobblestone.

> First of all, it was a rumbling every night, a rumbling of the cannons…We heard the shooting. We were sitting in the school class…All of a sudden we heard explosions. Everybody, the teacher, everybody was like paralyzed. Everybody was running here and running there. The parents were running after the children, "Where are they?!"…until finally we found home.

The railroad station in Vizhnitsa had been destroyed, so those who could afford it hired donkeys or horses and fled toward Hungary. Schapp and his family were poor, so they had no choice but to remain in town as Russian and Austrian soldiers drove each other back and forth across the region. Finally, Max recalled, "We came to a point that the military authorities told us, 'You have to leave. There's going to be a big battle. We'll give you twenty-four hours.'" So the family packed up their belongings and started walking.

> Where could we walk? Up towards the Hungarian Mountains…there was no other way out…I was with my sisters, and they were in danger of being raped by our own soldiers. And they claimed that I did not understand, I was ten years old. They held onto me, they clawed their nails in on me to make sure to hold onto me, and this scared me…But anyway we travelled up until a place we were safe. Where we were safe, then we were, thousands of people from all over, refugees, and the Austrian government started to distributing us [sic] in different places in Austria.[1]

For millions of citizens of the Habsburg Empire, the First World War was a war of unprecedented mobility and immobility.[2] While soldiers were notoriously paralyzed in trenches on the Western Front and held captive as POWs, the armies of

---

[1] Interview of Max Schnapp by Paul E. Sigrist, Jr., August 26, 1991, in *Ellis Island Oral History Project*, Series EI, no. 075.
[2] Wolfram Dornik, "A School of Violence and Spatial Desires? Austro-Hungarian Experiences of War in Eastern Europe, 1914–1918," in Joachim Bürgschwentner, *Other Fronts, Other Wars? First World War Studies on the Eve of the Centennial*, ed. Matthias Egger and Gunda Barth-Scalmani (Leiden: Brill, 2014), 220–1.

the Central Powers and the Russian steamroller pushed each other back and forth across contested territory, sending civilians into flight. Max Schapp was one of at least 600,000 Austrian civilians who fled or were evacuated from the front during the war. State officials scrambled to address the crisis with an ambitious network of refugee camps scattered throughout the Empire's interior. But once refugees were sorted, counted, and contained in camps, it became difficult for them to leave, as the Habsburg state increasingly aimed to control the mobility of its citizens during the war.

The refugee crisis inside of Austria was part of a much larger mass displacement of civilians across the continent. An estimated 10 million people were forced to flee their homes in Europe during the war, including those individuals displaced internally and across state borders, along the Western and Eastern Fronts.[3] This mass upheaval generated new forms of local, imperial, and international relief. In the Habsburg Empire, for both the Austro-Hungarian military and civilian bureaucracy, the massive displacement of citizens represented both a crisis and an opportunity. The unprecedented movement of civilians, soldiers, and state borders during the Great War was a humanitarian and logistical catastrophe, but one that reshaped the relationship between citizens and their Empire. It brought people in contact with new regions and people, furnished them with new entitlements and expectations, and enabled them to experiment and at times to subvert prewar social norms. Although most hoped to return home after the war, many discovered that they could not, as their homes had been transformed beyond recognition.[4] Meanwhile, new ideas about how to care for and control

---

[3] For an overview see Peter Gatrell, "Refugees," *1914–1918—Online International Encyclopedia of the First World War*, 2014, https://doi.org/10.15463/IE1418.10134.

[4] A literature is beginning to emerge on the refugee crisis during the First World War in Austria Hungary. See for example Doina Anca Cretu, "Securitized Protection: Health Work in Wartime Austria-Hungary and the Making of Refugee Camps," in *Out of Line, out of Place: A Global and Local History of World War I Internments*, ed. Rotem Kovner and Iris Rachamimov (Ithaca, NY: Cornell University Press, 2022); Panikos Panayi, Pippa Virdee, and Julie Thorpe, "Displacing Empire: Refugee Welfare, National Activism and State Legitimacy in Austria-Hungary in the First World War," in *Refugees and the End of Empire: Imperial Collapse and Forced Migration in the Twentieth Century* (New York: Palgrave Macmillan, 2011), 102–26; Francesco Frizzera, "Population Displacement in the Habsburg Empire During World War I," in *World War I in Central and Eastern Europe: Politics, Conflict and Military Experience*, ed. Judith Devlin, John Paul Newman, and Maria Falina (London: I.B. Taurus & Co, 2018), Kamil Ruszała, *Galicyjski Eksodus: Uchodźcy Podczas I Wojny Światowej w Monarchii Habsburgów* (Kraków: Towarzystwo Autorów i Wydawców Prac Naukowych Universitas, 2020); Frizzera, *Cittadini Dimezzati*; Jernej Kosi, "Less than 'Verwaltungsobjekte'? Testimonies of the Slovenian-Speaking Inhabitants About the Retreat to the Austrian Hinterland During the Battles of the Isonzo," in *U Sjeni Velikoga Rata. Odraz Ratnih Zbivanja Na Život Istarskoga Civilnog Stanovništva* (Pula, Croatia: Istarsko povijesno društvo—Società Storica Istriana—Istrsko zgodovinsko društvo, 2019), 327–45; Rebekah Klein-Pejšová, "Beyond the 'Infamous Concentration Camps of the Old Monarchy': Jewish Refugee Policy from Wartime Austria-Hungary to Interwar Czechoslovakia," *Austrian History Yearbook* 45 (April 2014): 150–66; Tara Zahra, "'Condemned to Rootlessness and Unable to Budge': Roma, Migration Panics, and Internment in the Habsburg Empire," *The American Historical Review* 122, no. 3 (June 1, 2017): 702–26.

refugees became models for governments and agencies responding to mass displacement throughout the remainder of the twentieth century and beyond.

The refugee crisis began on the Eastern Front in August 1914 with the Russian occupation of Austrian Galicia and Bukovina. The following May (1915), as we will see in the next chapter, it extended to the southern edges of the Empire, when Italy declared war on Austria-Hungary and citizens fled or were evacuated from the contested Italian-Austrian borderlands. Almost as soon as Austrians abandoned their homes, Imperial authorities began to reflect on the unprecedented nature of the situation. A government publication from 1915 declared that there was "no model, no precedent in Austrian history" for the efforts being undertaken to provide for dislocated Austrians. There was only the terrifying example of Russia, where reports were emerging that the chaotic flight of starving citizens from the hinterland was weakening the "power of the Empire to resist the enemy troops."[5]

In Austria, the refugee crisis was immediately linked to a broader set of social and political issues as well as to success or failure on the battlefield. "This flood from the hinterland created a new social and ethnic problem," officials declared in 1915, "the solution to which would determine far more than the individual fates of the refugees themselves." On the one hand the internal displacement of hundreds of thousands of people highlighted social, religious, and cultural differences among the Empire's large and diverse population. But by bringing citizens into contact with one another, often for the first time, some reformers hoped that the encounters created by displacement would actually cultivate a greater sense of imperial solidarity.

The refugee crisis initially threw together citizens from vastly different social backgrounds. In Galicia, special refugee trains transported civilians from the war zone. These trains, officials reported, were "filled to the last patch" with "civil servants, the wives of officers, the families of city merchants and artisans, railway and postal workers, laborers, and an unbelievable number of children, with which Galicia is so rich, all jumbled together, unified by their common fate."[6] As these refugees streamed into Vienna, the Romanian-born, Jewish journalist Marco Brociner observed, "Since the overwhelming majority of these refugees grew up in their own peculiar cultural zones, they appear to be from a foreign world, and since these uprooted people face us with fearful shyness, or even mistrustful secretiveness, we must first of all create a spiritual bridge between us and these masses."[7]

---

[5] K.K. Ministerium des Innern, *Staatliche Flüchtlingsfürsorge im Kriege 1914/15* (Vienna: Hof- und Staatsdruckerei, 1915), 26.
[6] Ministerium des Innern, *Staatliche Flüchtlingsfürsorge*, 3.
[7] Marco Brociner, "Wir und die Flüchtlinge," in *Ein Jahr Flüchtlingsfürsorge der Anitta Müller* (Vienna: Rollinger, 1915), 4.

While flight initially jumbled refugees together from different backgrounds, Imperial authorities almost immediately intervened to segregate them. Through its own social policies, it therefore reinforced, rather than effaced, divisions of class, language, nationality, and religion. A new Center for Refugee Welfare in Vienna rushed to create a network of camps throughout the Empire's interior. The most significant factor determining a refugee's fate was social class. Those with financial resources to support themselves were generally granted the privilege of mobility and allowed to live wherever they could find housing (the cities of Vienna, Prague, Brno, Linz, and Graz were eventually "closed" to refugees, but the prohibition was completely ineffective). Those in need of support, by contrast, were sorted and confined to camps according to their nationality and religion. Socially "higher-standing" refugees who needed state assistance were typically allocated a daily allowance and allowed to live in private housing.

This sorting process was far from simple, however. Confusion reigned not only about how individual refugees should be classified, but also about who counted as a refugee in the first place. Many people fled their homes without official orders. Initially, they were not eligible for refugee welfare support. Olga Pogorelz was a 15-year-old resident of Trieste when the war broke out. Her mother was dead, and her father, a railway employee, was ordered to evacuate the city. She was sent to Marburg/Maribor to live with an older sister. Three years later she was still petitioning the state to be officially recognized as a "refugee" so that she could receive a small payment.[8]

In 1917, the Interior Ministry finally ruled that individuals could receive state support regardless of whether they had fled "of their own will" or on military orders. Support for refugees was also expanded to include those who were not officially Austrian citizens, such as loyal non-Austrian Poles and Italians, so long as they "appear to be assimilated in terms of their lifestyle and inclinations."

Initially, refugee relief also depended on an individual's official Heimat or legal domicile. Refugees who happened to live in an official war zone but were domiciled elsewhere were supposed to return to their hometown for financial help. But by the turn of the twentieth century, thanks to rural–urban migration within the Empire, only 61.7 percent of individuals actually had pertinency (and were entitled to assistance) in the place in which they lived. The numbers were even lower in large cities like Vienna and Prague. And when people fled their hometown because of an advancing army, they were not keen to return to receive welfare benefits.[9]

---

[8] Pogorelz Olga, Flüchtlingsunterstützung, Statthaltereirekurs, May 10, 1918, Busta 2814, LL (Luogotenza del Litorale), GEN (Atti generali), AST.

[9] On Heimatrecht, see most recently Dominique Kirchner Reill, Ivan Jeličić, and Francesca Rolandi, "Redefining Citizenship After Empire: The Rights to Welfare, to Work, and to Remain in a Post-Habsburg World," *Journal of Modern History* 94, no. 2 (June 2022), 326–62. See also Heindl and Saurer, *Grenze und Staat*, 164–70; Andrea Komlosy, *Grenze und ungleiche regionale Entwicklung:*

Figure 4.1 Refugee barracks under construction in Mitterndorf, 1914–15.
Source: Austrian National Library: https://onb.digital/result/11135634

Figure 4.2 Life inside a refugee camp in Landegg, 1914–15.
Source: Austrian National Library: https://onb.digital/result/11135656

Figure 4.3 Refugees outside of a camp in Gmünd, 1914–15.
Source: Austrian National Library: https://onb.digital/result/1113566F

Figure 4.4 Women learn to sew in a refugee camp in Grieskirchen, 1914.
Source: Austrian National Library: https://onb.digital/result/10BA4FA5

Figure 4.5 Inspection of refugees in the snow at a camp near Salzburg, 1915.
Source: Austrian National Library - https://digital.onb.ac.at/rep/osd/?1127A50B

Figure 4.6 Street in a refugee camp in Porhlitz/Pohořelice Moravia, 1915.
Source: Austrian National Library: https://onb.digital/result/1127A7F7

These rules only changed in July 1917, when authorities officially recognized that refugee relief was distinctive from normal poor relief and uncoupled the two forms of assistance. For the first time, the state created welfare benefits that were accorded to individuals as citizens of the Empire, rather than as individuals or families attached to a locality, or as veterans of the army and their dependents.[10]

From the beginning, state officials saw the creation of camps or barracks as the preferred (as well as the most modern) solution to the refugee crisis. Camps would keep refugees contained and prevent the kind of chaotic wandering that characterized refugee movements in Russia. Camps would enable the state to centralize provisioning, prevent cities from becoming overcrowded, and supposedly prevent rivalries and conflicts between locals and refugee newcomers.

The Interior Ministry, which controlled the new Center for Refugee Relief, scrambled to open the first barracks for Galician refugees in Moravia near Nikolsburg/Mikulov in the fall of 1914. These were followed by camps in Pohrlitz, Gaya, and Bruck an der Leitha for Jews; camps for Ruthenes in Gmünd and Wolfsberg; and camps for Poles in Leibnitz and Chotzen. In the summer of 1915, additional camps were constructed to accommodate refugees from the Italian front, with Italian camps in Pottendorf, Mitterndorf, Braunau am Inn and Deutschbrod, and a camp for Slovenes in Steinklamm. Systematic repatriation to Galicia began in July 1915, and by November 1, 2015, 250,000 refugees from the north had already been returned home. Bruck an der Leitha was hastily converted into a Slovene camp and Gmünd into a camp for Croatians. The entire network could accommodate around 130,000 people in 1915. The remainder of refugees was housed privately. As of October 1, 1915, for example, 73,028 refugees were housed in camps and another 317,118 lived in private accommodations.[11]

Camps were popular in 1914–15, and not only as a solution to the refugee crisis. Swept up in the wave of patriotic paranoia that infected all of Europe at the outbreak of war, Austrian officials (like those of the other Great Powers at war), rushed to intern various suspect populations, including accused traitors, "enemy aliens" and POWs. The internment camp and the refugee camp developed in tandem, and it is hardly surprising that the distinction between the two was lost on many refugees, who were not happy to find their freedom of movement restricted.

Binnenmarkt und Migration in der Habsburgermonarchie (Vienna: Promedia, 2003), 100–1. On Budapest, Robert Nemes, *The Once and Future Budapest* (Dekalb, IL: Northern Illinois University, 2005), 182; Susan Zimmermann, *Divide, Provide, and Rule: An Integrative History of Poverty, Social Policy, and Social Reform under the Habsburg Monarchy in Hungary* (Budapest: Central European University, 2011), 148.

[10] Flüchtlingsfürsorge. Unterbringung, Unterstützung und Übersiedlung von Kriegsflüchtlinge, generelle Regelung, January 13, 1917, Busta 2811; Flüchtlingsfürsorge, Unabhängigkeit von der Heimatzuständigkeit und von der Armenfürsorge, July 7, 1917, Busta 2812, LL (Luogotenza del Litorale), GEN (Atti generali), AST. On Heimatrecht, see also Dominique Kirchner Reill, Ivan Jeličić, and Francesca Rolandi, "Redefining Citizenship After Empire," 326–62.

[11] Instruktion betreffend die Beförderung und Unterbringung von Flüchtlinge aus Galizien und der Bukowina, September 15, 1914, Karton 341, Fach 36, AR, MdA, HHstA.

The defining features of camp life were scarcity, dirt, and illness. In 1916, for example, a group representing refugees from Istria requested that the state minimize the number of refugees confined to camps. They complained that sanitary conditions and infant mortality rates were atrocious, noting that camp life also took a serious psychological toll on residents. "In the barracks...refugees only see repressive measures and hardships and develop the dark suspicion that things are better on the outside, that their internment is not a wartime necessity, but a punitive measure directed expressly at them." Allowed to live like normal citizens, by contrast, refugees retained a feeling of "freedom and equality with other citizens," however poor their material conditions might be.[12]

In light of such complaints, why did the refugee camp become the default "solution" to the refugee crisis? After all, it was cheaper to simply give refugees money and let them fend for themselves. Camps were an expensive undertaking. In the first fourteen months of the war, building and maintaining refugees in camps cost the Habsburg state 41,652,641 crowns, while supporting refugees with direct payments in private dwellings cost only 1,014,835 (this difference explained in part by the fact that those outside of camps generally had resources to support themselves). One official estimated that "every refugee in the concentration camps" cost the state 70 hellers a day.[13]

The reality was that camps were always more than containers for refugees. Officials quickly came to imagine them as potential solutions to social and political problems ranging from disease, to provisioning, to nationality conflict and economic development. Authorities especially hoped that the system of refugee camps would help to integrate the Empire economically, politically, and socially. A government publication from 1915 explained that the education and training offered to refugees in camps would even advance the "cultural and economic development of the borderlands of our Empire."[14] Camps were to achieve these goals by transforming the most vulnerable victims of war into a captive audience for the state's program of cultural uplift. As in its wartime occupied territories, discussed in the next chapter, Austria's citizens were targets of the state's own wartime "civilizing" mission. And camps were also seen as promising venues for social experimentation.

Only refugees of "lesser means" were considered appropriate subjects of these experiments. Camps were deemed wholly inappropriate for the "socially higher-standing elements" of the population, who were allegedly "particularly sensitive"

---

[12] Landesausschuss der gefürsteten Grafschaft Görz und Gradisca, March 11, 1916, Carton 1955, MdI, 19 allg, AVA, OestA.

[13] Ministerium des Innern, *Staatliche Flüchtlingsfürsorge*, 46–7; Unterstützung galizischer Flüchtlinge, May 16, 1915, Karton 341, Fach 36, AR, MdA, HHstA.

[14] Ministerium des Innern, *Staatliche Flüchtlingsfürsorge*, 22, 15. See also Wolfgang Burghauser, "Zweckmässigkeit der Flüchtlingsbaracken," *Neue Illustrierte Zeitung: Sondernummer Flüchtlingsfürsorge*, December 15, 1917, 41–2.

to the loss of personal freedom that camp life entailed. Such refugees were also to be spared the "more or less unavoidably disturbing intrusion of strangers into family life." By contrast, camps were considered ideal habitats for the lower classes, who supposedly had little need for privacy or individual liberty and were in greater need of the state's care and supervision.

Wolfgang Burghauser, who directed an Austrian refugee camp during the war, admitted that infectious disease was at first rampant in refugee camps, and that camp rules constrained the "personal liberty" of refugees. But he insisted that camps served the greater interest of "humanity," the state, and refugees themselves, particularly when it came to the lower classes. "One should not forget which sector of the population we are talking about. It is normally the lowest social classes who are held by the state in camps...These are all people who are not yet sufficiently culturally formed and developed to undertake the struggle for life's necessities with money in their own hands." Camps, he claimed, also served the psychological needs of refugees, who preferred to live collectively with other individuals from their own hometowns, "so that they don't have to give up their daily habits, so that they can continue to develop and protect some part of their Heimat even in a foreign land."[15]

Of course, camps also served the more general purpose of controlling mobility, a longstanding (and often frustrated) goal of the Austro-Hungarian state. Individuals who refused to remain in their assigned camp were deprived of social assistance, and strict rules regulated and limited requests for transfers. Officials were particularly determined to prevent unruly and uncontrolled movements across state borders. In Hamburg, for example, an Austrian consul insisted that Galician refugees who had crossed the border into Germany should be interned, and that those who refused to remain in camps should be denied welfare benefits. "Whoever willfully leaves the inland refugees camps or wanders around aimlessly must be deprived of regular assistance," he demanded.[16]

In keeping with this goal of controlling unruly mobility, officials even created a special camp for Roma in Hainburg. While the camp was ostensibly for Roma refugees, many officials and commentators immediately seized on the idea of the concentration camp as a more general "solution" to what they called the "Gypsy problem." The idea of interning Roma had circulated before the war, but no one wanted to pay for it. The fact that the central state and the Imperial War Ministry was now in the business of financing internment camps eliminated this obstacle. In occupied territories as well, the army High Command took measures to

---

[15] Wolfgang Burghauser, "Zweckmässigkeit der Flüchtlingsbaracken," 41–2.
[16] Unterstützung galizischer und bukowinischer Flüchtlinge im Deutschen Reich, 16 August 1915, Fach 36, Karton 341, AR, MdA, HHstA.

impede Roma mobility. For example, Roma in occupied Serbia were confined to "Gypsy quarters" unless they had long been settled and exercised a trade.[17]

In general, the war offered an opportunity to take harsh measures against Roma. In June 1916, for example, newspapers reported that the Hungarian government, seeing the war as "a chance to resolve the Gypsy question," had decided to "put an end to the free Gypsy lifestyle." The Ministry decreed that all Roma men would be drafted into the army and that women should be forced to work for the war effort. All Gypsies were required to register with the police and their wagons and animals were confiscated for the war effort. Every Roma individual over age 12 or was to be issued an identity card, without which they could not leave their locality. A German language newspaper in Budapest welcomed these measures, proclaiming, "The Gypsies, who already failed to fulfill their civic duties in peacetime, are now avoiding military service, eking out a living through begging, thievery, or even robbery. In today's difficult circumstances it can no longer be tolerated that a segment of the population detracts from the defense of the fatherland and from the common good."[18] In general, the repressive impulses that shaped the camps were inextricable from their alleged civilizing mission.

But a civilizing mission could include many elements. And as Austrian officials scrambled to meet the social, medical, psychological, educational, and spiritual needs of refugees, camps expanded into miniature societies. By the fall of 1915, many were equipped with massive kitchens, bakeries, slaughterhouses, chapels, hospitals, schools, and workshops. Some published camp newspapers. There were also initiatives to prevent infant mortality, improve child welfare, and offer schooling to refugee children in their native language.[19]

Idle girls were of particular concern to government officials, as they were allegedly most at risk of "demoralization" (i.e. prostitution). Special homes were therefore erected for refugees in Vienna, Prague, and Aussig/Ústí nad Labem. In Vienna, charitable organizations also created an impressive network of social institutions specifically designed to meet the needs of female refugees and their children. Marco Brociner was particularly concerned about the fate of pregnant women displaced by the war:

> In wild flight she left her home. Upon arrival in Vienna, this woman…ends up in some dark mass accommodation, or a back room, that she often shares not only with her husband and child, a makeshift shelter. No means exist for the gentle care that her

---

[17] Scheer, *Zwischen Front und Heimat*, 191. On the internment of Roma during the First World War, see also Marcus Weigl-Burnautzki, *Internierung und Militärdienst. Die "Lösung der Zigeunerfrage" in Österreich-Ungarn im Ersten Weltkrieg* (Vienna: Böhlau, 2022).

[18] "Konec cikánského života," *Dělnické Listy*, June 7, 1916, 4; "Die Konskription der Zigeuner," *Pester Lloyd*, June 5, 1916, 6.

[19] Cretu, "Securitized Protection."

condition demands...her physical and mental power of resistance is broken. How many sleepless nights, in which she is tormented by anxious worry about the life germinating in her womb.[20]

Relief efforts included birth clinics and convalescent homes for refugee mothers, maternal and infant welfare clinics, day nurseries, soup kitchens, and finally, handicrafts schools where refugee girls could keep their fingers busy and avoid the "danger of physical atrophy and in some cases moral derailment" that ostensibly threatened them in the capital city.[21]

The expansive nature of refugee relief reflected concerns about the psychological condition of refugees as well as their material needs. Austrian authorities worried about encouraging a pathological state of dependency and inactivity in camps—a concern that would dominate the United Nations' refugee relief efforts after the Second World War as well. Almost as soon as the state introduced welfare support for refugees, officials fretted that it would encourage "payment for inactivity."[22] A lack of purposeful occupation, they feared, would induce depression, which in turn threatened the "confident mood of the population on the home front" and posed a "moral threat to the refugees themselves." But the obvious solution, allowing refugees to work for pay, carried its own risks. Local populations would not respond well if refugees began to compete with them for scarce jobs or resources. To resolve this tension, officials created facilities for handiwork and artisanal crafts and organized vocational training to encourage "useful activity."[23]

In 1915, officials generally remained confident that the entire system of refugee welfare (and perhaps the war itself) would only enhance the overall cohesion and patriotism of the Empire's population. Refugee relief, officials insisted in 1915, was creating "a bridge over all that divides us," and strengthening the sense of "common citizenship, mutual trust and reciprocal gratitude of all of Austria's nations."[24] There was some evidence that the state's efforts bore fruit. In March 1917, for example, officials reported that many non-German speaking refugees, interested in their economic advancement and educational enrichment, were eagerly attending German language classes and even requesting German language elementary schools for their children. "These efforts deserve the most emphatic support of the state administration," officials reported. "They further the development of active economic and social relationships between the borderlands and

---

[20] Brociner, "Wir und die Flüchtlinge," 6–7.   [21] Brociner, "Wir und die Flüchtlinge," 12–13.
[22] Unterstützung galizischer und bukowinischer Flüchtlinge in Deutschen Reich, August 16, 1915, Fach 36, Karton 341, AR, MdA, HHstA.
[23] Ministerium des Innern, *Staatliche Flüchtlingsfürsorge*, 15.
[24] Ministerium des Innern, *Staatliche Flüchtlingsfürsorge*, 27.

the interior of the Monarchy and indirectly deepen harmonious feelings of togetherness."[25]

But as the war dragged on, the morale of refugees declined precipitously along with that of the rest of the population; resentment and depression began to trump feelings of Imperial solidarity, and relations between locals and refugees became strained. When the refugees in question were Jewish, this resentment crystallized into anti-Semitic incidents. In Prague, the city council even attempted to ban Jewish refugees from riding trams in 1917, claiming that they spread disease.[26]

The writer Joseph Roth recalled that during the war many Jewish refugees from Galicia came to Vienna. "For as long as their homelands were occupied, they were entitled to 'support.' Not that the money was sent to them where they were. They had to stand in line for it, on the coldest winter days, and into the night. All of them: old people, invalids, women, and children." In these conditions of hardship (and growing shortages of foodstuffs in the city), "They took to smuggling. They brought flour, meat, and eggs from Hungary. They were locked up in Hungary for buying up food stocks. They were locked up in Austria for importing unrationed foodstuffs. They made life easier for the Viennese. They were locked up for it."[27] Jewish organizations both within the Empire and beyond mobilized on behalf of displaced coreligionists, motivated by solidarity, Imperial loyalties, anxieties about anti-Semitism, and a view that saw the Russian Empire as the enemy of Jews. But this aid itself also sometimes generated resentment from non-Jews.[28]

In Hungary, Jewish refugees from the Carpathians initially received a relatively warm welcome from locals, as the refugees were seen as fellow Hungarians. Locals even collected funds to help rebuild Carpathian villages. But the solidarity was short-lived. The Hungarian government worried that refugees would undermine the war effort and drain public funds and wanted them quickly repatriated to their homes. In the provincial town of Nagyvárad, Hungary, Hasidic refugees were scapegoated as disease carriers, draft dodgers, and war profiteers, and attacks on Jewish refugees soon spilled over into attacks on all Jews in the community.[29] As in Germany, anti-Semitism also flourished on false accusations that Jews were draft dodgers or profiteers.

---

[25] Kulturelle Flüchtlingsfürsorge, deutscher Sprachunterricht, Vienna March 14, 1917, Carton 15, Kriegsflüchtlingsfürsorge, BMsV, AdR, OestA.

[26] Morelon, *Streetscapes*, 148–50.

[27] Joseph Roth, *The Wandering Jews* trans. Michael Hoffmann (New York: Norton, 2001) (originally published in 1927), 67.

[28] Marsha L. Rozenblit, *Reconstructing a National Identity: The Jews of Habsburg Austria During World War I* (Oxford: Oxford University Press, 2001).

[29] Robert Nemes, "Refugees and Antisemitism in Hungary During the First World War," in *Sites of European Antisemitism in the Age of Mass Politics, 1880–1918*, ed. Robert Nemes and Daniel Unowsky (Waltham, MA: 2014), 236–54.

Right-wing Catholic leaders like the Bishop Ottokár Prohászka and other Christian nationalists in Hungary encouraged anti-Semitism by evoking the alleged threat posed by "Judeo-Bolshevism" to Hungary's Christian identity. While the government of István Tisza in Hungary attempted to counter anti-Semitic rumors and celebrated the service of Jews serving in the military, his government fell in early 1917. He was replaced by more conservative leaders, and the Hungarian Interior Ministry soon ordered all Austrian refugees to leave Hungarian territory, reflecting fraying ties between the two halves of the Dual Monarchy as well as the escalation of anti-Semitism.[30]

Some refugees made their discontent known. Refugees from the Italian front protested in March 1916 that they were tired of being treated like enemies in their own state. Camps, they insisted, should "shed the character of penal colonies." They should instead be organized more along the lines of large asylums or humanitarian institutions. Refugees especially resented restrictions on entering and exiting the camps, the use of military personnel to keep order, and the fact that so few camp doctors or personnel could speak their languages. They also demanded that meals be prepared according to local tastes and customs, that bathing facilities take into account their "feelings of shame and morality," and finally, that the personnel of the camps approach their jobs "not only with reason, but also with their hearts… that they keep in mind that the point is not simply to implement decrees but also to help reconcile fully-fledged citizens who have fallen into misfortune to their hard fate, to strengthen and increase their love for their fatherland for the sake of a better future."[31]

Nelly Mauro, a refugee from Pola, had even harsher words for the Viennese authorities. In the Steinklamm camp, she claimed, seven thousand refugees were living under the arbitrary rule of four gendarmes, "who claim to be the judges of everything." The camp residents rarely received the bread rations to which they were entitled, and often dined on rotten or inedible meat. Families that complained were threatened with internment, and the gendarmes even beat their children.[32] Camp authorities replied that the accusations were false, that the members of the Mauro family were all troublemakers, and that they should be interned in a penal camp.[33] But Mauro's outrage was not isolated. Similar complaints emerged from other camps across the Monarchy in 1917, particularly as the provisioning crisis deepened. In a camp in Jičín, Bohemia, in June 1917,

---

[30] Rigó, *Capitalism in Crisis*, 111–12; Paul Hanebrink, "Transnational Culture War: Christianity, Nation, and the Judeo-Bolshevik Myth in Hungary, 1890–1920," *The Journal of Modern History* 80, no. 1 (March 2008): 55–80.
[31] Wünsche und Vorschläge betreffend die staatliche Flüchtlingsfürsorge für Angehörige des Landes Görz-Gradisca, March 2, 1916, Karton 1955, MdI 19allg, AVA, OestA.
[32] An löbliche Direktion des Kriegsfürsorgeamts der Flüchtlinge Wien, January 7, 1917, Karton 1985, MdI 19allg, AVA, OestA.
[33] Flüchtlinge aus den südlichen Kronländern in Steinklamm, Beschwerde, May 30, 1917, Karton 1985, MdI 19allg, AVA, OestA.

several hundred refugees reportedly received only one meager meal per day for weeks. Ration cards were meaningless since the necessary foodstuffs were never delivered. In several camps there was no flour, meat, potatoes, or fat. In early 1917 in the Gmünd camp for Ukrainians, refugees had cabbage soup for dinner for two months. At least 1,300 out of 25,000 residents were sick, mostly from undernourishment. In another camp, refugees received about half the rations to which they were entitled and resorted to scavenging the trash for food; dead bodies remained unburied for a week because no one had the energy to bury them. Riots broke out in the camp in Brück an der Leitha in June 1917.[34]

Nor did the return home end this misery. If the refugee camps were bad, home was often worse. Upon return (often under the order of military authorities), many citizens found their homes completely ransacked, if they were still standing. In October 1916, Chaja Rösetbaumer was ordered to return home to Galicia with her five children. Upon discovering that her house had been plundered and destroyed and that she had no place to live, she promptly returned to a refugee camp in Bohemia.[35] In 1918, the mayor of Zablotow in Galicia appealed to the Ministry of Public Works to stop ordering refugees to return to the town. There were hardly any homes standing, as the majority were burnt down or plundered during the war, and those that remained were not fit for habitation. "The refugees who have been returning for weeks are living 20 or more to a room, no fewer in cellars, and some families are outside under the open sky. The building of barracks is proceeding slowly and there is almost no prospect that these poor people will have a roof over their heads before winter comes."[36]

After the war, the refugee camps of the Austrian Empire were mostly forgotten or remembered with mixed feelings. In 1920, when Jewish refugees fled the civil war in Eastern Poland, Jewish agencies insisted that Czechoslovakia do better than the "infamous camps of the old Monarchy." Czechoslovakia attempted to distinguish itself from the Habsburg Empire through its more generous treatment of Jewish refugees.[37] Yet misery is relative: some refugees later remembered the camps created by the wartime Austrian state with gratitude. Their memories depended largely on where the refugees were coming from, their experiences before and after the war, and how they fared during the height of the provisioning crisis.

---

[34] 27555/17, Flüchtlingsfürsorge in Böhmen, unbefriedigende Approvisionierungsverhältnisse, June 4, 1917; Bericht der delegierten des ukrainischen Hilkskomitees über die Inspizierung des Barackenlagers Gmünd, March 18, 1917; Abschrift, February 16, 1917; Flüchtlingslager Bruck a.d.L.; Unruhen, June 9, 1917, Karton 1985, MdI 19allg, AVA, OestA.

[35] K.K. Ministerium des Innern, March 22, 1916, AVA, MdI, 19 allg, Karton 1955, OestA.

[36] Quoted in Beatrix Hoffmann-Holter, *Abreisendmachung: Jüdische Kriegsflüchtlinge in Wien 1914 bis 1923* (Vienna: Böhlau, 1995), 70.

[37] Rebekah Klein-Pejšová, "Beyond the 'Infamous Concentration Camps of the Old Monarchy': Jewish Refugee Policy from Wartime Austria-Hungary to Interwar Czechoslovakia," *Austrian History Yearbook* 45 (2014): 150–66.

The state's efforts to provide for hundreds of thousands of displaced citizens failed mostly due to the state's inability to provide for refugees' basic needs. And yet despite these failures, the Austrian state's refugee relief campaign "succeeded" in another way: it established a model for refugee relief for the remainder of Europe's violent twentieth century. The "infamous camps of the Monarchy" represented an expansion of the state's obligations and ambitions with respect to its citizens and reflected the intersecting priorities of control and care that would dominate humanitarian relief and welfare states for decades to come. But they also failed to inculcate those patriotic feelings of solidarity that idealistic social reformers and bureaucrats had hoped for. Rudolf Schwarz-Hiller, a leader of the relief effort in Vienna concluded in August 1918 that the experiment had been a failure. "Instead of the expected deepening of feelings of commonality and the great Austrian idea, conflicts became greater, and bitterness is vastly increasing each day."[38]

Captivity

Refugees were, of course, not the only citizens of the Empire who spent much of the war in camps. Captivity was the defining experience of the war for the 2.7 million Austro-Hungarian soldiers (11 percent of the total male population), who were taken prisoner during the First World War. The vast majority of these men (around 2 million) spent the final years of the war in Russia. Almost as soon as the war began, their experiences became the subject of anxiety, mythmaking, and contention. Did captive soldiers remain loyal to the Empire? Or did they form the backbone of nationalist and Bolshevik uprisings that precipitated the Empire's collapse? How, if at all, did the experience of captivity shape these men and their loyalties?

During the First World War, being taken prisoner was often seen as de facto evidence of disloyalty or cowardice. As the Russian army swept large numbers of Austro-Hungarian soldiers into captivity, anxieties about their reliability festered back home. Paranoid military authorities worried about deserters and about POWs being turned against the Habsburg state. Nationalists who wrote the first histories of the Habsburg successor states intentionally reinforced these narratives. Ironically, both groups had an interest in portraying some soldiers—particularly Czechs, Serbs, Italians, and Ruthenes—as disloyal. Franz Conrad von Hötzendorf, the Chief of staff of the AOK, was convinced that soldiers belonging to certain nationalities were deserting the army en masse. In the context of the abandonment of the rule of law in 1914–15, the army High Command introduced

---

[38] Quoted in Hoffmann-Holter, *Abreisendmachung*, 71.

extremely harsh measures to deter desertion, including the death penalty without trial. The High Command also tried to mix units composed of troops of "suspect" national origins with those believed to be loyal (German, Hungarian, Croatian). From the very beginning, the military's lack of faith in its own citizens bred mistrust among Austro-Hungarians and their government leaders.

It is highly unlikely that many soldiers allowed themselves to be captured voluntarily. The risks were simply too great. To start with, there was dishonor associated with captivity. When soldiers wrote their memoirs they usually began by trying to exculpate themselves. Rumors of brutal Russian treatment—of POWs being executed or maimed—also surely deterred soldiers from surrendering.[39] Nor was entry into captivity pleasant. Although severe abuse was rare, many POWs recall being deprived of their personal possessions, down to their shoes and clothing. Then they began to march toward an unknown destination—sometimes spending three months en route to the Russian interior. One Czech infantryman reported to his family:

> We were prodded hungry from the Carpathians to Lemberg. We marched for nine days, each day making 25 km. Because of weakness we could hardly walk or step on our feet. They gave us something to eat after two days and indeed only a small amount of soup and a piece of bread. Those of us who had some money could buy here and there a little piece of bread, but this was very expensive. How I and others who had no money fared you cannot even imagine.[40]

Travel by train was hardly better. POWs were packed into modified boxcars, thirty to forty-five men per car, with bunks and a bucket as a latrine. It was nearly impossible to sleep and easy to contract disease. One man recalled that he did not get a bath or change of sheets for three months.

Upon arrival at their destination, the fate of POWs depended mostly on their rank. Russia generally followed the rules of the Hague Conventions of 1899 and 1907, which meant that officers (around 2.5 percent of all POWs) were provided with the same treatment as officers in the army that had captured them. This translated into superior living quarters and food, a monthly stipend, and exemption from forced labor. For officers, life as a POW usually meant a standard of living well above that of the local population, in conditions that sometimes resembled summer camp rather than an internment camp. An officer stationed in Omsk wrote a letter home describing the delicious cakes and doughnuts he enjoyed for dessert each night. Sports teams, theaters, woodworking, shoemaking, basket-weaving, and printing rounded out the extracurricular activities on offer.

---

[39] Iris [Alon] Rachamimov, *POWs and the Great War: Captivity on the Eastern Front* (Oxford: Oxford University Press, 2002), 45–6.

[40] Quoted in Rachamimov, *POWs and the Great War*, 50.

Figure 4.7 Advertisement for an exhibition of handicrafts made by Austro-Hungarian prisoners of war, 1917.
Source: Austrian National Library: https://onb.digital/result/11310A3C

These activities were considered therapeutic antidotes to idleness, apathy, and depression. But as Iris Rachamimov has argued, they also enabled soldiers to establish a feeling of "normalcy," middle-class respectability, and domesticity within camps. This recreation of domestic spaces and activities in a world without women could simultaneously reinforce and subvert norms of masculinity, for example, in the many drag performances that took place in camps, both on and off the stage.[41]

Contemporary observers feared the impact of captivity on the morals, masculinity, and psychological stability of interned men. Elsa Brandström, the daughter of the Swedish Ambassador to Petrograd, provided relief to POWs in Russia as a representative of the Swedish Red Cross. She described men afflicted with "POW psychosis," which consisted of "nagging restlessness, a desperate feeling of emptiness, discontent and loathing of everything." As with refugees, middle- and upper-class men were believed to suffer most from the loss of personal freedom. "The more culturally developed the prisoner, the more he suffered," Brandström observed. But these men also allegedly possessed the greatest capacity to develop the "hard will" necessary to master their surroundings, "to maintain self-respect, and sometimes even to deepen their character."[42]

Austro-Hungarian censors back home worried about the alarming sexual and moral laxity of POWs, which they saw as a consequence of captivity. As soon as POWs settled into their life and realized that they had enough to eat, one censor reported, their thoughts turned to sex. They started writing sexually explicit letters to friends and family back home, including their wives, girlfriends, and mothers. These titillating letters naturally ended up in the hands of the censors. At a party to celebrate Italian King Victor Emmanuel's Birthday, one group of POWs reportedly donned women's clothing, "and it came to shameless and disgusting scenes," a censor reported. Another officer wrote in a letter home, "You can well imagine in what kind of environment I am living in: there are 250 officers here together, vocal wolves, who thirst for dirty pleasures and suffer greatly in their absence."[43] Another POW, Enrico Pizzini, wrote in his wartime memoirs that many of his imprisoned comrades had already been "living like monks for months before they were taken prisoner, and suffered terribly. The result was that

---

[41] Alon Rachamimov, "The Disruptive Comforts of Drag: (Trans)Gender Performances Among Prisoners of War in Russia, 1914–1920," *The American Historical Review* 111/2 (April 2006): 362–82; Iris Rachamimov, "Small Escapes: Gender, Class and Material Culture in Great War Internment Camps," in *Objects of War: The Material Culture of Conflict and Displacement*, ed. Leora Auslander and Tara Zahra (Ithaca, NY: Cornell University Press, 2018).

[42] Elsa Brandström, *Unter Kriegsgefangenen in Rußland und Sibirien, 1914–22* (Berlin: Deutsche Verlagsgesellschaft für Politik und Geschichte M.B.H. 1922), 51.

[43] Märzbericht 1917 über die Angelegenheiten der italienischen Kriegsgefangenen in Österreich-Ungarn, Folder 4563, Box 3749 1917, GZNB, Kriegsarchiv, OestA.

many sought refuge in same-sex love, and above all many very young men were ruined for life."[44]

Much like the refugee camp and wartime occupations, captivity was seen as a social experiment—with the potential to transform individuals and to reveal something fundamental about individual character and human nature. "The first period of captivity often produced a strong development of individual peculiarities. There was plenty of time at hand for reflection about life's most profound questions," Elsa Brandström noted.[45] Hans Kohn, later historian and theorist of nationalism, was taken prisoner as an Austrian officer in March 1915, and was not released until early 1920. He recalled his five years in captivity as "the decisive years of my life," as they changed his outlook in unpredictable ways. While he recalled privations, including a winter in Khabarovsk during which he survived on tea and dry macaroni, it was also a period of intellectual and political development. Kohn got to know Russian people, learned languages, and reflected on the nature of war, empire, and colonialism. Paradoxically, he explained, a captive officer during the First World War "enjoys freedom. True, he is physically confined, but very few people, even outside prison camps, are completely free to move about and be wherever they wish at the moment...But a prisoner of war is master of his own time; he may spend it reading good books, in conversation, or in thought and reflection."[46]

In reality, only the small minority of officers had time to reflect on the meaning of life. Captivity was a far more grueling experience for the rank and file. In Russia, as in all warring states including Austria-Hungary, POWs were used as a source of labor to replace mobilized soldiers. Conditions varied greatly for the 1.64 million Austro-Hungarian POWs who worked in Russian agriculture or industry during the war. Those assigned to small farms were typically best off, as they were likely to be treated the same as other Russian workers, provided with regular meals, and able to interact closely with Russians. Some even married Russian women, much to the distress of Habsburg authorities.

Fraternization was a two-way street, of course. Between 1.8 and 2.3 million Allied POWs were held as prisoners on Habsburg territory, and at least a million of these soldiers were mobilized for forced labor in the Austro-Hungarian economy, beginning in 1915. This included grueling work building railroads, work that was sometimes deadly. The vast majority were soldiers from the Russian Empire, but there were also thousands of Italians, Serbs, and Romanians. The treatment of these POWs depended on their nationality. As long as the resources were available (which was not very long), Ukrainian and Polish POWs from Russia received

---

[44] Enrico Pizzini, *Durch! März bis Dezember 1917* (Graz: Lenkam Verlag, 1934), 127–8. Our thanks to Tamara Scheer for providing this reference.
[45] Brandström, *Unter Kriegsgefangenen*, 51.
[46] Hans Kohn, *Living in a World Revolution: My Encounters with History* (New York: Trident Press, 1964), 99.

better rations, housing, and other privileges, because Austrian authorities hoped to turn them against Russia. In general, however, conditions in Austro-Hungarian POW camps were abysmal, with widespread epidemics and ever more dire shortages of food.[47] Increasingly, however, POWs were housed outside of camps, on farms and in labor barracks, where they inevitably entered into relations with local women. In Linz in 1915, for example, local authorities decreed,

> There have been many cases in which women and girls have been unmindful of nationality, race and family honor in interacting with POWs. For this reason, every interaction...between civilians and prisoners that is not necessary for the work relationship is forbidden. In particular, women and girls are warned not to enter into a love affair or to maintain forbidden contact.

These relationships were forbidden by law, and women caught violating the prohibition against "forbidden contact" were sentenced to up to fourteen days' imprisonment, fined, and publicly shamed, as their names were published in the newspapers. Military and civilian officials feared the consequences of fraternization both for the morale of men on the front as well as the morals of women at home.[48] Austro-Hungarian officials also feared the political consequences of fraternization, initially banning the deployment of POWs for labor in regions with largely Slavic populations. But the desperate need for workers eventually ended those restrictions.[49]

Back in Russia, conditions for POWs on large estates or in industry tended to be harsh. "We are here in a remote corner of a south Russian gubernia, completely cut off from the rest of the world. We must drudge here restlessly for a Russian estate owner, from sunrise to sunset...I worry about my health but what can we do when we are treated here like slaves," one Czech POW wrote in a letter home.[50] The most unfortunate POWs were deployed to construct the Murman railway, linking Petrograd with the Murmansk port on the Artic. Some 70,000 prisoners joined Russian, Chinese, Finnish workers and convicts on the line between July 1915 and October 1916. Accommodations for these workers often

---

[47] Verena Moritz, "The Treatment of Prisoners of War in Austria-Hungary, 1914/15," in *1914: Austria-Hungary, the Origins and the First Year of the World War I*, ed. Gunter Bischof, Ferdinand Karlhofer, and Samuel Williamson (New Orleans: University of New Orleans Press, 2014), 233–48.

[48] Julia Walleczek-Fritz, "The Social Degeneration of the Habsburg Home Front: 'Forbidden Intercourse' and POWs During the First World War," *European Review of History: Revue européenne d'histoire* 24/2 (April 2017): 273–87, quotation, 273. On use of POWs for forced labor in Austria-Hungary see also Watson, *Ring of Steel*, 388–92.

[49] Moritz, "The Treatment of Prisoners," 244.

[50] Rachamimov, *POWs and the Great War*, 108–11.

consisted of huts or bare ground, and there was a near total absence of fresh food. An estimated 25,000 men died.[51]

In addition to hard labor, epidemics raged in many POW camps. Brandström described plagues that killed thousands. In ten months in Omsk, 16,000 died; in Totzkoje, she described barracks housing up to eight hundred men, "sick and healthy mixed together, nearly naked, infested with vermin and undernourished." Out of 25,000 men imprisoned there, 17,000 died.

And yet, contrary to accounts that describe Russian POW camps of the First World War as "mini-gulags" that prefigured the concentration camps or gulags of later decades, Russian authorities mostly followed the rules laid out by the Hague Conventions. Even the prototypical "camp" (with enclosed areas, barbed wire, and watch towers) developed relatively late in the war. Many POWs were housed in barracks similar to those used for the Russian army; others were housed in whatever accommodation could be found, including, in Omsk, a liquor distillery, a former circus, and a slaughterhouse.[52]

There was actually no "typical" POW experience, since conditions varied so much from locality to locality. "The bread is black as earth and sour as vinegar," wrote private Jonica Gonta from Siberia in February 1915. In June of that year, Romanian language censors noted that one soldier complained of being treated "as badly as slaves," while another reported that he received "excellent food" in Moscow.[53] As Iris Rachamimov has argued, perhaps the best evidence that the camps of the First World War differed qualitatively from those of the Second World War is the survival rate. In spite of serious outbreaks of typhus and other illnesses, 90 percent of POWs survived captivity.[54]

Throughout this ordeal, and contrary to the fears of the High Command and postwar nationalist accounts, most Habsburg soldiers remained loyal to the Empire. Even the most famous anti-Habsburg units in Russia, like the Czech Legion, represented a very small fraction of the POWs. Units that deserted, such as Prague Infantry Regiment 28, were often acting more in response to abusive and incompetent officers than out of longstanding anti-Habsburg convictions.[55] This is not to say that the Russian army did not attempt to divide and rule. Its official policy favored "Slavic" and Alsatian POWs, with the intention of sowing nationalist divisions within Austria-Hungary. But until the last year of the war, these policies were generally ineffective.[56]

---

[51] Rachamimov, *POWs and the Great War*, 112; Brandström, *Unter Kriegsgefangenen*, 62–3.
[52] Brandström, *Unter Kriegsgefangenen*, 46–7.
[53] Bericht pro Juni 1915, KA, AOK, GZNB, Karton 3728.
[54] Rachamimov, *POWs and the Great War*, 125.
[55] Rachamimov, *POWs and the Great War*, 31–3. See also Richard Lein, *Pflichterfüllung oder Hochverrat? Die tschechischen Soldaten Österreich-Ungarns im Ersten Weltkrieg* (Vienna: Lit Verlag, 2011).
[56] Cited in Rachamimov, *POWs and the Great War*, 58.

We know so much about the experiences and attitudes of these POWs because their patriotism (and everything else) was closely monitored through one of the most ambitious censorship operations in world history: 1,150 Austro-Hungarian censors, divided into fifteen language groups, read up to 455,000 articles of mail each day by the end of the war.[57] These censors used very different standards as they evaluated the patriotism of national groups deemed "loyal" to the Monarchy and those suspected of disloyalty. Whereas Magyar, German, and Polish POWs were considered loyal even if they expressed nationalist sentiments, any hint of nationalism from Czech or Slovak prisoners was deemed suspect.[58]

Censors feared that many Austrian POWs in Italy preferred captivity to the front. Such sentiments actually existed, but they were not confined to "suspect" nationalities. One German-speaking POW wrote from captivity in the Piedmont, "Now I don't hear any more cannons screaming or bullets whistling. If I had not been taken prisoner, I would have been dead a long time ago. I am healthy, doing well, and I have as much to eat as in Austria, I am also sleeping well."[59] And from Alexandria, Egypt, another German-speaking officer reported, "We have a tennis court in the camp. Twice a week we go on outings in the region, once a week swimming in the sea," adding that the weather and food were excellent.[60]

When soldiers did become embittered with the Habsburg state, it was often a result of disappointed expectations. Austria-Hungary launched an ambitious relief program for POWs, which aimed to address material shortages, improve morale, and monitor loyalties. In purely numerical terms, the campaign was significant, with more than 14 million crowns worth of food and 8 million crowns of medical supplies distributed to soldiers. Habsburg officials dispatched Red Cross nurses, mostly aristocratic women, to fulfill relief functions. The duties of these "nurses" went far beyond nursing, however: they were charged with inspecting camp conditions, negotiating with Russian authorities to address severe issues, distributing supplies, and reporting back on soldiers' morale.[61]

By the end of the war, however, as shortages intensified at home, many POWs came to believe that they had been forgotten at home, or that the state was indifferent to their fate. Prisoners compared the care packages received by German POWs to their own meager provisions. One soldier imprisoned in France wrote to a friend in Vienna in March 1918. "It is really grand how little our government and our countrymen do for us. You should see everything that is done for the

---

[57] Rachamimov, *POWs and the Great War*, 142.
[58] Rachamimov, *POWs and the Great War*, 149–53.
[59] Sonderbericht. Österreich-ungarische Kriegsgefangene in Italien, July 14, 1915, KA, AOK, GZNB, Karton 3728.
[60] L. Baron Unterrichter, Kgf. in Alexandria, to Thayda Baronin Unterrichter in Wien 25.IV.1918, Unsere Kriegsgefangenen und Internierten in Frankreich, England und den neutralen Staaten, Mai-Bericht, May 31, 1918, G.Z.N.B. Zensurabteilung, HHstA, MdA, AR, Fach 36, Karton 582.
[61] Rachamimov, *POWs and the Great War*, 163–72.

Germans! Don't we also suffer for our fatherland?"⁶² When a Red Cross nurse turned up at his camp in Russia empty-handed, another complained:

> We were very happy to learn of a planned visit of a Red Cross nurse. During the waiting days before the visit, everybody was in a festive mood, however what disappointment and bitterness after the visit. The person did not seem to know why she was here. Perhaps it is now a sport to travel and visit POW camps.⁶³

Homecoming was often the greatest disappointment of all. After years of waiting and longing to return home, many soldiers were deeply embittered by the cool reception that they received. When POWs first began to stream back into the Empire after Russia's defeat in the summer and fall of 1918, they were often greeted as suspect traitors rather than returning prisoners. This reception had a lot to do with the fact that Russia had erupted in revolution in 1917. Returning POWs were suspected of being Bolsheviks, accused of bringing disorder, criminality, and disease home with them. One report from Trieste in May 1918 claimed, "The majority of POWs returning from Russia experienced the revolution and have been infected by revolutionary tendencies…Some even regret that they returned, because according to them things were better for them in Russia than here."⁶⁴ Already in February 1918, Hungarian parliamentary deputy (and later government minister) Károly Huszar voiced concerns raised by several politicians and journalists in both Hungary and Austria at the time, regarding the possible infection with Bolshevism of the returning POWs. "He asked the government to take the severest possible security measures."⁶⁵

Returnees were therefore subjected to a repatriation process that entailed ten to twenty-one days of medical quarantine and "disciplinary re-education." One POW recalled how much this homecoming disaffected him and his fellow soldiers: "We were overjoyed to be again in the fatherland after so many difficult experiences. The unbelievable suspicion with which we were greeted struck us as very peculiar." This reception, he reported, "made us sick and embittered."⁶⁶ In reality, moreover, most soldiers were not eager to bring revolution home with them. But they were deeply disappointed by the harsh welcome they received.

---

⁶² Gaiger Komomann, St. Tropez, Var to Filip Gaiger in Wien, 13. March 1918, Unsere Kriegsgefangenen und Internierten in Frankreich, England und den neutralen Staaten, Mai-Bericht, May 31, 1918, G.Z.N.B. Zensurabteilung, HHstA, MdA, AR, Fach 36, Karton 582.
⁶³ Rachamimov, *POWs and the Great War*, 212.
⁶⁴ MdI, Min für Landesverteidigung, May 4, 1918, Bolschewikische Agitation (Heimkehrer), Busta 439, LL-AP, AdstT. On the treatment of POWs returning from Romania, see Ionela Zaharia, "For God and/or Emperor: Habsburg Romanian Military Chaplains and Wartime Propaganda in Camps for Returning POWs," *European Review of History: Revue Européenne d'histoire* 24, no. 2 (March 4, 2017): 288–304.
⁶⁵ Quoted in Galántai, *Hungary*, 300.
⁶⁶ Rachamimov, *POWs and the Great War*, 194; Zaharia, "For God and/or Emperor"; Watson, *Ring of Steel*, 509–12.

And they were even more distressed by the abominable conditions in which they often found their family members, above all the massive ongoing food shortages.[67]

In the end, the state's mistrust of its own citizens became a self-fulfilling prophecy. The Habsburg state, like all of the warring powers, extended its powers during the war, particularly its powers to manage mobile populations and newly acquired territories. Occupied territories were initially seen as sites in which the Empire could expand and strengthen its civilizing mission, grounded in its multinational character. Even in POW camps, ambitious relief efforts were initially intended to shore up loyalties to the Empire, inoculating soldiers against nationalism and later against Bolshevism.

In practice, however, the experience of occupation and captivity ended up alienating and dividing citizens. The military was mistrustful to the point of persecuting "suspect" nationalities, violating longstanding traditions of equality before the law. Efforts to secure the loyalties of occupied populations were weakened by rapacious extraction and chronic shortages; and many citizens and soldiers were profoundly disappointed with how the state provided for them. In many ways, Austria-Hungary was defeated by its own ambition during the war. But these "failures" were not isolated incidents. Taken together, they had a lasting impact. The Empire's wartime rulers set the terms of its own destruction, with wartime policies that deepened national divisions and resentments. But it also invented new forms of population policies and politics that carried on in the interwar successor states.

The Great War and the Transformation of Habsburg Central Europe. Pieter M. Judson & Tara Zahra,
Oxford University Press. © Pieter M. Judson & Tara Zahra 2025. DOI: 10.1093/9780191842306.003.0005

---

[67] Zaharia, "For God and/or Emperor," 190.

5
Entitled Citizens
Empire, Citizenship, and the Welfare State

In July 1914, when Austria-Hungary declared war on Serbia, vacationers in Carlsbad, Austria-Hungary's most posh and international spa town, reveled in the excitement. The "atmosphere seemed surcharged with electricity" on July 28, so much so that even American visitors "have fallen under the spell of the restless, excited feeling of being in the war zone."[1]

With the outbreak of war, however, citizenship, a legal status that had rarely intruded in daily life, also erupted on the scene in Carlsbad. Suddenly, one's citizenship became a powerful source of emotion. Initially, even if the emotions didn't last long, those feelings were largely positive. Even Sigmund Freud succumbed to contagious patriotism. He wrote in a letter on July 26, "It is perhaps the first time in thirty years that I feel [sic]to be Austrian, and I'm willing to give it another chance," and then hurried home to Vienna.[2] The trains were full of Austrians rushing home. German nationalist writer and theater director Adam Müller-Guttenbrunn wrote that in the days after the declaration of war,

> Vienna is attracting everything and everyone like a magnetic mountain...it's impossible to stay away. Everyone wants to commiserate and sympathize with one another in the great magical circle that has encircled us all today and made us once again into a nation of brothers. Nothing is more beautiful than such a feeling of unity, such a collective will.[3]

But citizenship in a time of war was not all magical feelings, and not everyone could rush home to their loved ones. Mr. William Shmidlap of Cincinnati, who had been enjoying a summer holiday in Europe's spas for forty-four years, was dismayed to discover that he would need a passport to return home, for the first time since the Franco-Prussian war.[4] Moreover, as we have seen, a culture of denunciation quickly swept through the Empire, and holiday towns were no

---

[1] *The New York Herald*, European Edition, July 30, 1914.
[2] Sigmund Freud to Karl Abraham, Carlsbad, July 26, 1914, Lutecium, accessed August 17, 2014, https://www.lutecium.org/1914/07/1914-07-26-freud-a-abraham-2/2539.
[3] Adam Müller-Guttenbrunn, *Volkerkrieg! Österreichische Eindrücke und Stimmungen* (Graz: Moser, 1915), 22.
[4] *The New York Herald*, European Edition, July 30, 1914.

exception. Four French cooks in one Carlsbad hotel were denounced by hotel guests and interned. While French and British women and children were allowed to return home immediately, men of military age had their holidays involuntarily extended, as they were detained.[5]

This new attention to citizenship—as both a feeling and a status—raised several questions and conflicts for both Habsburg authorities and citizens. In the decades leading up to the war, Habsburg citizens had become accustomed to an ideal of citizenship that guaranteed equal treatment before the law. During the First World War, this ideal of citizenship both expanded and shattered. On the one hand, citizenship became fuller: it mattered more, brought more entitlements and duties, brought individuals in closer contact with the state, and was infused with new feelings of solidarity against common enemies. But just as quickly, the wartime regime undermined Austrian traditions of "unity in diversity" and "equality before the law." The military gained control of the state and treated citizens differently and arbitrarily based on their apparent nationality. The state made ambitious efforts to expand the welfare state, but it could not always fulfill its promises, especially when it came to food provisioning. Citizenship itself, it turned out, was not a binary legal category. More a feeling than a status, Maureen Healy has argued, citizenship came to be seen as "a spectrum."[6] An individual's position on this spectrum, their relationship to the state, sometimes depended on traditional categories, such as gender, age, nation, language, religion, or class. But other categories and divisions were new or fleeting. The war divided combatants from noncombatants, peasants from urban dwellers, those with access to food from those without it, the people who lined up in the cold outside the shops and those who were suspiciously well-fed inside. By the end of the war, the dominant posture of the Empire's citizens toward their state combined an expectation of fairness, a sense of entitlement thanks to sacrifice, with disillusionment, outrage, and mistrust.

From the moment the peace ended, questions arose about who counted as a legal citizen of the Habsburg Empire, and about what to do with noncitizens. Initially, male enemy aliens of military age were to be interned and women and children were to be expelled. In Vienna, 1,300 French citizens and 1,254 British citizens were apprehended at the outbreak of the war. Those deemed untrustworthy were held in Karlstein and Gosau castles. But what about their Austrian wives? These women, reported the Austrian Embassy, had "married British, French or Italian subjects, continue to reside within the limits of the Monarchy and do not speak the language of their husbands nor have any interests outside of Austria-Hungary." Many were now destitute, and while they were entitled to reside in their husband's countries, most had no desire to live in countries where

---

[5] Information, 11713, Vienna September 5, 1914, HHstA, MdA, AR, Fach 36, Karton 582.
[6] Healy, *Vienna*, 10.

they were total strangers and would be treated as enemy aliens, in spite of their legal status.[7] Would the Empire really deport women who had known no other homeland?

The screening process was only softened in June 1915, when the army High Command decreed that exceptions could be made for citizens of foreign states "who are only formally citizens of an enemy state, but were actually born and raised here, are totally assimilated to natives, in some cases don't even know the language of their homeland, as well as those who only lost their citizenship through marriage and are now widowed or live separately from their spouses." Rigorous screening would, however, continue for Italian citizens, in order to "eliminate Italian influence once and for all"—there was much more fear of Italian subversion on the southern borders of the state than French or British agitation.[8]

Gender remained critical to the assessment of citizenship throughout the war, however. Although considered full citizens in some contexts, Austrian women generally enjoyed citizenship rights only as they pertained to their husbands, fathers, and brothers. The degree of a woman's commitment to Austria did not always carry the same weight as her husband's citizenship or her brother's wartime accomplishments. This ambivalence produced contradictory results. On the one hand, patriotic Austrian women married to foreigners were sometimes denied access to state or charitable welfare benefits, or even the right to work (regardless of the official law). On the other hand, the same gendered assumptions held that women were fundamentally ignorant of public affairs, and this saved many women from legal prosecution for traitorous outbursts or violent acts in public places.

The citizenship and loyalties of millions of Austrian citizens abroad also came under heightened scrutiny. In October 1915, authorities in the Austrian Foreign Ministry reported that Polish-American committees were encouraging Polish emigrants in the United States to return to Poland, where they could contribute to the reconstruction of their war-devastated homeland. The news sparked alarm in the Austrian Interior Ministry. One official warned that given the "unfriendly" propaganda that had already infected wide circles of Slavic emigrants in America, there would doubtless be "numerous questionable elements with respect to state security" among return migrants.[9] Austrian officials were justifiably worried, as Czech, Slovak, and Polish nationalist movements in the United States were sometimes far more radical than those at home. As early as November 1914, the *Dziennik Związkowy*, organ of the Polish National Alliance in the US, urged Polish-Americans to return to Poland after the war, where they could use their

---

[7] Note verbale, Vienna, June 23, 1915, HHstA, MdA, AR, Fach 36, Karton 582.
[8] Kriegsüberwachungsamt, 31.064 an das k.u.k. Ministerium des Äussern, June 17, 1915, HHstA, MdA, AR, Fach 36, Karton 582.
[9] Aktion zur Rückwanderung der Polen aus Amerika, Interior Ministry, November 29, 1915, Haus-Hof und Staatsarchiv, Ministerium des Aussern, Administrativ Registratur, Fach 15, Carton 55.

newfound knowledge and skills to build an independent Poland and combat alleged Jewish trickery. "American business properly understood, free of humbug and advertising tricks, can enjoy great success in the homeland and in time may become the best medicine for Jewish bargaining methods—that awful plague of the poorest classes of our society."[10]

In Galicia and Carniola, meanwhile, authorities plotted to prevent emigrants' wives from joining their husbands in America, concluding that such emigration would damage the war effort.[11] Many men in America were avoiding their duty to serve in the Austrian military, military authorities reasoned, and if they had their wives with them, they'd be even less likely to come home to serve.[12] At the same time, citizens abroad represented resources: valuable labor, funding for the war effort, and even military power, if only they could be enlisted, lured home, and trusted. And some Austrians did want to return home to fight for their emperor. In 1914, a 70-year-old immigrant from Austrian Galicia, now living in America with her two sons, wrote to the *Jewish Daily Forward* in New York for advice. When the war began, she wrote, her two sons, "who are ardent patriots of Kaiser Franz Josef, announced that they were sailing home to help him in the war." The woman was despondent. "When I heard this, I began to cry and begged them not to rush into the fire because they would be shortening my life. But so far they have not given up the idea of going to fight for the Kaiser." (The editor responded that the boys should stay in New York and "thank God that they are in America, where they are free and can't be forced to shed their blood for the Austrian Kaiser.")[13]

Her sons may have remained in the United States, but when the United States joined the war on the side of the Allies, hundreds of thousands of Austro-Hungarian citizens like them faced a lose–lose situation. While many immigrant organizations (including Hungarian organizations) rushed to declare their loyalties to their adopted homeland, citizens or former citizens of the Habsburg Empire were often treated as enemies of the state. Austro-Hungarian consuls reported that many emigrants were considering a return to Europe, feeling depressed or threatened by anti-Austrian sentiment in the American population.[14] Authorities also worried, however, that Austrians were spreading dark rumors about the situation in the Empire among their relatives in the United States. The darker

---

[10] Ibid.

[11] Holland Amerika Line Auswanderungsbewegung nach Amerika, Ministry of Interior, April 17, 1916, c.k. Starostwo powiatowe w Chrzanowie, 1869–1918, Sig. 128, Archiwum Państowe w Krakowie.

[12] Kuk 5. Armeekommando, Schwaiger, Marie, Reise nach Nordamerika An die kk Landesregierung in Laibach, May 30, 1916, LL, AP, Busta 401, Archivio di Stato, Trieste.

[13] Letter from "A Suffering Mother," 1914, *A Bintel Brief: Sixty Years of Lettes from the Lower East Side to the Jewish Daily Forward*, comp. and ed. Isaac Metzger (Garden City, NY: Doubleday, 1971), 128–9.

[14] Aufzeichnung über die am 15. Juni 1917 abgehaltene Besprechung über die nach Friedenschluss zu erwartende Rückwanderung der österreichischen und ungarischen Staatsangehörigen aus Nordamerika, Fach 36, Karton 607, MdA, AR, HHstA.

Figure 5.1 Wounded soldiers taken off a train.
Source: Austrian National Library: https://onb.digital/result/1124272F

the spin they put on their situation at home, the bigger the care packages the Americans sent.[15]

Xenophobia in the United States sometimes escalated into violence. Nicholas Babinski, an emigrant from Austria, was drafted into the U.S. army although he had never declared his intention to become a U.S. citizen. When he protested he was summoned to a "kangaroo court" in Fort Snelling, Minnesota. Along with several fellow Austrian soldiers, he was subjected to a mock trial and beaten, and threatened with more violence if he refused to remain in the army and to take out citizenship papers. In Johnstown, Pennsylvania, twenty immigrants, all citizens of Austria-Hungary, were tarred and feathered and paraded through town when they allegedly refused to contribute to a fund to raise money for the purchase of army uniforms and liberty bonds.[16]

Representatives of the Austrian government complained that Austrian citizens were arbitrarily interned, "thrown together with felons and murderers, whites and negroes, exposed to ill treatment and undernourishment, housed in cages like animals or in unsanitary, vermin-infested and filthy cells with open

---

[15] Unwahre Gerüchte im Auslande. Verbreitung, October 22, 1915, LL, AP, Busta 401, AdS Trieste.
[16] "Mob tars twenty aliens," *Washington Post*, April 28, 1918; Affidavit, In the matter of the Petition of Nicholas Babinski, for Correction of Certain Abuses in Company F, 36th Infantry, Fort Snelling, Minnesota, Fach 36, Karton 607, MdA, AR, HHstA.

sewers... although absolutely innocent of any crime or offense against the laws of the United States."[17] In one case, an Austrian mining engineer in Salt Lake City was tossed into jail because the local sheriff had eyes on his wife. The sheriff then attempted to persuade the wife to leave her husband. "Austrians are not classified amongst white people; they are black and if I were you, I would not tell your babies later on that their father was an Austrian," he counseled.[18] Anti-Austrian sentiment in the United States created an atmosphere of fear and depression among many Austrian immigrants during the war, consuls agreed. A Hungarian-American newspaper, the *Magyar Tribune*, advised Hungarian immigrants, "Keep your thoughts to yourself." Deference to authority was the best strategy. "Do not take part in any political movement. Trust the people whose duty it is to think for you."[19] While some migrants accepted this advice, others began to talk about returning home, as "America ceased to be a land of hope and opportunity for them."[20]

Back at home, as the war dragged on, deference to authority was certainly not the dominant posture. Mass starvation, above all, transformed the meaning of citizenship and the relationship between citizens and the state. As we saw in chapter 2, a crisis of provisioning followed fairly quickly after the first dreadful year of war, severely straining social relations and compromising the state's legitimacy. Worried authorities (and observers) linked hunger and a growing social crisis to a broader breakdown of the family. Children and youth spent their nights and days standing outside in bread lines and participating in protests, rather than attending school. Schools were soon closed anyway, due to lack of teachers and coal to keep them warm (or were turned into hospitals). The absence of fathers and mobilization of mothers for war work left many unsupervised for hours on end. A preoccupation with family breakdown during the war was not unique to the Austrian Empire. Across Europe, citizens and state officials saw the war as an unprecedented threat to the unit of the family and feared an epidemic of juvenile delinquency.

The war transformed "threatened" children into imagined threats to public safety and order. Children and youth allegedly lurked in the streets, hung out in cabarets and movie theaters, stole food and provisions, threw rocks at store windows, and begged in railway stations. Teenagers who found employment in war factories had plenty of money but nothing to spend it on, since shops were empty. Instead, claimed officials in the Austrian Defense Ministry, they developed adult

---

[17] Verhandlung mit den Vereinigten Staaten von Amerika in Ansehung von Zivilpersonen, Konferenz in Bern, October 20, 1918, Fach 36, Karton 607, MdA, AR, HHstA.

[18] Erich Pohl to Swedish Ambassador, February 10, 1918, Fach 36, Karton 607, MdA, AR, HHstA.

[19] "The Ten Commandments for Immigrants in Time of War," *Magyar Tribune*, April 21, 1917. CFLPSR, Box 26, Section I G.

[20] Aufzeichnung über die am 15. Juni 1917 abgehaltene Besprechung über die nach Friedenschluss zu erwartende Rückwanderung der österreichischen und ungarischen Staatsangehörigen aus Nordamerika, Fach 36, Karton 607, MdA, AR, HHstA.

Figure 5.2 Vienna breadline in Ottakring district, 1915.
Credit: Polizeifotografie (1914–1918) (Fotograf), Warteschlange vor Anker-Brot-Verkaufsstelle (Ottakringer Straße), 1915, Wien Museum Inv.-Nr. 41233/4, CC0 (https://sammlung.wienmuseum.at/objekt/105843/)

vices as "a lack of oversight and parental instruction encourages the imitation of bad adult habits." The Defense Ministry was convinced that the perceived rise in youth delinquency would sap the state's military power.

As the food crisis dragged on, overworked and undernourished parents reached their wits' end. In 1917 censors reported rumors of mothers who threatened to kill themselves along with their children, diagnosing a massive "destruction of family life and the burial of motherly instincts." The German Provincial Commission for Youth Welfare in Bohemia reinforced popular fears about the wartime destruction of familial bonds: "The war has revealed the sad truth, that the pretty picture of the family as a force of social education has been destroyed by hard economic realities, and a certain wildness has emerged in its place. Feelings of parental duty are considerably stunted." As we have already seen in earlier chapters, along with any notion of childhood innocence, the war upended traditional ideals of masculinity and femininity, motherhood and fatherhood. While mothers were feared to be incapable of caring for their children, many fathers were absent (or had returned home physically or mentally disabled). Symbolic fathers (including Emperor King Francis Joseph himself) meanwhile proved incapable of providing for their subjects.[21]

---

[21] Healy, *Vienna*, 209–10, 298–300.

Women developed a more direct relationship with the wartime state as they demanded food and support when their husbands were called up, returned wounded, or never returned at all. But even as they made new (and sometimes violent) claims, their relative status often remained unchanged. Women's protests and strikes were often dismissed as "apolitical" food riots (even as they threatened the state's very legitimacy). Women's war work, too, was often described as a temporary, emergency measure. Welfare support payments were structured to reinforce women's status as dependants. On the other hand, it is hardly coincidental that women acquired the right to vote in Austria, Czechoslovakia, Poland, and Hungary immediately after the war ended.

As the social crisis expanded to threaten the well-being of middle-class families, working-class families, and almost all consumers, the stage was set for a broader rethinking of the state's relationship to its citizens. Experiments with canteens and soup kitchens had revealed that middle-class Austrians resisted any form of assistance that felt like charity, even if they desperately needed it. While some forms of state assistance continued to distinguish between Austrians based on need or social class (like refugee relief) other welfare benefits were reformulated and universalized as social rights or entitlements, owed to all citizens in return for their sacrifice and service to the war effort; or as eugenic policies aimed at improving the health and welfare of the entire population. In this it is important to recognize the ways that citizens themselves forced these changes on the state.

Yet even as state officials became aware of (and sought to respond to) escalating demands for social services, they lacked the resources and know-how necessary to intervene effectively. As a result, much of the "welfare state" that emerged in response to the wartime social crisis in Austria-Hungary was funded by private donations and staffed by volunteers, a product of cooperation between public and private initiatives. The Austrian Red Cross, for example, boasted twenty-two provincial organizations and 661 local branches at the war's outset; Red Cross nurses delivered medical care to wounded veterans in 874 military hospitals, provided transport to wounded veterans, and provided assistance and refreshments to hundreds of thousands of Austrian refugees and veterans as they traveled through the Empire's train stations.[22] Viennese Mayor Richard Weisskirchner acknowledged the public–private mix at the outset of the war: "War welfare is partly ruled by laws, regulations, and decrees from the central government organs, and partly organized by voluntary charities, without designation of any strict division between their respective fields of work."[23]

---

[22] Ke-Chin Hsia, "Who Provided Care for Wounded and Disabled Soldiers? Conceptualizing State-Civil Society Relationship in First World War Austria," in *Other Fronts, Other Wars? First World War Studies on the Eve of the Centennial*, ed. Joachim Bürgschwentner, Matthias Egger, and Gunda Barth-Scalmani, History of Warfare, volume 100 (Leiden: Brill, 2014), 307–11; Hsia, *Victims' State*.

[23] *Kriegsfürsorge: Ein Jahr Kriegsfürsorge der Gemeinde Wien* (Vienna: Gemeinde Wien, 1915).

Figure 5.3 A Favoritenstraße Breadline in Vienna, ca. 1918.
Source: Austrian National Library - Wien 10, Favoritenstrasse 128, ca. 1918 https://onb.digital/result/10BBB021

Indeed, a great deal of the work carried out by the thirty-four branches of the Imperial War Relief Office (Kriefsfürsorgeamt) amounted to exhorting private citizens to give donations—of food, cigarettes, metal, textiles, and time. Under the banner of "war welfare," the welfare relief office carried out a highly modern and sophisticated fundraising and recycling operation. In a 1917 report, the Relief Office boasted, "There was not a single household in the country that was not solicited for a contribution." These efforts relied on armies of unpaid women and children who thumped on doors with collection boxes, using their charm to their advantage. "The request from a child's mouth…cannot be resisted, and so everyday there were plentiful donations."

The Imperial recycling operation was particularly ambitious. By 1916, the naval blockade and heightened border controls meant that the Empire was no longer able to import textiles, paper, or powder; the military also faced a massive shortage of metal, rubber, and leather. Kids had collected close to 8,000,000 kilos of recyclable materials by March 1917. These scraps and rags were assembled at factories staffed by POWs, women, and girls, who sorted them into seven categories, from material destined to fabricate soldiers' uniforms to scraps intended to insulate feet during Alpine marches. A massive shoe repair and recycling operation kept shoes on at least some of these feet shod in spite of a severe leather shortage.²⁴ The war effort also relied on the "hardworking hands" of the girls and women to knit trainloads full of socks, hats, and scarves for soldiers in the field. In the first two years of war alone, Viennese women sewed no less than 2,538,761 pairs of pants and 25,227 gas masks.²⁵

Even as officials worried about the capacity of mothers to care for their own children, the state clearly relied heavily on the volunteer and paid labor of women to keep the Empire running and the army fighting. As Belinda Davis and Maureen Healy have shown, women were essential to the war effort in ways that fundamentally altered their relationship to the state and status as citizens during the war. In addition to their sewing, knitting, collecting, and sorting, countless women went to work in factories, with large increases in the numbers in war industries like metalworking. In March of 1918, the state even planned to introduce compulsory labor conscription for all women between the age of 18 and 40, as well as non-enlisted men, but the measure was never put into force.

Between 33,000 and 50,000 women even served as uniformed volunteers on the front in a Women's Auxiliary Service in 1917–18. Many of these women considered themselves to be an essential part of the front community. Demanding "direct participation in the care of the wounded on the field," for example, Red Cross sister R.M. Konrad requested a transfer to a hospital directly on the front at the end of 1915. A few women went further, dressing as men in order to fight alongside them. Ludwika Daszkiewiczowa, an elementary school teacher from Bukovina, joined the military under the pseudonym Slanisław Kepisz in September 1914. She was taken prisoner by the Russians in November 1915 and released in a prisoner exchange in June 1916. After a brief stay in the hospital following a suicide attempt, s/he returned to the front, and was eventually awarded medals by the Austrian and Polish armies.²⁶ And yet, these women in uniform were often ridiculed for being unfeminine or neglecting their domestic duties, and were suspected to be prostitutes. Ultimately, women were expected to contribute to the war effort in sharply gendered ways.²⁷

The flurry of inventive fundraising schemes and volunteer efforts testified to a modern philanthropic operation: in addition to the collection cans that appeared on every street corner and in every town square, customers at restaurants and taverns were encouraged to add a small donation to their tab in exchange for a black and gold receipt. Every woman in the Empire was exhorted through

---

²⁴ *Kriegsfürsorge*, 37.
²⁵ Bericht über die Tätigkeit des Kriegsfürsorgeamtes während der zeit von seiner Errichtung bis zum 31 März 1917. Wien, 1917, quotations 28, 46.
²⁶ Angelique Leszczawski-Schwerk, "Amazonen, emanzipierte Frauen, 'Töchter des Volkes': Polnische und ukrainische Legionärinnen in der österreich-ungarischen Armee im Ersten Weltkireg," in *Glanz-Gewalt-Gehorsam: Militär und Gesellschaft in der Habsburgermonarchie (1800 bis 1918)*, ed. Laurence Cole, Christa Hämmerle, Martin Scheutz (Essen: Klartext, 2011), 68–9.
²⁷ Christa Hämmerle, *Heimat/Front: Geschlechtergeschichte/n des Ersten Weltkriegs in Österreich-Ungarn* (Böhlau: Wien, 2014), 12–39, (p. 39); Healy, *Vienna*, 204–9.

"intensive and systematic propaganda" to contribute a single crown to the "woman's crown fund" for disabled veterans. Wartime memorabilia also sold well: the welfare office produced and sold 250,000 iron rings with portraits of Kaiser Franz-Joseph, along with commemorative medals, badges, toy weapons, postcards, and portraits of military leaders. These products enabled citizens to consume and own a piece of the Empire's history and contribute to the war effort at the same time.[28]

Another one of the state and military's most pressing and immediate obligations was the care of those injured or left behind by war: veterans, widows and orphans. And there were a lot of them in the first six months of the war. As of January 1915, some 189,000 men had died on the battlefield, 491,200 were wounded, and 291,800 had taken ill.[29] Something clearly had to be done for these soldiers and for the family members who relied on them for support.

There had been some baby steps toward the reform of veterans' welfare in the years leading up to the war. A 1912 law specified that wives, children, parents, grandparents, great-grandparents, and even the unmarried companions and nonmarital children of enlisted soldiers (not, however, mistresses) were entitled to receive support if they were dependent on the enlisted man's income. This support continued for six months after a soldier's death or disappearance in service. The amount depended on the soldier's rank but could not total more than his average salary. Widows and orphans were entitled to a yearly pension, the sum of which depended on the soldier's rank and whether or not he had died in combat.[30]

This 1912 law, passed during the Balkan Wars, represented a real improvement, since it allocated the same fixed allowances to enlisted men and officers rather than basing pensions on rank or time served. In 1915, the law was further amended so that families of reservists who were killed in combat or who returned as invalids continued to receive state support for the duration of the war, and in the case of invalids, based on the degree of disability they had suffered. For the first time, payments were based on the disabled veteran's ability to return to his or her former civil occupation or profession, using principles adopted from the relatively new field of accident insurance/worker's compensation, which attempted to calculate the precise economic value of a missing arm or leg, the ability to see or walk.

In fact, there was a major shift in the way the state understood the plight of disabled veterans shortly after the outbreak of war—a shift that anticipated a broader transformation of the welfare system. Before the First World War, officials generally had imagined bleak futures of dependence on family or charity for

---

[28] Bericht über die Tätigkeit des Kriegsfürsorgeamtes während der Zeit von seiner Errichtung bis zum 31 März 1917. Wien, 1917, 23.
[29] Glaise-Horstenau ed. *Österreich-Ungarns letzter Krieg*, Beilage 4, Tabelle 2, cited in Hsia, *Victims' State*, 47.
[30] Hsia, *Victims' State*, chap. 2.

disabled veterans. The initial response to the war was to take up charitable collections for injured veterans and their families, reinforcing a view of them primarily as objects of poor relief. But not long after reports of massive casualty and injury rates began to arrive home, Habsburg leaders and experts began to articulate a new vision of relief and rehabilitation for wounded veterans. As early as December 1914, Austrian Prime Minister Stürgkh declared that it was incongruent with a "modern understanding of the state" that injured veterans, widows, and children be forced to rely on charity, and requested the Interior Minister, Baron Karl Heinold von Udyński, to come up with a plan for a state-financed welfare system.[31]

Alongside a new understanding of the state's role in assisting soldiers and their families, however, came a new conception of the objectives of relief. Instead of charitable support, the goal was to rehabilitate and reintegrate disabled veterans into the economy and society. A Hungarian social scientist and government advisor, Emerich/Imre Ferenczi, argued that this was both a matter of preserving "the highest possible amount of labor" for the economy and an important defense against "impending social threats" that could result from mass disability and idleness.[32]

As Ke-Chin Hsia has shown, the 1915 law represented a major shift in the way the Habsburg welfare state worked, in that it now entailed a direct expenditure by the Monarchy, rather than (as in the case of social insurance) a system based on private contributions or local obligations. But it arguably did not go far enough. Men without families and young men who were first completing their military service received nothing according to this schema. High inflation rates also meant that the real value of payments constantly declined. Disabled soldiers were known to try to extend their stay in hospitals as long as possible simply to receive free food and shelter; upon discharge, many ended up begging in the streets. There were a few improvements to the system during the war, but substantial reform was delayed until the war's end. Once again, divisions between the two halves of the Monarchy were partly to blame. Military finance laws required Austria to pay 63.6 percent of war expenses, although only 56 percent of wounded soldiers came from Austria.[33]

---

[31] Austrian State Archive [OeStA], Allgemeines Verwaltungsarchiv [AVA], Ministerium des Inneren [MdI], Präsidium [Praes.], 19, Kt. 1862, 19093/1914 Bekämpfung der Kriegsschäden für die Angehörigen der Wehrmacht und ihre Familien./: Militärversorgungsgesetze und Anregung einer präventiven Hilfsaktion :/, Stürgkh an den Minister für Landesverteidigung, 1–4, Zitat Stürgkh: 3.

[32] Emerich Ferenczi, "Die Zukunft der Kriegsverletzten als volkswirtschaftliches Problem," *Pester Lloyd*, December 12, 1914, 12, cited in Thomas Süsler-Rohringer, *Krisenindizierte Kontinuität. Soziale Sicherung und die Re-Integration Kriegsversehrter im Habsburgerreich 1880–1918* (Kritische Studien zur Geschichtswissenschaft Bd. 248), Göttingen 2023, 213–214.

[33] For more on pensions and war victim relief, see Hsia, *Victims' State*. See also Verena Pawlowsky and Harold Wendlein, "Die normative Konstruktion des Opfers," in *Glanz, Gewalt, Gehorsam: Militär und Gesellschaft in der Habsburgermonarchie (1800 bis 1918)*, ed. Laurence Cole, Christa Hämmerle, and Martin Scheutz, 1. Aufl, Frieden und Krieg, Bd. 18 (Essen: Klartext, 2011), 359–83.

Each crownland also established a commission to facilitate the reintegration of veterans after their return home, but these state organizations were heavily reliant on private donations and charity. They served more as umbrellas that coordinated the services of private organizations and initiatives rather than providers of welfare services in their own right.[34] The state's heavy reliance on private initiatives molded post–First World War welfare states as well. Locally, nationalist organizations and associations were often far ahead of the central state, and they built the foundation of the wartime welfare apparatus. In the two decades preceding the war, local nationalist associations had created a politically powerful link between the idea of health and welfare of children and the demographic power of the nation. They had also abandoned an old-fashioned view of social services as a form of charity. Instead, they promoted social welfare as a form of nationalist population politics intended for all social classes, a strategy for elevating the eugenic quality and demographic power of the national community.

During the war, provincial and local nationalist associations were particularly enterprising in raising funds and providing services to families and children. By the time authorities in Vienna caught on, they had little choice but to rely on the existing nationalized [private] infrastructure. This in turn contributed to the further fragmentation of the Austrian state and society along national and regional lines. For example, in Bohemia, nationalist organizations like the Sokol, České Srdce, and the Czech Provincial Commission for Child Welfare were charged with distributing state welfare funds. Members of these organizations were particularly embittered when the government returned the favor with suspicion and persecution for alleged disloyalty.[35]

When the government created a new Ministry of Social Welfare in November 1917, that Ministry immediately recognized the principle of national autonomy and national representation in its bureaucracy. During the parliamentary debates surrounding creation of the new Ministry in 1917, Minister Heinrich Mataja declared, "The new Ministry for Social Welfare will strive to be national/popular [*volkstümlich*]. It will be open and accessible to everyone and will in particular strive to attract the enthusiastic cooperation of private associations and autonomous organizations." The Ministry convened a Youth Council (*Jugendbeirat*), charged with developing a new centralized Imperial youth welfare policy. This council was explicitly designed to facilitate national representation and included Czech, Polish, Italian, Croat, and Jewish delegates, many of whom represented private nationalist social welfare institutions in their respective crown lands.

German and Czech nationalist activists in the Bohemian Lands were at the forefront of these efforts to create a nationalized welfare state. They stood at the vanguard of a broader movement toward the establishment of a nationally

---

[34] Hsia, *Victims' State*, 54–63.   [35] Morelon, *Streetscapes*, chap. 2.

divided social welfare system throughout Habsburg Central Europe. In 1917, policymakers in Vienna officially adopted the system established in the Bohemian Lands, whereby each national community managed its own public social welfare institutions and funds, as the model for an expanding public child welfare system in all multilingual regions of Habsburg Austria, including Galicia, Bukovina, Southern Styria, and Silesia. In each of these regions, government officials in the new Ministry for Social Welfare pledged to create nationally segregated city and regional youth welfare offices, guardian councils, and provincial commissions to care for the physical and moral welfare of the Empire's children and youth. They also empowered nationally segregated welfare offices to administer the Imperial Widow and Orphan Fund, the Empire's largest wartime welfare fund.

Jewish organizations also mobilized to provide relief specifically to Jewish refugees, orphans, and families. In 1917, for example, Zionists planned orphanages for an estimated 15,000 Jewish war orphans in Galicia and Bukovina. They also planned a children's home in Vienna, fearing that Jewish children there would otherwise be "lost" to the nation in foster care with Christian families, or bullied in orphanages in which Jews were a minority.[36] Jewish citizens of the Monarchy also received relief from local Jewish communities and from international organizations like the Zionist organization and the American Joint Distribution Committee founded in 1914.

One of the most lasting and significant consequences of the First World War throughout Europe was the conviction that states owed something to citizens who worked, fought, lost their homes, and died for the war effort. This transformation was a product of citizens' own demands for compensation for their patriotic sacrifice, which they equated to the sacrifice of soldiers on the front. But who would control this welfare state, and who would receive credit for its successes and failures? In Austria-Hungary, Imperial authorities in Vienna and Budapest were often forced to follow the lead of local nationalists and to work through their voluntary organizations.

This was only one of many ways in which the Habsburg state itself contributed to the gradual national segregation and division of the Empire's population and institutions during the war. Already, refugees had been divided into camps based on nationality; a censorship regime had tracked the loyalties of citizens based on nationality, and censors and military authorities assumed that some national communities were more loyal than others.

One outcome of this further national division was that, when it came to the successes of the new welfare measures, local nationalists were poised to take credit. But when it came to failures and disappointments, Imperial authorities often took the blame. Censors reported complaints that state welfare payments

---

[36] Rybak, *Everyday Zionism in East-Central Europe*, chap. 2.

ENTITLED CITIZENS 117

Figure 5.4 "Brothers in America! Why don't you join our army?"
Source: Herder-Institut: https://www.herder-institut.de/bildkatalog/iv/257522

were distributed unfairly or unequally. From Styria, one citizen protested, "Those people who own large plots of land get the support, while we poor people get nothing." Sarcasm and bitterness were endemic, with writers mocking the pretense of "justice" in state allocations. "In America there is a different kind of justice," one letter writer noted. Others speculated that perhaps the situation was better in Russia after the Revolution.[37] The sarcasm, mockery, and outrage that permeated citizens' letters indicated another transformation in citizenship during the war. There was a decided lack of deference in citizens' interactions with the state, along with a heightened sense of entitlement.

The consequences of these wartime transformations in citizenship would long outlast the Empire itself. The fracturing of the welfare state into nationally segregated institutions facilitated the breakup of the Monarchy into self-declared nation-states and created the foundation for institutions that survived well beyond 1918. Continuity, rather than rupture, would characterize social institutions across the caesura of 1918. Citizens' outrage and entitlement, their disappointment in the state's ability to provide, contributed heavily to the fall of the Habsburg Empire. But the same feelings would pose serious challenges for the successor states. Their very legitimacy would hang on their ability to satisfy the unmet social and political demands of hungry, exhausted, and radicalized men, women, and children.

The Great War and the Transformation of Habsburg Central Europe. Pieter M. Judson & Tara Zahra, Oxford University Press. © Pieter M. Judson & Tara Zahra 2025. DOI: 10.1093/9780191842306.003.0006

---

[37] Gegenstand: Unregelmässigkeiten bei der Auszahlung von Unterhaltsbeiträgen, Folder 4614, Box 3751, GZNB, AOK, KA, OestA.

6
Revolutions

In March 1917, food riots in several Russian cities provoked a severe political crisis that turned into a full-scale revolution, forced the abdication of the Tsar, and very quickly ended the rule of the autocracy. For eight months, a so-called "provisional government" drawn from parties in Russia's Duma or parliament exercised official power. This so-called "provisional government" was joined by spontaneously organized soldiers and workers' councils called "soviets" that sprang up in several cities during the March revolution and that claimed a measure of local political authority. Under pressure from its British and French allies, the provisional government decided to keep Russia in the unpopular war, however, and in early November the Bolshevik or Communist Party that promised Russians both bread and immediate peace took power and toppled the provisional government. With the Bolsheviks in control of Petrograd and Moscow, a destructive civil war broke out, pitting them against several different enemy armies, some of which were supported by Russia's erstwhile wartime allies.

As the Bolsheviks struggled to consolidate their rule in Russia, they sought a quick end to the unpopular war that had led to revolution in the first place. Peace, however, would come only at a terrible price. Holding all the cards, the Central Powers imposed draconian terms on Russia at the Peace Treaty of Brest-Litovsk in March of 1918. At the same time, however, the Bolsheviks used several forms of propaganda to induce the workers and peasants in Europe's other armies to lay down their arms, turn on their masters, and to create a truly global revolution.

The powerful example of successful revolution in Russia posed a stark warning to the other warring states: find a quick end to the war or risk revolutionary turmoil themselves. Exhausted populations could only take so much misery in the service of a cause that by 1917 seemed both hopeless and futile to most Europeans. What was the point of the war, asked many people across Europe? Austria-Hungary's rulers, too, faced a dire domestic situation, and they could hardly afford to ignore the stark warning from Russia.

In fact, the Russian Revolution was neither the first nor the only uprising to threaten the war efforts of the great powers; it was merely the biggest and the most successful of them. A year earlier in April 1916, an Irish nationalist uprising in Dublin, the Easter Rebellion, had forced Great Britain to deploy thousands of troops and heavy artillery away from the war effort on the continent to Ireland. For six days the British military fought Irish nationalist rebels in battles that raged through urban neighborhoods and produced thousands of civilian casualties.

When the British military finally re-established order after close to a week of fighting, the cost was 485 dead, over 2,600 wounded, three thousand taken prisoner, 1,800 deported to internment camps, and several rebel leaders executed.[1] Barely a year later, in the wake of yet another failed military offensive against the Germans, thousands of French troops mutinied and left the front lines to demonstrate for peace, thereby jeopardizing the entire allied war effort.[2] At the same time in 1917 and especially in 1918, each combatant state including Austria-Hungary faced mass strike movements at home that crippled war industries and threatened to destroy what remained of a fragile social peace on the home front. The years 1917 and 1918 were indeed a dangerous time for a wartime Austro-Hungarian regime that devoted its remaining resources to achieving a military victory in the hopes of avoiding social revolutionary collapse.

Austria-Hungary never experienced a nationalist revolt on the scale of the Irish nationalist Easter uprising, nor military mutinies on the scale of the French in 1917, and certainly no revolution like the one that toppled the Tsar in March of 1917. Nevertheless, the ongoing pursuit of an unpopular war that placed intolerable strains on society meant that Austria-Hungary constantly experienced serious and repeated strikes and hunger riots, especially in the years 1917 and 1918. By the summer of 1918, as we will see, Austria-Hungary's rulers also faced a storm of desertions and mutinies among the troops, the complete collapse of what was left of its food supply systems, the inability to feed or clothe the troops, the gradual disintegration of the front lines, and a possible social revolution. At the same time, regional bureaucrats and civil servants in several of the crownlands took matters into their own hands and simply ignored orders from Vienna and Budapest. As the Austrian and Hungarian governments deadlocked over what to do about the war, and what to promise for the future, their states drifted into a kind of no-man's land, where local and regional authorities increasingly took responsibility from a paralyzed central state for feeding people and maintaining security. By late summer 1918 the lines of authority that connected the Imperial state to localities simply ceased to function. They were replaced by the efforts of hastily organized regional authorities and so-called "national councils." In early November, what was left of the Habsburg Empire came to an end.

The Russian, British, and French experiences all show that by 1917 at the latest, grim wartime conditions could produce rebellion and even revolution. Every regime worried about the ripple effects of the Bolshevik Revolution on its own societies. Yet there are at least three points to keep in mind when we consider the possible influence of the Russian Revolution on Austria-Hungary. In the first

---

[1] On the Easter Rebellion generally, Charles Townshend, *Easter 1916: The Irish Rebellion* (Lanham: Ivan R. Dee, 2006).
[2] On the French mutinies, Leonard V. Smith, *Between Mutiny and Obedience: The Case of the French Fifth Infantry Division During World War I* (Princeton: Princeton University Press, 1994).

place, it should be clear that for many people, the war experience up to 1917 had already revolutionized every aspect of economy, social relations, and cultural values. Mobilization, militarization, mass internment, incitement to every kind of sacrifice, transformation of gender roles; by 1917, each of these had unintentionally but dramatically revolutionized daily life. Austria-Hungary may not have undergone a formal political revolution, but by 1917 it had already experienced several social, economic, and cultural revolutions.

Secondly, the radicalizing experiences of war also produced a range of very different revolutionary hopes for the postwar future. After almost three years of continuous mobilization, most people believed that postwar society could and should never return to the social status quo that had existed in July 1914. Many believed that a postwar world would have to be fairer and more just. They sought a world where the state would equalize burdens among all citizens regardless of class, rank, or perhaps even sex, while offering tangible relief to those who were hardest hit by sacrifice. This was certainly the view among political liberals, socialists, and radical socialists, but it was also a view shared by many consumers and veterans who had otherwise supported the social status quo. As we will see, influential government elements in Austria and Hungary including a new emperor king also accepted much of this dream for the postwar world, in part to stave off the specter of worse revolution. As Julius Andrassy bluntly declared for the opposition in a speech to the Hungarian parliament in February of 1917:

> If the [Hungarian] government and the leading circles think that they may continue things where they left them before the war, if they think that they need not conduct an entirely new social policy for which the first step must be taken now, then there really will be a revolution.[3]

But pictures of a more just world were hardly the only visions indulged in by Austro-Hungarians. Others dreamt of vast Imperial territorial and economic expansion to the east and south that would allegedly create limitless opportunity for personal enrichment. In 1916, for example, a Hungarian journal for legal scholars argued that "We [Hungarians] go to Germany to study. In the Balkans, however, we must become teachers ourselves." As Maté Rigó argues, this Hungarian Imperial civilizational mission might include anything and everything from creating Balkan rail links or capturing new markets to physical occupation. In preparation for its country's postwar role, for example, the Hungarian Oriental Academy offered three-month courses for businessmen and artisans on the culture, economy, and customs of southeastern Europe.[4]

---

[3] Quoted in Galántai, *Hungary*, 225.   [4] Rigó, *Capitalism in Chaos*, 72.

Still others envisioned a reformed empire where their national community would gain significant political and territorial autonomy for itself and its people. Many South Slav nationalist, for example, imagined an empire reorganized on a trialist principle (an Austria-Hungary-South Slav state). Polish nationalists, some of whom fought in a Polish Legion against Russia, sought an independent Poland loosely connected to Austria-Hungary, perhaps with a Habsburg as Polish king. Czech nationalists in Bohemia agitated for an autonomous Bohemian kingdom while German nationalists there hoped through legislative coercion to establish permanent political dominance. These diverse visions often intermixed nationalist ambitions with a promise of a better economic future. With their "own" nation firmly in control of a region, nationalists argued, the population could expect better economic conditions. Given the level of wartime privation, this argument was highly persuasive.

Still another distinctive group of visionaries—the various nationalist exiles—abandoned the Empire altogether. Some surrendered intentionally to the enemy at the front, as did the ill-fated Italian nationalist Cesare Battisti. Others sought aid from the enemy in Paris, London, and later from emigrant communities in the United States, hoping to create a series of independent nation-states after the war, as did Czech nationalists Tomáš Garrigue Masaryk and Edvard Beneš. What these exile women and men shared was a powerful dedication to forge a radically different future made up of new states, if nevertheless their vision was often rooted in social and cultural ideas from the pre-1914 world.

The third consideration regarding the possible influence of the Russian Revolution on Austria-Hungary was that it did indeed influence Austria-Hungary's war effort and its people's expectations for immediate change. In policy terms, the revolution added urgency to the warnings of those civil servants and politicians who demanded a loosening of the military dictatorship, a reform of labor conditions, and a range of new welfare initiatives. Others also saw in Russia's surrender a solution to the problem of food procurement. Early in 1918, there was much talk in the newspapers about access to allegedly enormous grain supplies in Ukraine and the Treaty of Brest-Litovsk was popularly—if ultimately misleadingly—dubbed the "Bread Peace." The Russian Revolution also created new opportunities for some in the government to argue for concluding a separate peace from Germany with the Entente powers and leaving the war altogether. Although Austria-Hungary's leaders repeatedly failed to extricate their country from the war, the revolution in Russia and the subsequent peace made visible the degree to which their wartime goals differed radically from those of their German ally. For Germany, the war remained one of Imperial conquest, while for Austria-Hungary, ending the war increasingly became understood as necessary for the very survival of state and society. Nevertheless, and despite these efforts, during its final years Austria-Hungary came increasingly under the economic, military, and political dominance of its German ally.

Still others on the ground and in many of the factories hoped to replicate a communist-style revolution within Habsburg lands. This they hoped—and government officials feared—might take place through the intervention of hundreds of thousands of Austro-Hungarian POWs returning from Russia, men recently freed—and perhaps indoctrinated?—by the new Bolshevik regime.

A New Era?

Already at the end of 1916, some governmental reform and peace efforts had been set in motion before revolution in Russia changed military and domestic calculations. These internal changes were partly the products of two unexpected deaths. Their ultimate effect was to loosen the grip of the Military High Command on society, and to create reasonable hopes for political change. One death was a political assassination and the other resulted from natural causes. Both shocked Austro-Hungarian society. On October 20, 1916 Friedrich Adler, son of Socialist Party leader Viktor Adler, approached the Austrian Prime Minister Count Stürgkh in the Viennese Hotel *Meissl und Schadn*, just as the latter was finishing his lunch. Adler shot the Prime Minister four times at close range and then allowed himself to be taken into custody by the police. Adler had planned this action for months, betting that only a spectacular assassination like this could shake up Austria's leadership (including the moderate Social Democrats) enough to end both the military dictatorship and the war. As Maureen Healy points out, however, it was a blatant sign of the general misery in Vienna, that public discussion about the assassination centered far more on what Stürgkh had been eating for lunch on that fateful day, than on the celebrity identity of the assassin or his aims.[5]

The second death took place in much quieter circumstances just one month later, and its effects were even more consequential. On November 21, 1916 the old Emperor King Francis Joseph died after a sixty-eight-year reign. His death at age 86 was received with considerable shock across the Monarchy, both because of his general popularity even during wartime, and because he had been the only ruler most citizens could remember. In the first decades of his reign following his installation in 1848, he had been massively unpopular. Yet over time, Francis Joseph had become something of a popular grandfather figure who was venerated as a symbolic protector by people from among all the Monarchy's social, linguistic, and religious groups.

---

[5] Rauchensteiner, *The First World War*, 627, 631; Healy, *Vienna*, 32. Stürgkh's last lunch consisted of soup, boiled beef, mashed turnips, plum pudding, and a wine spritzer, as Healy points out, a far better meal than most Viennese had enjoyed since before the war.

Some historians have argued that because the old emperor/king had been the only real object of public affection and loyalty in the last decades, his death weakened the Monarchy decisively and left it ripe for revolution and collapse. With Francis Joseph gone, they asked, what could possibly hold this Empire together? This was certainly a question that many contemporaries asked of each other. The fact that the Monarchy did not fall apart at this difficult wartime juncture suggests, however, that the legitimacy of the state rested on far more than simply loyalty to a beloved grandfather figure. It also suggests that a ruler who was less subservient to the state's military rulers and more flexible and reform-minded in his outlook might be able to improve Austria-Hungary's dire situation.

The new emperor king, Francis Joseph's great nephew the Archduke Charles, could possibly fit that bill. At a mere 29 years of age, and despite his inexperience, Charles nevertheless brought refreshing personal qualities to the table. These included a generally more dynamic and youthful style of leadership, a much greater interest than his great uncle had shown in twentieth-century technologies and their use to present the dynasty to the public, an attractive young wife and family, and a vigorous drive to travel to the various fronts to visit the troops. Charles strongly believed that Austria-Hungary would only survive in the long term if it could somehow extract itself from the war. In his accession manifesto Charles assured his peoples that, "I will do everything to banish in the shortest possible time the horrors and sacrifices of war."[6] Unlike the German Emperor Wilhelm II, Charles openly expressed support for a peace without annexation, and privately, at times, he occasionally even considered giving up some small territories of Austria-Hungary to buy an end to the war. He was less clear, however, about his intentions for reforming the domestic structures of his empire.

Yet despite his intentions, Charles found his ability to maneuver constantly constrained by a powerful web of circumstances, and above all, by Austria-Hungary's increasing military and economic dependence on its German ally. Try as he might—and he tried often—this state of affairs made it impossible for him to withdraw Austria-Hungary from the war. It also became clear to many of those who witnessed his actions first-hand, that despite his objectives, Charles's character was ultimately indecisive. He often found it difficult to contradict the powerful and older establishment figures who surrounded him. Perhaps this should not surprise us in a relatively inexperienced young man who came to power under impossible circumstances, and whose older, more experienced, and aggressive military and political advisors constantly bombarded him with their strong opinions.

At the beginning of his reign, however, Charles immediately shook things up, and these efforts did buy him some credit and time from the suffering citizens of his realms. Several key political actors, among them Hungary's strong man Prime

---

[6] Quoted in Gordon Brook-Shepherd, *The Last Habsburg* (London: Weidenfeld & Nicolson, 1968), 49.

Figure 6.1 Emperor King Charles and Empress Queen Zita.
Source: Alamy: https://www.alamy.com/emperor-charles-i-of-austria-1887-1922-with-empress-zita-museum-private-collection-author-anonymous-image407166738. html?imageid=FA8498D6-4C57-423D-B28C-109EA8D40D3F&p=697458&pn=1&searchId=fdc378b4692bf5944052f6d28daa654d&searchtype=0

Minister Count Tisza, watched with mounting concern as the new ruler threatened to implement major political changes. In his very first month in power Charles fired both the Foreign Minister and the highest military officials, replacing them with men who held very different views. He made himself Commander in Chief of the military, replacing the old Archduke Friedrich, and he removed

Figure 6.2 Emperor King Charles inspects the Polish Legion, 1917.
Source: Austrian National Library: https://onb.digital/result/10D3E45

the man responsible for Austria-Hungary's failed military strategies, Franz Conrad von Hötzendorf, from the General Staff.

Charles appointed Count Ottokar Czernin (1872–1932) to the influential post of Foreign Minister. Czernin had been a close associate of the assassinated Archduke Francis Ferdinand, whose critical views on Hungary's power and influence within the Dual Monarchy were well known. Before the war, Tisza and others had worried that Francis Ferdinand wanted to reform the Empire in favor of Austria-Hungary's South Slav populations and at Hungary's expense. For these reasons, an anxious Tisza insisted on an immediate coronation for Charles in Budapest. A quick coronation, he claimed publicly, would bolster Charles's legitimacy in Hungary, introduce him to his Hungarian subjects, and rally them for the war effort. The bigger reason for Tisza's haste, however, had more to do with his fear that Charles might share the anti-Hungarian sentiments of his dead uncle, the Archduke Francis Ferdinand.[7] Whether or not Charles in fact shared these views, taking the Hungarian coronation oath would at least bind him to the status quo and prevent him from imposing radical structural reform on the Hungarian regime. Before the year was out—and before he could propose any changes to the dualist system—Charles and his young wife Zita brought their

---

[7] Dániel Szabó, "Die Agonie des historischen Ungarns," in *Die Habsburgermonarchie 1848–1918*, vol. 11/1/2, *Die Habsburgermonarchie und der Erste Weltkrieg*, ed. Helmut Rumpler and Anatol Schmidt-Kowarzik (Vienna: Verlag der Österreichischen Akademie der Wissenschaften, 2016), 698–9.

4-year-old son and heir, Archduke Otto, to Budapest, where together they took part in the elaborate coronation ritual on December 30.

Almost immediately Charles did try to change Austria-Hungary's situation, and not simply by shaking up the military command and the civil administration. In March 1917 he announced his intention to reopen the Austrian parliament in May, and he agreed to create a complaint commission with representation for workers in war industries who were subjected to harsh military discipline.[8]

In Hungary, the new King lobbied an unwilling Prime Minister Tisza vigorously throughout the spring to enact suffrage reform. On April 28, the King ordered him to propose legislation for social relief measures and an extension of the suffrage that would be "equal to the present great moment and to the sacrifices made by the people."[9] At the very least, Tisza should support enfranchising war veterans with a bill referred to as the "heroes' right to vote." The political opposition had already twice introduced this legislation to reward Hungary's veterans with the vote.[10] In April and May of 1917 its adoption seemed imperative in the face of growing unrest among Hungary's miners, metalworkers, and railway workers, all of which imperiled the war effort. When Tisza refused to budge on franchise reform Charles accepted his resignation. It was largely amid these shake-ups in Austria-Hungary that news of revolution in Russia began to sink in.

For all the fears it raised of possible social revolution, the events in Russia did little to produce new revolutionary rumblings in Austria-Hungary. Nor did the news apparently weaken the resolve or discipline of Austria-Hungary's frontline troops in the east, as military leaders worried that it might. Most people on the home front in Austria-Hungary were far more concerned with daily survival than with the news of a successful revolution in a neighboring state. The revolution did offer some hope that the war could be ended more quickly, and that with peace, food from the east might relieve suffering from starvation. But for most Austrians and Hungarians, the revolution did not call into question the continued existence of their own Empire. The Habsburg Monarchy and its institutions, rather than its possible destruction, remained the common viable starting point for most efforts to achieve the many different visionary futures mentioned above. Many of those who might have welcomed the possibility of breaking up the Empire also feared that its destruction could produce decades more of fighting (and starvation) in East Central Europe once warring nationalist factions were

---

[8] Margarete Grandner, *Kooperative Gewerkschaftspolitik in der Kriegswirtschaft: die freien Gewerkschaften Österreichs im ersten Weltkrieg* (Vienna: Böhlau, 1992), chap. 6.

[9] Galántai, *Hungary*, 244.

[10] Gabor Vermes, "Leap into the Dark: The Issue of Suffrage in Hungary During World War I," in *The Habsburg Empire in World War I: Essays on the Intellectual, Military, Political and Economic Aspects of the Habsburg War Effort*, ed. Robert A. Kann, Béla K. Király, and Paula Sutter Fichtner, East European Monographs 23 (Boulder, CO: East European Quarterly, 1977).

released from Imperial control.[11] In the short term at least, for much of 1917, news of revolution in Russia had little effect on the continued legitimacy of the Monarchy.

The Russian Revolution did, however, accelerate two revolutionary trends in Austria-Hungary, trends that marked off clear differences between Austria-Hungary and the failed Russian autocracy. In Vienna, the highly placed diarist, historian, and politician Josef Redlich noted in March 1917 that while revolution in neighboring Russia did not seem likely to spread, nevertheless, "'up here' where we are, things are becoming very social democratic out of sheer fear."[12] What he meant by this was that events in Russia had brought a new legitimacy and political influence to Austrian Social Democracy. In 1917 and 1918 the Austrian government paid increasing attention to the demands of Social Democratic leaders, supporting their participation in a peace conference in Stockholm and even on occasion offering them positions in the cabinet, positions that they turned down. This effort to pacify Social Democrats wherever possible sought to avoid something much worse—communist revolution. In the spring and summer of 1917 in Austria, this effort culminated in several reforms including, most notably, the creation of a new and well-funded Ministry for People's Health and Social Provision. Already in December 1916, the government had drawn up plans to increase social provision for the elderly and sick while creating special homes for soldiers and youth.[13] As Foreign Minister Czernin—whose business this was not—wrote to the skeptical Hungarian Prime Minister Tisza before the latter's resignation, "after the war we shall be obliged to implement a social welfare policy, whether any one individual wants this or not, and it is in my view essential to enlist the Social Democrats for this purpose. Social policy is the valve that we must open to vent the excess steam—otherwise the gasket will explode."[14]

This support for social democracy by some in the Austrian government—however indirect—may indeed have resulted from real fears about the potential for social revolution in the Dual Monarchy. But it also tells us something about the accomplishments and weaknesses of organized socialism and labor by 1917. The Social Democratic Party leaderships in both Austria and Hungary had originally supported the war as a defensive fight against a reactionary, oppressive, and anti-Semitic Russian autocracy. In return for their support of the war, the Social Democrats had expected to gain a greater voice in labor and economic policy

---

[11] Rauchensteiner, *The First World War*, 707. [12] Quoted in Rauchensteiner, 707.
[13] On the creation of the Ministry, see Tara Zahra, "'Each Nation Only Cares for Its Own': Empire, Nation, and Child Welfare Activism in the Bohemian Lands, 1900–1918," *The American Historical Review* 111, no. 5 (December 1, 2006): 1378–402. See also Hsia, *Victims' State*; Thomas Süsler-Rohringer, *Krisenindizierte Kontinuität: Soziale Sicherung Und Die Re-Integration Kriegsversehrter Im Habsburgerreich 1880–1918* (Göttingen: Vandenhoeck & Ruprecht, 2023).
[14] Letter from spring 1917, quoted in Rauchensteiner, *The First World War*, 723. Also quoted in Margarete Grandner, *Kooperative Gewerkschaftspolitik in der Kriegswirtschaft: die freien Gewerkschaften Österreichs im ersten Weltkrieg* (Wien: Böhlau Verl, 1992), 309.

both during and after the war. And indeed, by spring 1917 leading Czech, German, and Polish Social Democrats had earned positions on Austrian government commissions and gained some voice in shaping social policy. This influence, however, came at a steep price. As conditions for workers and consumers drastically worsened, as younger unskilled or female labor replaced traditionally unionized skilled male labor, party and union discipline often broke down. Social Democratic and union leaders faced mounting challenges to their authority from workers who often struck, despite the efforts of union leaders to keep striking to a minimum.[15]

After Russia exited the war in 1918, more party leaders increasingly opposed the war. Even with their participation on government commissions, leading Socialist Party politicians nevertheless maintained a formal distance from the government for ideological reasons. Some, like Karl Renner, whom the government viewed as useful, still showed an informal willingness to cooperate in the expectation that this would bring them a significant voice in shaping the postwar order. But by 1917, workers were also being pressured in brutal new ways to fulfill the massively increased and unrealistic production targets set by the ambitious German Hindenburg Program. Austria-Hungary's participation in Germany's intensified efforts to mobilize all members of society for the war effort proved even more destructive to the economy in Austria.[16] Its increased demands on workers in war industries severely impacted the productivity of an already exhausted workforce.

At the very same time, workers' job and living conditions worsened considerably, and their access to food became even more precarious. Strikes unauthorized by the Social Democratic Party broke out with greater frequency in both halves of the Monarchy. Governments habitually turned to the more moderate Social Democrat and union leaders to rein in working-class radicalism. These latter worked hard to control their clients but found themselves increasingly helpless in the face of worker anger by 1917.[17] In October 1917, for example, a revolutionary offshoot of the Hungarian Social Democratic Party published a pamphlet calling on workers to undermine war production and support a general strike. "Governments, foreign ministers, and diplomats representing the ruling classes

---

[15] Kučera, *Rationed Life*, 141–52 provides a superb analysis of a major strike against Škoda in Plzen/Pilsen in the summer of 1917; Sabine Schmitner, "Sabotage?! Passive Resistenz von Rüstungsarbeiterinnern in der k.u.k. Munitionsfabrik Wöllersdorf während des Ersten Weltkrieges," *Österreich in Geschichte und Literatur* 3 (2012): 259–71.

[16] Watson, *Ring of Steel*, 508. Watson points out that the increased targets of steel and iron for munitions diverted those materials from needed repairs of rolling stock and meant that munitions industries could not be supplied with coal.

[17] Wolfgang Maderthaner and Alfred Pfoser, "Die Enttäuschung des Krieges. Kulturelle Transformationen während der 'Grossen Zeit,'" in *Die Habsburgermonarchie 1848–1918*, vol. 11/1/1, 647; Sabine Schmitner, "Local Politics During the First World War: Political Players in the Armaments Center Wiener Neustadt," *European Review of History: Revue européenne d'histoire* 24, no. 2 (March 4, 2017): 229–49, 242.

are unable to give back peace to the people...Neither can we expect any longer that those whose task it is [i.e. Social Democratic Party leaders] should force a peace." Arguing that the recent failure of the international conference in Stockholm of Social Democratic leaders ("Even those official party chiefs...would not have been at variance had they all stood on the basis of class struggle") meant that workers should take matters into their own hands.[18]

If the growing recognition of social democracy by conservative government officials constituted one wartime revolution, another revolution in 1917 and 1918 shook the realm of diplomacy. Many Imperial officials believed that the Russian Revolution offered Austria-Hungary an excellent opportunity to extract itself from the war by means of a separate peace. One of the ongoing justifications for war in the east—especially for Social Democrats—had been the need to defeat Europe's most authoritarian and anti-Semitic regime. After March 1917, with Russia apparently on the road to democracy, not only the legitimation for the war but also the basic argument for continuing the social truce among the various political parties suddenly vanished. The autocracy had been defeated. Why continue the war? All the more reason to make peace with Russia and try to keep the Social Democrats and their constituents committed to the ongoing war against Italy. In March 1917, therefore, many government officials actually encouraged the leading Austrian Social Democrats to participate in formal and informal negotiations with Russia's new provisional government to broker a peace that could also relieve harsh home front conditions back home in Austria-Hungary.

A diplomatic revolution to take Austria-Hungary out of the war, however, would put it radically at odds with its German ally. The question of how to solve this conundrum continued to baffle politicians and the emperor king himself. Anti-German feeling was clearly growing throughout the Monarchy, especially among those who did not see themselves as German nationalists. In Bohemia, for example, popular rumors and accusations abounded that food was being deliberately shipped from Austria-Hungary to benefit Germany.[19] In March of 1917 for example, the American *chargé d'affairs* in Vienna reported a popular joke, which claimed that while it might take five years before Germans would again be allowed to travel to France, and ten years before they could travel to England, it would be twenty years before they would be allowed into Austria.[20]

The Austro-Hungarian diplomatic approach to peace with Russia was not simply a product of popular resentment against Germany. It resulted more from a hard-nosed understanding in the highest circles that the very survival of the Monarchy depended on finding swift solutions to several other domestic political challenges that involved the lands to the east. Whereas Germany pursued an

---

[18] Quoted in Galántai, *Hungary*, 260–1.
[19] Morelon, *Streetscapes*, 24–5; Stimmungsberichte Folder 5024, February 1918, Beilage 42.
[20] Rauchensteiner, *The First World War*, 710.

expansionist policy of annexation in the east, Austria-Hungary's goals focused more on food procurement on the one hand and attempts to satisfy the conflicting territorial demands of Polish and Ukrainian nationalists on the other. Ukrainian nationalists hoped to create an autonomous territory in East Galicia, perhaps with the addition of Ukrainian territory from Russia. Polish nationalists, who had been promised a state by the Central Powers in 1916, sought to maintain all of Galicia for a new Polish state (that might also have a Habsburg King). As long as the war in the east continued, deciding these questions could be postponed. Now with peace looming, at least one of these nationalist groups, if not both, would be bitterly disappointed by the outcome.

A Separate Peace?

As we have seen, Charles had openly expressed hopes for a quick end to the war at his accession. He repeatedly searched for a way out of the war, even at the possible cost of abandoning his Germany ally. His willingness publicly to support a peace without annexation also worried his German ally, as did his efforts to reform domestic policy. These developments drew criticism in much of the press in Germany, and in May 1917 the Austrian War Surveillance Office even prevented German newspapers from entering Austria.[21]

In fact, early in 1917 Charles did undertake a highly risky set of undercover negotiations with the enemy. He secretly communicated his wishes for peace to his wife's brothers, Princes Sixtus and Xavier of Bourbon Parma, who served in the Belgian army. In his reply to Charles's first letter, Sixtus asked whether Charles could agree to the restoration of Belgian and to Serbian independence, to a German renunciation of the border provinces of Alsace-Lorraine, and to the Russian occupation of Constantinople? Interestingly, this first message from Sixtus made no mention of Italy and its desire to obtain considerable Austro-Hungarian territory along the Monarchy's Adriatic coast and in Tyrol. Charles's reply suggested—in appropriately vague terms—that he was willing at least to consider the French conditions (restoration of Belgium and Serbia, adjustment of the Alsace Lorraine border).

Sixtus then traveled secretly to Vienna to meet with both Charles and Czernin. Afterwards, in a note dated March 24, 1917 that he did not show to his Foreign Minister, Charles asked Sixtus to convey "secretly and unofficially to M. Poincaré, President of the French Republic, that I will support the just claims of France concerning Alsace Lorraine with all means at my disposal and exert all my personal influence with my allies to this end." Charles also promised his support to

---

[21] Rauchensteiner, *First World War*, 709.

restore German-occupied Belgium with its colonial empire, and to preserve an independent Serbia.[22] He could not comment on any questions regarding Russia because the recent revolution there made future developments unclear.

Soon thereafter Charles and Zita traveled to German Headquarters at Homburg to meet with Kaiser Wilhelm and his generals. Charles hoped to impress on his German allies the critical importance of concluding some kind of peace in the very near future. While there, however, he found his German counterpart—and the generals Hindenburg and Ludendorff—completely convinced that their recent policy of unrestricted submarine warfare would soon bring England to its knees before the United States could join the war.[23]

The British and French leaders reacted positively to Charles's note of March 24, partly because the strategic situation seemed especially bleak for their side at that moment, especially given the uncertainty surrounding the future of their ally Russia. The Italians, however, were unwilling to renounce their claims to Austro-Hungarian territories that the British and French had secretly promised them in return for entering the war, promises of which Charles was entirely ignorant. Sixtus did convey yet another secret letter hinting that Charles might consider making some minor territorial adjustments in Trentino for Italy, but given the extravagant promises of Habsburg territory the Treaty of London had guaranteed them, this small concession could hardly have satisfied the Italian government.[24] At the same time, both Charles's efforts to guarantee the territorial integrity of the Monarchy and the general contempt in which the Austro-Hungarian military held for its Italian foe, made compromise with Italy impossible.[25] And as it turned out, once the United States declared war on Germany (April 6, 1917) the British and French suddenly had fewer reasons to seek an immediate peace. The negotiations now ground to a halt and that might well have been the end of the story. But as we will see with the peace of Brest-Litovsk that formally ended the war in the east a year later in March 1918, the secret negotiations would return to haunt both Charles and Czernin in the worst possible way.

This was not the only effort Charles made to find a way out of the war. At various moments in 1917 and 1918, his government also negotiated with the United

---

[22] The entire note is reproduced in Brook-Shepherd, *Last Habsburg*, 72–3. Charles also offered to allow Serbia access to the Adriatic but demanded in turn that Serbia renounce and suppress groups that supported the dissolution of the Habsburg Monarchy. See also Rauchensteiner, *The First World War*, 898.

[23] Brook-Shepherd, *Last Habsburg*, 77–8.

[24] Italian intransigence on the territorial issue was strange because it came at a time when General Luigi Cadorna (1850–1928), the Italian Chief of Staff, indicated in separate talks with Austria-Hungary in Switzerland that Italy would indeed be satisfied with a slice of Trentino as the price for achieving a separate peace. Watson, *Ring of Steel*, 467.

[25] Watson, *Ring of Steel*, 467. Watson paints a very different picture of Charles's efforts, arguing that the emperor king did not contemplate a separate peace, but merely a general peace without annexation, while at the same time negotiating with the Germans over war spoils in the east.

States. It was a testament to how seriously the United States took these informal discussions that it did not declare war on Austria-Hungary until December 7, 1917, a full eight months after it had declared war on Germany. Nor did the Fourteen Points that President Woodrow Wilson (1856–1924) articulated a month later as the basis of the United States' war aims call for the dismemberment of Austria-Hungary, to the disappointment of many of the émigré nationalist politicians from Austria-Hungary. Wilson's Point Ten read: "The Peoples of Austria-Hungary, whose place among the nations we wish to see safeguarded and assured, should be accorded the freest opportunity to autonomous development." Larry Wolff has noted that the deeper purpose of Point Ten was to hint at the possibility of destabilizing the Monarchy through nationalist agitation, as a way to detach it from the German alliance.[26] For an exile activist like Czech nationalist Edvard Beneš, the Fourteen Points demonstrated that Wilson was "not a partisan of the destruction of the Monarchy, and his plan for the liberation of the peoples of Austria-Hungary did not call for the creation of independent national states but only for the organization of self-government or some sort of federation."[27] Even after Wilson articulated the concept of political self-determination in a speech to Congress on February 11, 1918, he still understood it in terms of a reformed Habsburg Empire.

The American hope that the threat of increased national instability might help detach Austria-Hungary from its German alliance still could not alter the inescapable reality that Austria-Hungary depended increasingly on Germany for military and food assistance. This increased dependence made any separate peace almost impossible to achieve. For this reason, it is difficult to imagine what might the consequence have been had Charles proceeded more openly with these separate peace efforts? Most historians argue that Germany would almost certainly have attempted to occupy Austria-Hungary, to overthrow its governments, and to use its economic influence to punish the Monarchy as well. Alexander Watson, however, has argued persuasively that Germany could have ill afforded the troops necessary to occupy Austria-Hungary effectively. Still, the question is not easily answered by recourse to statistics alone. The psychology of the situation and the many ways in which both Austro-Hungarian society and the military had come to depend on its German ally made it difficult to imagine an effective strategy for leaving the war. Moreover, it was largely thanks to German military assistance—and the presence of German units interspersed with Habsburg ones on all the fronts—that Austria-Hungary would win its most impressive and decisive victory of the war in the fall of 1917.

---

[26] Larry Wolff, *Woodrow Wilson and the Reimagining of Eastern Europe* (Stanford, California: Stanford University Press, 2020), 66–71.
[27] Quoted in Wolff, *Wilson*, 70.

Figure 6.3 Italian POWs, 1917.
Source: Wikimedia Commons: https://commons.wikimedia.org/wiki/File:Italijanski_vojni_ujetniki_po_bitki_pri_Kobaridu.jpg

On October 24, 1917, Austria-Hungary and Germany began a highly successful offensive operation against Italy on the Isonzo front near the town of Kobarid/Caporetto. The operation ended on November 19, with a massive defeat of Italy's forces. The Austro-Hungarians and Germans advanced ninety miles, took over 250,000 Italians prisoner, and captured valuable stores and military equipment. The defeat brought down the Italian government.[28] With this stunning victory, activity on the Italian front ended. Austria-Hungary had essentially defeated Italy.[29] But this victory came at an enormous price. It had required most railway cars to be diverted to supply the front and away from delivering food to Austria's cities, and of course it also meant the responsibility for feeding and housing some 250,000 Italian POWs.[30]

---

[28] John Gooch, *The Italian Army and the First World War*, Armies of the Great War (Cambridge: Cambridge University Press, 2014), 245–6. The advance included an effective deployment of poison gas by the Germans.

[29] The Italians lost 11,000 killed and at least 29,000 wounded. The Austro-Hungarians and Germans suffered casualties of 20,000–70,000 killed or wounded. Anna Grillini, "Battle of Caporetto," *1914–1918–Online International Encyclopedia of the First World War*, 2015, https://doi.org/10.15463/IE1418.10630.

[30] Watson, *Ring of Steel*, 476; J. Robert Wegs, "Transportation: The Achilles' Heel of the Habsburg War Effort," in *The Habsburg Empire in World War I*.

On the Edge

The censored press touted Austria-Hungary's glorious victory at Caporetto/Kobarid, but it hardly affected the dangerously low public morale. Already seven months before, in an April 1917 memorandum, Czernin had warned Charles (and German Emperor Wilhelm II) bluntly that if they "could not conclude peace within the next months, then the peoples will make it over their heads, and then the waves of revolution will sweep away everything for which our brothers and sons are still fighting and dying today."[31] In domestic terms, this period saw institutional efforts to improve conditions with the creation in May 1917 of a new Welfare Ministry by the Austrian government. Then in July, Charles issued an amnesty for political prisoners. These included several leading Czech nationalist parliamentarians who were being held in prison on trumped up charges of treason, as well as Friedrich Adler, the assassin of Count Karl Stürgkh. The amnesty incurred the wrath of several establishment figures as well as of many German nationalists who feared the emperor was catering to Slav-nationalist or socialist traitors. But Charles would not be deterred in this new course. By the end of 1917, Charles had even ended the harsh military censorship in Austria, in the process, also weakening the control over domestic information exercised by the Austrian and Hungarian propaganda bureaus.[32]

Taken together, and by the standards of earlier times, these acts by a conservative ruler might have seemed revolutionary to some. And at the time, they may have inspired some people, however briefly, with hope for a swift end to the war and a just settlement. But after three years of harsh wartime conditions, Charles's efforts could hardly meet with popular gratitude and support. As we will see, in taking steps to dismantle the military dictatorship, it was as if he had removed the pin from a grenade. Instead of expressing willingness to work with the new regime, frustrated and angry politicians and journalists took advantage of their new rights to criticize these measures as too small, too long overdue, and barely meaningful.

More to the point, increased rights and welfare payments could not solve the fundamental problem of food supply, for which there simply were no solutions. Urban popular opinion blamed corruption, hoarders, Hungary, Germany, black marketeers, refugees, and always Jews for the starvation. For years, government officials and local civil servants had loudly and repeatedly announced new laws to crackdown on hoarders and black marketeers. But the fact was that the country and the occupied territories simply did not produce anywhere near the amounts of food necessary to feed the population. Urban women and children resorted increasingly to foraging trips to the surrounding countryside, scavenging for what

---

[31] Watson, *Ring of Steel*, 351; Fritz Fischer, *Germany's Aims in the First World War* (New York: W. W. Norton, 1968), 468.
[32] Cornwall, "Das Ringen," 423.

little food might be left to local farmers. In Lower Austria outside Vienna, for example, this foraging practice culminated in a so-called "potato war," as an estimated 30,000 urban Viennese attacked the surrounding potato region. The authorities discouraged these trips, often confiscating the contents of knapsacks and baskets in the regional railway stations as exhausted women and children returned from their forays.[33] This harsh governmental response only produced more outrage and anger.

If the new emperor king and his advisors feared for the survival of the state in 1917, society itself showed every sign of collapse at the beginning of 1918. On January 14, 1918 the Austrian government found itself forced to announce that already meager Austrian flour rations would be halved, thanks to a lack of coal to transport supplies from Hungary. Immediately, the largest industrial strikes in Austria's history broke out in Vienna. These strikes quickly spread in waves to cities across both halves of the Dual Monarchy. On January 15, Cracow was hit by serious unrest. From Budapest, where striking workers destroyed streetcar rails, the German consul reported that the movement was beginning to take on a revolutionary character. For several days, over 600,000 industrial workers struck, rioted, caused hundreds of thousands of crowns worth of damage, injuries to both strikers and the police, and hundreds of arrests.[34]

These massive strikes were only the most egregious example of the many small and large ways in which people had created space to make their demands known even in the context of wartime dictatorship. This development, however, also brings into greater focus the situation of municipal administrators and district civil servants who occupied critical positions between the military or the central governments in Austria and Hungary on the one hand, and local society on the other. Even under the worst of the dictatorship it was clear that the military often depended on these administrators at all levels for their expert knowledge, and to carry out basic functions, from organizing local economies to surveilling populations to administering justice.[35] Their public roles became even more critical in the months before the collapse of the Empire. As the central and often provincial governments became increasingly incapable of supplying localities, district and municipal civil servants often had to take matters into their own hands to maintain order. This trend became particularly acute in the summer of 1918, as we will see, when local officials especially in Galicia and Bohemia no longer intervened to protect local Jewish communities from violent popular attacks on them and their property.

---

[33] Healy, *Vienna*, 53–6; Morelon, *Streetscapes*, chap. 4; Martin Moll, *Die Steiermark im Ersten Weltkrieg: der Kampf des Hinterlandes ums Überleben 1914–1918* (Vienna: Styria Premium, 2014), 158.
[34] Rauchensteiner, *The First World War*, 873–4.
[35] Schmitner, "Local Politics During the First World War," 229–49.

Given its own reliance on home-front production, conditions in the military also worsened severely in the spring of 1918. Every necessity was in dangerously short supply, from boots, uniforms, and ammunition, to food. The number of available military physicians fell to 5,500 from 7,500.[36] At the same time, mass desertion from the military increasingly became a factor undermining efforts to maintain strength at the front. Among the returning POWs from Russia, fear of being remobilized to the front was a far greater factor in their subsequent desertion than any alleged indoctrination by Bolshevism during their time in Russia.

Not surprisingly, Conrad and his circle blamed this dangerous and increasing trend of desertion on Charles's very leniency, his amnesty of political prisoners of the previous year, as well as on his reforms of brutal military discipline. When military courts lost the right to confirm death sentences in May 1917, for example, Charles had also ended certain extreme physical punishments for minor infractions. All these examples and changes had allegedly weakened discipline and encouraged desertion. The fact was, however, that frontline conditions themselves explained the massive increase in desertion statistics.[37]

On February 1, 1918, only a few weeks after the outbreak of the urban strike wave, the crew of the cruiser *Sankt Georg*, anchored at the Adriatic military base in Cattaro/Kotor, mutinied. The mutineers who took over the ship demanded, among other things (like extra time off and cigarettes), an end to the war, democratization of the Empire, autonomy for its many nations, and especially an improvement in the food supplies that had been promised by the flagging peace negotiations with Russia. When reinforcements arrived from Pola, the mutiny collapsed. Eight hundred men were arrested and four executed.[38]

The final straw for the public may have been the futile hopes for food raised briefly by the so-called "bread peace" of Brest-Litovsk with Russia, discussed below. According to its terms, the Treaty required occupied regions of Ukraine to ship grain west to both Austria-Hungary and Germany in return for their support for Ukraine's newly independent governments. But as we will see, ultimately, there was little grain to be had from the east, especially after the two militaries had taken their shares.[39] At the same time factory workers across the Monarchy continued throughout the spring of 1918 to strike in increasing numbers, agitating for food and an end to slave-like labor conditions. As strikes and insufficient coal

---

[36] Rauchensteiner, *The First World War*, 887.
[37] Watson, *Ring of Steel*, 508–9. Watson points especially to the extreme harshness of Habsburg military discipline up to July 1917 compared to that of other powers. The Habsburg military executed 754 of its soldiers during the war as opposed to 600 for the French, 346 for the British, and forty-eight for the Germans. With regard to desertion, Watson reports that "in the first quarter of 1918, the Hungarians alone were searching for 20,000 absconded soldiers."
[38] Rauchensteiner, *The First World War*, 888. The commander of the fleet was subsequently replaced by the relatively young ship captain Miklos Horthy who later ruled Hungary as "regent" after the war.
[39] Rauchensteiner, *The First World War*, 880.

and food supplies ground production in key war industries to a halt, the transport infrastructure too collapsed, the military now starved as well, and desertion and mutinies multiplied. And after barely twelve months as emperor king, Charles's efforts at political reform had produced the very opposite effect than what he had intended.

Years' worth of pent-up public anger at the abandonment of legality, the brutal excesses of the military dictatorship, and enforced starvation exploded. The reopening of parliament in May 1917 and the subsequent relaxation of censorship simply created more public opportunities for politicians to articulate public outrage over conditions of the past three years and government incompetence regarding the food crisis. This anger was made more poignant by the fact that in May 1917, before Charles announced his amnesties, close to forty parliamentary deputies had languished in prison. Although Charles's original purpose in recalling parliament had been to resolve the food crisis, the angry deputies and parties had other ideas in mind.

At the opening session of parliament various nationalist groupings seized the opportunity to renew their highly public efforts to wring promises of increased autonomy from the Austrian government. Speaking for the thirty-three parliamentary deputies representing Slovene-, Croatian-, and Serb-speaking regions of Austria, deputy Anton Korošec presented the May Declaration of the newly formed South Slav Party. The petition demanded the unification of all territories of the Monarchy—both Austria and Hungary—inhabited by Slovenes, Croats, and Serbs. This new territorial unit, to be ruled by the Habsburg dynasty, would have an independent status comparable to that of Hungary. When the deputies received no answer from the government, they soon resorted to a petition drive to demonstrate the popularity of their demands among both women and men.[40] At the very same opening session of parliament, a "Czech Union" that combined all but two of the Czech nationalist parties read out a statement that blamed the dualist system for the structural ills of the Monarchy and demanded the transformation of the Dual Monarchy into a federal union of "free and equal national states." Additionally, the statement demanded the unification of Czech lands in Austria with the "Slovak branch" in Hungary, arguing for a common nation-state of Czechs within a Habsburg federation.[41]

Most dangerous for the Monarchy among the nationalist demands, however, were the ongoing negotiations with Polish nationalists over Galicia and a future

---

[40] On the May Declaration and later petition movement, see Peter Štih, Vasko Simoniti, and Peter Vodopivec, *Slowenische Geschichte: Gesellschaft—Politik—Kultur*, Veröffentlichungen der Historischen Landeskommission für Steiermark 40 (Graz: Leykam, 2008), 301–10; Rok Stergar, "'We Will Look Like Fools If Nothing Comes of This Yugoslavia!': The Establishment of Yugoslavia from the Perspective of Slovene Contemporaries," *Hiperboreea* 10, no. 1 (June 1, 2023): 82–101.

[41] Ivan Šedivý, "Der Einfluss der ersten Weltkrieg auf die Tschechische Politik," in *Die Habsburgermonarchie 1848–1918*, vol. 11/1/2, 730–1; Watson, *Ring of Steel*, 470.

Poland. Since 1916, as we saw in chapter 3, both Austria-Hungary and its German ally had sought to win support from Polish nationalists both by promising to create some kind of quasi-independent Polish state after the war and by promoting a Polish legion under Polish socialist and nationalist Josef Piłsudsky to fight against the Russians. Polish nationalists in Austria, too, had sought for some time to establish an independent Poland after the war that would include all of Galicia, possibly under the rule of a Habsburg archduke. Austria-Hungary and Germany had given people in the occupied Russian Polish territories the right to schooling in their own language, even if other local measures of self-rule turned out to be disappointingly symbolic in character. By late 1917, however, with the collapse of Russia, negotiations with the Austrian Poles ran afoul of the demands of Ukrainian nationalists for a state or autonomous unit of their own within the Empire, one that demanded territory in Galicia and Russian Poland that Poles also claimed. Given the food situation in Austria-Hungary, Ukrainian nationalists now gained new negotiating leverage, as we will see below in the peace negotiations with Russia.

This revival of the Austrian parliament, which unleashed loud recriminations about the depredations of the previous three years and radicalized nationalist demands, had two further noteworthy effects. First, the debates occasioned by the reopening of parliament had a strong effect on politics in Hungary. Indirectly, the demands by Austrian politicians increased pressure on the recalcitrant Hungarian government to carry out a long overdue reform of the restricted suffrage and to respect the fundamental rights of national minorities in Hungary. Secondly, the debates also renewed intense public criticism of Austria-Hungary's German ally.

The "Bread Peace"

If the politics of nationalism made it next to impossible to develop a broad structural reform proposal for even the Austrian half of the Dual Monarchy to which the major political parties could agree, it remained the politics of food that most corroded popular support for the Monarchy. As we saw in chapter 5, the issues of food—or welfare provision—and nationhood came together in 1917 with the creation of the new Ministry of Social Welfare. That linkage of welfare provision with the various local nationalist committees dangerously challenged the legitimacy of the Imperial state. On the ground, for example, it was not clear whether welfare relief came from the emperor king's government or from the nationalist bodies that in fact disbursed the benefits.[42] At the start of 1918, however, peace

---

[42] Zahra, "Each Nation Only Cares for Its Own."

negotiations with Russia raised some hope for an Empire-wide resolution to the unsolvable issue of food provision.

Negotiating this peace was not easy for Austro-Hungarian Foreign Minister Czernin, not simply because of the positions adopted by the USSR, but because of the attitude of his German ally and of his own domestic critics. At the beginning of 1918, with the peace negotiations at hand, Czernin found himself hamstrung between opposing claims, particularly because in 1918 a newly proclaimed Ukrainian People's Republic on formerly Russian territory seemed to promise the only viable solution to Austria-Hungary's food crisis. On January 12, 1918 the Central Powers recognized the Ukrainian People's Republic delegation to the peace negotiations and on the 25th, the Republic officially declared its independence from the USSR.[43] On February 9, Austria-Hungary and Germany signed the First Treaty of Brest-Litovsk, promising to provide the Ukrainian Republic with military assistance against the Bolsheviks in return for desperately needed agricultural supplies. The Ukrainian Council in turn promised to deliver a million metric tons of grain by August 1. However, the Council also demanded the territory around Chelm in formerly Russian Poland, a territory also claimed by Polish nationalists, and the Council demanded national autonomy for Eastern Galicia. Desperate to conclude negotiations swiftly so that grain could reach Austria-Hungary, Czernin agreed to Ukrainian demands for Chelm, and agreed secretly that Galicia would later be partitioned between Polish (western) and Ukrainian (eastern) halves. When on February 11 it became known publicly that the Treaty promised the Chelm region to Ukraine, enraged Polish nationalists rioted in Cracow and declared a "day of Polish mourning" and a general strike for February 18. Polish nationalist soldiers returned their medals and demonstrators attacked local German institutions, blaming Austria-Hungary's ally for the betrayal of the Polish nation. In Austro-Hungarian occupied Lublin, angry demonstrators burned the portrait of the emperor king and the Austrian flag. Schoolchildren replaced portraits of Emperor King Charles with those of Piłsudski.[44] Czernin could not even present the Treaty to the Austrian and Hungarian parliaments for official ratification. Had he done so, the secret agreement to divide Galicia would also have become public.

Meanwhile, Soviet negotiators led by Leon Trotsky (1879–1940) had balked at the harsh terms offered by the Central Powers, and abandoned the peace talks on February 10, 1918. Trotsky declared a Soviet policy of "no war, no peace," meaning that the Soviets would not agree to the peace, but neither would they continue fighting. This was a disastrous development for Czernin, who needed to secure

---

[43] Polish nationalists had also demanded to be represented at the Treaty negotiations, but to no avail.
[44] Piotr Szlanta, "Der lange Abschied der Polen von Österreich," in *Die Habsburgermonarchie 1848–1918*, vol. 11/1/2, 813–85 (pp. 839–43).

Figure 6.4 Signing of the Treaty of Brest-Litovsk, March 1918.
Source: Austrian National Library: https://onb.digital/result/110DF798

both peace and grain as swiftly as possible. His German ally, on the other hand, was in no rush to conclude peace, presuming correctly that the breakdown in negotiations would eventually give Germany an even stronger position against the USSR. When German and Austro-Hungarian forces swiftly advanced to take Kyiv from Ukrainian Bolsheviks on March 1, two days later the Soviets agreed to sign a second and even harsher Treaty of Brest-Litovsk.

The Treaty effectively ended Russia's engagement in the First World War. It also required that Russia sign over close to a million square miles of territory with a population of 50 million and a majority of Russia's industry and coal resources.[45] The Treaty was certainly a victory for the Central Powers. The German military believed that the Treaty would free up troops for the Western Front, where Hindenburg was planning a new spring offensive. And it was believed by many that the Treaty would swiftly provide food for the starving cities of Austria-Hungary. This, even though Austria-Hungary's powerful German ally had demanded a full three quarters of the occupied territory for itself.

In the following weeks, the forces of the Central Powers advanced further into Ukraine, expelling Bolshevik forces from the southern city of Odesa. However, this at first "friendly occupation" of Ukraine by German and Austro-Hungarian

---

[45] Watson, *Ring of Steel*, 494. Watson also notes that even given the draconian nature of the Treaty, it still would have left Russia with somewhat more territory than that of today's Russian Federation.

forces required that enormous numbers of the troops remain in Ukraine to oversee the occupation and especially the export of food to the west. The situation in Ukraine remained unsettled, and the occupying troops too few to enforce their will effectively on this large territory. Social relations in the Ukrainian countryside bitterly divided peasants from large landowners, and their social conflicts made it difficult for the Ukrainian Council to exert its rule over much of the territory or to fulfill its promises to deliver grain. The presence of the occupying forces and the need for grain also caused severe inflation in Ukraine. When Germans and Austro-Hungarians offered inflated paper currency to purchase grain, peasants balked, and the Austro-Hungarian military soon tried to requisition it by force. Peasants hid grain or even destroyed fields, because the future of their produce—whether they could use it, sell it, or would lose it to the occupying forces—was not clear.[46] The Central Powers needed grain as quickly as possible and could not wait for the implementation of land reform plans or the development of a more effective Ukrainian state administration. In a handwritten note from March 31, Emperor King Charles ordered that "requisitions need to be carried out ruthlessly, even by force." The mounting frustration with the situation was evident in a military note that counseled the use of force where necessary on April 9, "If we do not properly make use of Ukraine, something to which it has agreed in the peace treaty, then the whole operation in Ukraine is worthless."[47]

Eventually, the Central Powers reorganized the occupation several times to encourage purchases and increase deliveries. The fact remains, however, that Ukraine could not provide anywhere near the numbers the Council had originally promised. By August 15, 1918, Dornik and Lieb estimate that Ukraine had supplied only 102,000 tons of grain to the Central Powers, of which 52 percent went overland to Austria-Hungary and 28 percent to Germany. Of 400–500 million promised eggs, 60 million had been delivered. During the entire period of the occupation, Ukraine repeatedly gave overly optimistic promises, and as Dornik and Lieb argue, "The Central Powers also seemed to live in a dream world and did not want to see the country's limited capacity."[48]

Things Fall Apart

In a formal, diplomatic, and superficial sense, one might argue that in the spring of 1918 Austria-Hungary came extremely close to a final victory. The Treaty of

---

[46] For an excellent analysis of the occupation, Wolfram Dornik and Peter Lieb, "Economic Utilization," in *The Emergence of Ukraine: Self-Determination, Occupation, and War in Ukraine, 1917–1922*, ed. Wolfram Dornik et al., trans. Gus Fagan (Edmonton: Canadian Institute of Ukrainian Studies Press, 2015), 235–79.

[47] Both quotations in Dornik and Lieb, "Economic Utilization," 244, 245.

[48] Dornik and Lieb, "Economic Utilization," 269. See also the tables and statistics on 267–9. Ukraine did deliver close to 75 percent of the promised 50,000 tons of sugar, and 45 percent of 200,000 promised cattle.

Brest-Litovsk had imposed a harsh peace on defeated Russia, and the subsequent Treaty of Bucharest in May did the same against Romania. Italy had still not recovered from its devastating defeat at Caporetto/Kobarid the previous fall. Yet as the burgeoning strike movement, mutinies, and desertions suggest, Austria-Hungary was in fact close to complete collapse. An utterly misguided military decision to push for a new offensive against Italy, at a moment when the military could least afford it, now demonstrated openly the imminent collapse.

But first, a scandal with the young emperor king at its center broke in April 1918, and this too contributed to the already failing legitimacy of the state and dynasty. Soon after the signing of the Treaty of Brest-Litovsk, news leaked of Charles's negotiations for a separate peace with the Allies the year before. When Czernin publicly criticized the French for refusing to let go of their desire to regain Alsace Lorraine, the French Prime Minister Georges Clemenceau (1841-1929) published the text of Charles's letter to his brother-in-law Sixtus of Bourbon Parma. Among other damning concessions, that letter had suggested that Charles would consider the legitimacy of France's claim to the German provinces of Alsace and Lorraine. Charles now disavowed his actions, claiming that the letter was a forgery. Czernin, whose speech had provoked Clemenceau's anger, had of course known all about the peace feelers but had not seen the actual text of the letter that discussed Alsace Lorraine. The Foreign Minister was now caught in an impossible position. Either he had to confirm that Charles had lied, or he had to take the public blame himself. At first, the Foreign Minister actually sought to have the emperor king remove himself from politics or even abdicate. Soon, however, he himself resigned, assuming the blame for the scandal. At the same time, Charles was forced to reassure his German allies that he would not abandon them to a separate peace.[49] The scandal damaged the public reputation of both the emperor king and his wife, who could be seen as a traitor to the war effort thanks to the involvement of her brothers in the scandal.

There was still, however, some room for hope for victory among the Central Powers. By March 1918, Germany had moved thousands of troops from the Eastern Front to the Western Front in preparation for a carefully planned spring offensive in the west. That offensive was meant to finally break the stalemate on the Western Front, separate the British from their French allies, and open the way to Paris before the arrival of substantial numbers of troops from the United States. As the Germans put their hopes into this March offensive, Austria-Hungary was even more isolated after the Sixtus affair. With the support of the emperor king, the Austro-Hungarian military leadership now decided that it, too, would engage in a new military offensive against Italy, not that this was necessary after the

---

[49] Brook-Shepherd, *Last Habsburg*, 142-52 offers a detailed explanation of events based both on official documents and on Empress Zita's recollections. Rauchensteiner traces British, French, and Italian reactions to the scandal, pointing out that much of it had to be kept secret by the allied governments because the affair implied that the Allies, too, had ignored a real possibility to end the war in 1917. Rauchensteiner, *The First World War*, 894-905.

earlier Italian defeat six months before. An offensive, many argued, would solve the problems of declining morale, desertion, and the lingering effects of the Sixtus affair. Hindenburg, too, indicated that Germany would welcome an Austrian offensive that could keep allied troops pinned down on the Italian front at the start of Germany's March offensive on the Western Front.[50]

Despite several internal misgivings about the condition and preparedness of the troops as well as their supply situation, Conrad managed to persuade his successor as Chief of General Staff to authorize an attack on the front near the Piave river in mid-June. Within hours of the start of the offensive, however, it became an immediate disaster. At every level, poor planning, poor supplies, the poor health of the troops and their poor morale, to say nothing of poor weather and the preparedness of the enemy, destroyed any possibility of an advance. Within days the troops who had managed to cross the Piave river retreated and found themselves having to defend their original positions. Within a week the Austro-Hungarian forces had suffered 80,000 wounded and 11,000 dead. Twelve thousand had been taken prisoner or had deserted. Although the allied casualties were just as high, and the Italians could not yet take advantage of the Austro-Hungarian disaster, it was clear to the Allies that the Austro-Hungarian forces were spent. In the fall of 1918, Italy would take its revenge.

After this military disaster, Charles relieved Conrad of his command, but Conrad was hardly the only culprit. Charles also revoked the economic agreement he had been forced to make with Germany after the Sixtus debacle, that had tied the Austro-Hungarian economy even closer to Germany's economy. Thanks to the summer failure of their spring offensive, the Germans were no longer able to guarantee the promised food supplies and Charles now viewed the agreement as null and void. In July, parliamentary deputies in Austria openly attacked the military in a bitter debate about the June debacle.

In March, faced with increasing desertions, the military had also developed a special propaganda office charged with keeping up and defending the morale of the troops.[51] The task of this office for the defense of enemy propaganda [*Feindpropaganda-Abwehrstelle*] was to be directed not so much against domestic subversion, against which the military still fought actively, but against the intensifying propaganda directed at Austro-Hungarians externally from both the Bolsheviks and the Entente powers. Since the end of 1917, the Western Allies openly supported the emigré nationalist committees that sought to dismember Austria-Hungary and to replace it with a series of independent nation-states. The military tried to defend against these increasing propaganda attacks, creating special patriotism classes in Vienna and Budapest for officers who could then

---

[50] Rauchensteiner, *The First World War*, 909–11.
[51] On this new office, its intentions and actions, see insightful analysis by Cornwall, "Das Ringen," 431–4.

disseminate those ideas to the troops. Yet as Mark Cornwall argues in his analysis of these efforts, especially after the failed Piave offensive, the propagandists simply had no new and persuasive ideas. In early October 1918, the Austrian Ministry of the Interior, together with the military office for defense of propaganda and the war press office even sought to create a similar office to coordinate domestic propaganda. The head of the war press office pointed out, however, that by this point propaganda could not agitate for a return to the old ways, but that to compete at all effectively with nationalist propaganda it should look toward "the holding together of the various nations in a loose association of states." The real problem remained not so much the effect of foreign or nationalist propaganda, but rather impossible social and economic conditions across the Empire. As Cornwall argues, the battle against the decline of civil and military morale had already been lost by mid-1917.[52]

The efforts of the various émigré national committees to agitate for the destruction of the Monarchy and the establishment of independent states appeared to offer effective propaganda to demoralize citizens of the Empire and bring the war to an end. Nevertheless, it is important to understand that these efforts often masked considerable disagreement among the interested émigré parties. It would be wrong to imagine that the eventual postwar settlement was already clear in 1918. A year before, for example, negotiations for a Yugoslav "Corfu Declaration" in June and July 1917 exemplified the problematic relationship of the émigré activists among themselves and to the allied governments. For thirty-five days the different parties sought to align the interests of the Habsburg émigré Yugoslav committee with those of the Serb government by negotiating an acceptable compromise regarding a future Yugoslav state. The discussions foundered repeatedly on the question of that future state's form of government: should it be federalist or centralized? Serb Prime Minister Nikola Pašić, still thinking in terms of a greater Serbia, demanded a centralized solution under the Serb Monarchy. Croatian émigré activists especially wanted a Croatian state within a future federalist Yugoslavia. The fact that the 1917 "May Declaration" of parties within Austria-Hungary had sought a Yugoslav state under the Habsburgs forced the émigrés to come to some kind of accommodation with the Serb government, as did their fears of Italian expansion. In the end, all agreed to postpone the question of the state structure and to leave it to a future constituent assembly to decide.[53] The Corfu declaration—like efforts by other exile activists—sought to force the Allies finally to abandon the idea of maintaining the existence of Austria-Hungary after the war, something the Americans had not been willing to do until as late as the spring of 1918. Similarly, the so-called Pittsburgh agreement forged by Masaryk

---

[52] Cornwall, "Das Ringen," 434–5.
[53] Marko Trogrlić, "Die Südslawische Frage als Problem der österreichisch-ungarischen und internationalen Politik," in *Die Habsburgermonarchie 1848–1918*, vol. 11/1/2, 1006–1009.

and Slovak leaders in the United States in May 1918 sought to solve difficult challenges that potentially separated Czech and Slovak activists. The agreement promised Slovak autonomy in a future Czecho-Slovak state. However, it too postponed the thorny issue of the state form—whether federalist or centralized—until a later date.[54]

Throughout the summer of 1918 various advisors presented Charles with possible reform programs to federalize the Monarchy. The ministers debated versions of trialism or confederation, but Hungarian leaders remained adamantly opposed to any such reform that might include Hungarian lands and people. With the collapse of the Bulgarian front on September 25, however, Austro-Hungarian Foreign Minister Burián insisted in the common ministerial council of September 27 that "we are finished." He urged his colleagues that Austria-Hungary should make a peace offer. The domestic reform issues must also be settled if Austria-Hungary were to survive. "We must make decisions if we wish to prevent the peoples themselves from taking control and deciding about their future over the heads of the governments."[55] Still, two weeks passed before Charles finally announced a reform plan to his peoples on October 16, a plan that applied only to the Austrian half of the Dual Monarchy. Charles declared that Austria "shall become a federal state in which each national component [*Volksstamm*] shall form its own state organization in its area of settlement."[56] Now, when it was too late, Charles proposed the creation of so-called "national councils" that would then create new governments. These, in turn, would make up a loose confederation of nations, joined together to protect their common interests in Central Europe.[57] On October 25, when Charles appointed Heinrich Lammasch (1853–1920) to serve as Prime Minister—as it turned out, the Austrian Empire's last Prime Minister—Lammasch in fact saw his job as to "lead an Executive Committee of the United National Governments" in recognition of the federalization of the Empire.[58]

By that point, however, the Monarchy's inability to solve the food problem was far more decisive than the question of what structure the Empire should assume in the future. Why should these national councils look to a confederation under the dynasty to solve a problem that it had not been able to solve for the past four and a half years? As Rok Stergar has shown for Yugoslav agitation, the successful provision of food had become so closely bound up with the ideas of nationalism

---

[54] Dušan Kovać, "Die Flucht der Slowaken aus dem ungarischen Staatsverband," in *Die Habsburgermonarchie 1848–1918*, vol. 11/1/2, 763.

[55] Quoted in Galántai, *Hungary*, 320.

[56] For the German text of the manifesto, *Neue Freie Presse*, October 18, 1918.

[57] For a detailed analysis of the events leading up to the drafting of the manifesto and its reception, Helmut Rumpler, *Das Völkermanifest Kaiser Karls vom 16. Oktober 1918: Letzter Versuch zur Rettung des Habsburgerreiches* (Vienna: Verlag für Geschichte und Politik, 1966). Not surprisingly, Hungary's government responded to the manifesto by declaring the 1867 settlement void.

[58] Lammasch quoted in Watson, *Ring of Steel*, 544.

that in the fall of 1918 the two were barely distinguishable. Many argued that only national independence could solve the food crisis and end the war.[59] On the other hand, for example, Stergar has also shown how deeply uncertain Slovene activists were even in the summer and fall of 1918 about what national independence should look like. By then, more than 500 municipal councils and more than 327,000 individuals had signed the petition supporting the May Declaration demanding a South Slav state, but many of those people could not imagine the Yugoslav state without a Habsburg ruler. Even Slovene leaders like Korošec who had secretly abandoned the idea of Habsburg rule in the spring of 1918 nevertheless continued to maintain public support for a Habsburg solution.[60]

In fact, a federalization of power—although of a different and unplanned kind—had already happened on the ground anyway, without Habsburg acknowledgement, and well before 16 October. National councils had sprung up unbid across the Monarchy, but their purpose was not to begin a process of federalization within the Empire. By the late spring of 1918, local and regional crownland officials mobilized to find ways to supply their own regions, independently of the Imperial state.[61] On 17 August, for example, South Slav parliamentary leaders had met in Ljubljana/Laibach to issue a declaration again proclaiming the unity of Austria's South Slavs and setting up one such "Yugoslav national committee." A month before on 13 July Czech nationalists had already created a Czech National Council. Ironically, therefore Charles's manifesto was seen by some simply to legitimize the existing national committees that had already sprung up. Some saw them as the very units that his plan imagined would form the basis of a reconstructed federal Habsburg Monarchy. This perception gave further legitimacy to many of the regional councils, even though at this point none of them contemplated remaining in a Habsburg-led federation.

Concerned citizens and Imperial administrators increasingly prioritized the needs of the local over the orders they received from the Imperial center or the military. Whether nationalist or not, provincial and regional governments throughout the Monarchy now declared their unwillingness to supply neighboring provinces any longer and to work for their own people's survival. Local and regional committees combining politicians, businessmen and labor leaders organized to maintain order and provision. There was little the Imperial center could do about it except often to retroactively support it.[62]

Galicia was an extreme example of this process. By the late spring of 1918 it was no longer governable from Vienna. Both Imperial and local officials increasingly sided with the crowds and these increasingly resorted to violence and pogroms.

---

[59] Rok Stergar, "'Yugoslavia is worthless.... You can get neither sugar nor kerosene.' Food Supply and Political Legitimacy in the Slovene part of Yugoslavia, 1918–1924," *Austrian History Yearbook* (2023): 1–12.
[60] Rok Stergar, "We Will Look Like Fools," 85–7.   [61] Schmitner, "Local Politics."
[62] For a nonnationalist example in Styria, see Moll, *Die Steiermark im Ersten Weltkrieg*, 159–60.

Jan Rybak reports that in the summer of 1918, the military command in the Galician fortress town of Przemyśl informed the Ministry of the Interior in Vienna that not only did hunger lead "to attacks on grocery stores and in connection with that to pogroms against Jews," but that the local authorities "did not always intervene against the pogroms" and that this new development had led to "self-help by armed Jews."[63] In fact, Rybak documents the many ways in which local and Imperial officials repeatedly disappointed the Jewish communities in Galicia that had traditionally looked to the Imperial authorities for protection. Those officials now increasingly turned a blind eye to anti-Semitic violence, refusing to intervene to stop the violence and refusing to prosecute known offenders for fear of provoking the local population. In Cracow and the surrounding region, for example, Jews organized self-defense units in the spring and summer of 1918 to protect property and lives after particularly egregious incidents that had produced death and injury to community members and destruction of shops and homes while the authorities had done nothing. Everywhere, it seemed, crownland officials increasingly acted independently of the government. Officials didn't merely defect, they were often instrumental in bringing about regime change. In fact, only a day before Charles made his federalization announcement, Polish nationalist officials in Galicia pledged their loyalty to a new independent Polish government in Warsaw.

In Hungary the issue of federalization and the concept of a South Slav state also came to a head, but in a very different context, since Hungary's structure was that of a centralized nation-state that did not allow for federation (except nominally with Croatia and the city of Fiume/Rijeka). On October 8, activists from both Austria and Hungary meeting in the Croatian capital Zagreb established a "National Council of Slovenes, Croats, and Serbs" to represent the South Slav nations in both halves of the Dual Monarchy. On October 19, this same Council promulgated a provisional constitution for the Slovene-speaking lands, Croatia, Dalmatia, Vojvodina, and Bosnia Herzegovina. On October 29, the Croatian Sabor or parliament finally cut ties for Croatia and the city of Fiume/Rijeka with Hungary. On October 13, a Romanian deputy read a declaration to the Hungarian parliament declaring that "The national organization of the Romanian nation of Transylvania and Hungary does not recognize the legitimacy of this parliament and government to consider themselves the representatives of the Romanian nation." A day later, a Slovak deputy made a similar declaration for the Slovak nation in Hungary, rejecting the legitimacy of the Hungarian parliament and government.[64] The establishment of Slovak and Romanian national councils

---

[63] Jan Rybak, *Everyday Zionism in East Central Europe. Nation Building in War and Revolution, 1914–1920* (Oxford: Oxford University Press, 2021), 165.
[64] Quoted in Galántai, *Hungary*, 315–16.

decisively rejected the concept of a unitary political Hungarian state, but left many other questions about the future political organization of the regions in question.

In Budapest too, the aspirations of what was called the "national minorities" and the pressing issue of democratization and franchise reform left the government paralyzed and uncertain how to proceed. The majority inside parliament still seemed oblivious to the developments on the ground. Opposition leader Mihaily Károlyi supported democratization and negotiation with the leaders of the nationalist movements, but the majority resisted. Outside of the parliament, a Hungarian Social Democratic congress agreed to demands for "a Hungary based on the federation and free association of equal, free, and democratic nations."[65]

As negotiations in parliament and with King Charles for a new government produced an impasse, street demonstrations grew, Károlyi and his allies decided to declare the formation of a Hungarian National Council as a rival to the existing government. Among the twelve points of its program were the elimination of the current parliament and its replacement with a body elected by universal suffrage, a renunciation of the German alliance, the end of the war, and autonomy for the nationalities, hopefully within the new Hungary.[66] At the same time, revolutionary army officers organized a soldiers' council that prepared for revolution. On October 27, some 30,000 demonstrators gathered in front of the parliament to support the Hungarian National Council. The next day police fired on demonstrators who attempted to break through police lines to cross the chain bridge. When General Lukachich pleaded to the King to send military reinforcements, since troops in Budapest were no longer reliable, Charles told him that enough blood had already been shed, and on October 31, he appointed Károlyi Prime Minister. On that same day a group of soldiers assassinated former Prime Minister Tisza at his suburban home.

In Vienna both bourgeois (Christian Social, German nationalist) and Socialist parliamentary deputies who represented German-speaking regions, including in Bohemia, Moravia, and Silesia, met on October 20 to create yet another national committee—this time one representing German interests. Calling itself a "provisional national assembly," the group established the "German Austrian State Council" on October 29, to serve as the new authority for an Austrian German state. As John Boyer points out in his masterful account of the revolution in Vienna, days before the final collapse of Habsburg authority, the last Imperial Finance Minister, Josef Redlich, already met with the new provisional state

---

[65] Quoted in Galántai, 318. Szabo, "Die Agonie des historischen Ungarn," in *Habsburgermonarchie*, 704–5. Károlyi also participated that week in talks with King Charles about the formation of a new Hungarian government, but Charles did not want to appoint him Prime Minister.

[66] Galántai elaborates the 12 points, 321.

Secretary for Finance of the German Austrian State Council, to negotiate Republican German Austria's first public loan.[67]

Meanwhile, on October 28, in Prague, demonstrations produced an almost unexpected takeover of the city by the Czechoslovak national committee. Only two weeks before, on October 14, a planned demonstration and proclamation of a Czech Republic had failed when the military had encircled the city center and dispersed crowds from Wenceslas Square. Two weeks later, however, the authorities did not intervene as the crowd took over the center. Claire Morelon argues that the civil servants may not have intervened on the October 28 the way they had on the 14th because of the very publication of Charles's manifesto. Many of them perceived that what was happening in Prague was in fact a legitimate transfer of sovereignty to the Czech National Committee.[68]

Charles had issued his federalization decree in part with the hope of maintaining something of his Empire by fulfilling the earlier allied demands articulated in Wilson's fourteen points. However, on October 18, the United States informed the Austro-Hungarian government that because of changed circumstances since the January Fourteen Points speech—meaning the United States' recognition of the Czechoslovak national council as a legitimate government and the aspirations of the Yugoslavs for an independent state—Wilson no longer accepted the autonomy of the peoples of Austria-Hungary as a basis for peace negotiations.

The revolutionary events in Budapest, Prague, and Vienna had been relatively bloodless, and relatively politically moderate in character, when compared with contemporaneous events in Russia or Germany. However, the end did involve unexpected further bloodshed; the war was not yet over. Immediately following Charles's manifesto (and the American reply to the Austro-Hungarian note), the Italians chose this moment to engage a military offensive. Their hope was to gain a more favorable position when an armistice finally came. On October 24, the same day that demonstrations broke out in Budapest, Italy attacked the Austro-Hungarian lines. For almost three days the exhausted and badly provisioned Austro-Hungarian troops managed to hold their lines, but on the 26th the Italians broke through decisively in the final bloodletting of the war. In these last days of October in the senseless debacle, Austria-Hungary lost 30,000 killed and wounded.[69] The dimensions of this defeat convinced Charles to request an armistice on October 28. The Italian conditions were extreme. They demanded a complete Austro-Hungarian demobilization, a retreat of the military to the Brenner Pass, leaving the entire South Tyrol and Trentino open to the Italians, and the right of allied troops "to move freely inside Austria-Hungary and to

---

[67] John W. Boyer, *Austria, 1867–1955* (Oxford: Oxford University Press, 2022), 581.

[68] See Morelon's account in *Streetscapes*, 231–2, 254, 257–64 that focuses especially on control of the streets. Masaryk and other exile politicians had already published a declaration of Czechoslovak independence on October 18.

[69] Francesco Frizzera, "Battle of Vittorio Veneto," *1914–1918—Online International Encyclopedia of the First World War*, 2015, https://doi.org/10.15463/IE1418.10601.

occupy strategic points." Charles hesitated, but was forced to agree to the conditions, especially after the new Hungarian Minister of War ordered Hungarian troops everywhere to stop fighting. The news of his agreement arrived at Villa Giusti on the morning of November 3. The Italians, however, played for extra time, and did not confirm that an armistice would take place until 3 p.m. on November 4. During this extra day their units pushed into Austro-Hungarian territory, surprising the enemy, who presumed that the hostilities had already ended. Without a shot fired the Italians took prisoner 350,000 Austro-Hungarian troops, along with their weaponry. This constituted the Italian "victory" of Vittorio Veneto and the end of the war for Austria-Hungary.

A week later, at 11:00 a.m. on November 11, the war ended on the Western Front. Just after noon that same day, an exhausted Charles signed a manifesto drafted in part by the political leaders of the new Austrian Republic (Catholic, Socialist, Nationalist) in which he renounced his participation in the affairs of state. "Only an inner peace can heal the wounds of this war" he wrote, and clearly the Habsburgs had repeatedly failed to bring their peoples peace of any kind. Could anyone in fact do so, given the horrific conditions suffered by Habsburg society and the various nationalist groups poised to battle further to gain territory for their new states? With an uncertain future in mind, Charles emphasized that this document did not constitute an abdication, nor did it apply to Hungary. Then he and his family and their retainers drove east to a family hunting lodge in Eckartsau, northeast of Vienna, close to both Vienna and the Hungarian border. Later, Empress Zita recalled of that evening that, "It was dark by now, and a misty autumn night. We did not risk driving out of the main gate in front of the palace [Schönbrunn]....We slipped out of [the Eastern Gate] and left the capital by a special route. Late that night—without any trouble or incidents, we arrived at Eckartsau."[70]

On November 12, from exile in Eckartsau, Charles issued a manifesto for Hungary that also stated: "I resign my part in the business of state and accept this decision as regards the new form of Government." As we will see, the Hungarian story regarding a future form of government would be far more complicated and violent than Austria's, although through the interwar period Hungary remained formally a kingdom without a king. The two November manifestos essentially ended Charles's role in political decision-making for the Empire and its successor states. The Empire of the Habsburgs had been falling apart for weeks, but now it was definitively gone. Nevertheless, as it turned out, quite a lot remained of the Empire, and remains to this very day.

The Great War and the Transformation of Habsburg Central Europe. Pieter M. Judson & Tara Zahra, Oxford University Press. © Pieter M. Judson & Tara Zahra 2025. DOI: 10.1093/9780191842306.003.0007

---

[70] Quoted in Brook-Shepherd, *Last Habsburg*, 216. Besides its convenient location, they chose Eckartsau because it was a family property and not a state property.

7
The Enduring Empire

In November 1918, there was no good manual for disassembling an empire. In recent history, wars had ended with territories changing hands, empires expanding or contracting, and governments or rulers violently overthrown. But the wholesale dismantling of an empire was uncharted territory. Nor was it even clear that the war had ended. Violent struggle over borders, people, resources, and states continued for years after the armistice. There was no clear dividing line between "war" and "peace" in Central and Eastern Europe, as conflict spilled past the armistice and well into the 1920s.[1] And in spite of a common belief that proclaimed the definitive end to the age of empire in Central Europe, there was no clean sweep of Imperial debris in 1918 when it came to institutions, laws, personnel, and governmental practices either. This created a paradoxical situation where many continuities shaped the postwar era, while the rulers of the new nation-states loudly defined their states in opposition to imagined and real Imperial legacies.

In the new Habsburg successor states, nationalist politics and language dominated public rhetoric, thanks to the validation given by Woodrow Wilson, whose name soon adorned train stations, streets, and squares across the successor states of East Central Europe. There was a Wilson Train Station (Wilsonovo nádraží) in Prague, along with Wilson squares in Warsaw and Zagreb, a Wilson Park in Poznan, and briefly, a Wilson City (Wilsonovo Město).[2] But nationalist feelings and rhetoric could be harnessed to achieve different outcomes, and there was no clear consensus on what those outcomes should be.

Meanwhile, emotions and concerns other than nationalism also motivated citizens of the former Habsburg Monarchy: the struggle to secure basic needs; a desire for peace; anger at a state that had failed to provide or at (elite) groups that had (allegedly) shirked wartime sacrifice. These emotions were sometimes successfully harnessed and mobilized by nationalist politicians for their ends, but they could just as often subvert nationalist goals, particularly when revolutionary depictions of the nation-state as a promised land fell short of expectations.

---

[1] Healy, "Introductory Remarks"; Miller and Morelon, *Embers of Empire*; Payk and Pergher, *Beyond Versailles*; Cornwall and Newman, *Sacrifice and Rebirth*.

[2] Larry Wolff, "Woodrow Wilson's Name Has Come and Gone Before," *Washington Post*, December 3, 2015, https://www.washingtonpost.com/posteverything/wp/2015/12/03/woodrow-wilsons-name-has-come-and-gone-before/?utm_term=.e7d0f786b459.

Despite the rhetoric of radical rupture that framed the revolutionary transition of the immediate postwar years, the Empire lived on in Habsburg Central Europe. It was alive in domestic and international laws and institutions, in practices of social welfare, material culture, social and economic relationships and hierarchies, and even in the ways that new nation-states sought to "colonize" their own borderlands. Sovereign nation-states were supposed to have replaced the Habsburg Empire. But for better and worse the leaders of the Habsburg successor states often perpetuated Imperial relationships while drawing legitimacy from an imagined opposition between the Imperial past and the nationalized present and future.

"They blindfolded themselves, there in Paris and with knives in their hands they played at drawing a map. The new Europe, result of this blind game, is in a shape which cannot be maintained," Hungarian pacifist Rosika Schwimmer lamented in 1920.

It was common at the time (and has been since) to blame the problems of the successor states on the clueless Western diplomats and Ivy League experts who arrogantly remade Europe's borders. While the experts were indeed often arrogant and clueless, we should be skeptical of this narrative for several reasons. For one, it implicitly contrasts the "artificial" national borders of Eastern Europe with what are presumed to be more "natural" borders in the West. But it also downplays an important reality: the process of breaking up the Empire did not begin in Paris with maps, charts, and censuses, but on the ground, with armies and guns.

The war had ended for the Habsburg Monarchy on November 4, when the armistice for the Italian and Balkan fronts took effect.[3] But this did not mean that soldiers simply went home. In Central and Eastern Europe, the armistice was merely a prelude to more violence. Relying on returning veterans and new paramilitary groups, regional nationalist governments had begun to seize control of the state in Cracow, Lemberg/Lwow/Lviv, Zagreb, and Vienna, and a revolution was underway in Budapest. While the peace settlements were negotiated among the Allies, these proto states did their best to claim as much territory as possible with their new armies. They hoped to create a fait accompli on the ground that might be ratified in Paris.

The armies of the new successor states were recruited from demobilized soldiers. In Bohemia, for example, Czech nationalists enlisted demobilized Austrian soldiers as well as members of the Czech Legion returning from Russia. These soldiers occupied key government buildings, railway stations, and supply depots, and on October 28, 1918, Czech nationalist leaders proclaimed the founding of a "Czecho-Slovak Republic" in Prague. They soon occupied most of Bohemia and

---

[3] In fact, Charles did make two restoration attempts to regain the Hungarian throne in 1921. Brook-Shepherd, *Last Habsburg*.

Moravia, ending the existence of the local small states of German Bohemia and German South Moravia that German nationalists had proclaimed in the wake of the Empire's collapse. Soon the Czecho-Slovak military went on to invade northern Hungary—the region that would be called Slovakia.

To the south, the national Council of Slovenes, Croats, and Serbs invited Serb troops into Croatia on November 24–5 and proposed the creation of a new state, which they now called the Kingdom of Serbs, Croats, and Slovenes (the state was renamed Yugoslavia in 1929). The Slovene National Council in Ljubljana/Laibach, meanwhile, occupied Habsburg military installations there and to the east in Maribor/Marburg. Romanian forces also crossed into old Hungary, occupying what had been Transylvania, claiming that deeply contested region for their own state. Romania was the biggest winner in 1918, more than doubling its population and territory with the acquisition of Transylvania from Hungary, Bukovina from Austria, Bessarabia from Russia, and former territory lost to Bulgarian occupation in Dobruja. But these gains came at a cost: in "Greater Romania," a third of the population now belonged to minority groups, compared to only 8 percent before the war.[4]

Further to the east, a war broke out following the collapse of Austria-Hungary between unofficial Polish and Ukrainian armies. Ukrainian nationalist politicians in Austria aspired to achieve "self-determination" and on October 31, 1918, they seized key buildings in the Galician capital city of Lemberg/Lwów/L'viv and proclaimed a "West Ukrainian People's Republic." They were quickly attacked by the Polish units under Josef Piłsudski that as we saw earlier had been organized by the Germans during the war. In January 1919 the Western Ukrainian People's Republic united at least in name with the Ukrainian People's Republic that currently occupied formerly Russian Ukraine. The war with the Poles continued until July of 1919, when the Polish army defeated the Western Ukrainians. But immediately after emerging victorious from this Polish–Ukrainian war in 1919, Polish armies went to battle with Soviet troops over contested territory between the two states. The violence didn't end until the Soviets sued for peace in September of 1921, and the border was determined by subsequent negotiations. Only two thirds of the population of the new Polish state that emerged from these conflicts were Roman Catholic Polish-speakers.

The biggest losers were the Austrian and Hungarian rump states. Count Albert Apponyi, who led the Hungarian delegation in Paris, called the Treaty of Trianon a "death sentence" for the Hungarian people, as the loss of two thirds of territory and population would create a "reduced and impoverished rump" incapable of survival. The terms of the Treaty of Trianon would deprive Hungary of "almost all her woodland, pasture grounds, iron ore, salt, oil, bituminous gas,

---

[4] Irina Livizeanu, *Cultural Politics in Greater Romania* (Ithaca, NY: Cornell, 1995), 8–25.

water-power, of the greater part of her manufacturing establishment and her coal-mines." It would destroy "the natural economic interdependence of the lowland and the mountainous border districts and the whole system of communications based on it."[5]

In Vienna, German-speaking deputies in parliament created a Provisional National Assembly and the Republic of German Austria on November 12. Karl Renner, a Social Democrat, was named Chancellor and a governing coalition of Social Democrats, Christian Socialists, and German Nationalists took control. That government claimed chunks of Bohemia, Moravia, and Austrian Silesia that were populated by many German speakers, as well as the German-speaking regions of South Tyrol, and demanded to be joined to Germany (the so-called *Anschluss*), but the Allies, unwilling to increase Germany's size and population, rejected these demands.[6] As mentioned above, at the end of the war, nationalist activists from German-speaking regions of Bohemia and Moravia had banded together to declare the states of "German-Bohemia" and of "German Southern Moravia," maintaining Imperial civil servants in their pre-November positions of

Figure 7.1 German nationalist demonstration in Vienna, 1919.
Source: Austrian National Library: https://onb.digital/result/10BCE75B

---

[5] Count Albert Apponyi, *The Peace-Treaty Proposed to Hungary* (London: Low, W. Dawson & Sons, 1920), 4.
[6] Judson, *The Habsburg Empire*, 436.

authority and hoping eventually to join with the new Austrian Republic. However, by early spring of 1919 the Czechoslovak military had successfully occupied those regions.

Advocates of Austria's *Anschluss* to Germany vehemently invoked the right to national self-determination, but also insisted that Austria, deprived of its hinterland and regional trade, would simply starve. According to the *Neue Freie Presse*, Austria's leading liberal newspaper, the Austrian rump state was unviable. "We cannot become... a sort of poorhouse of Europe that is maintained by charitable donations. A state can only remain upright if it has the basic requirements for viability... The regions that once supplied us with food in exchange for industrial products are now closed off and have spiteful economic policies."[7]

To the south, the secret Treaty of London that the Allies had concluded with Italy in 1915 had promised the Italians significant Austrian territory in Tyrol and on the Adriatic as a reward for joining against Germany and Austria-Hungary. Naturally, Italy expected to cash in at the end of the war. But the Americans, who had not been party to the negotiations back in 1915, opposed the deal. Italy did not come out empty-handed, however, in spite of its nationalists' cries of a "mutilated victory." The state took the chunk of Austria called the South Tyrol, with a population of close to 300,000 German speakers, and also seized control of Istria and the Adriatic coast, including the port of Trieste.

Fiume, another important Adriatic port that had been part of Hungary had an Italian-speaking elite and significant Croatian-speaking working-class population. The city was contested by both Italy and Yugoslavia. Wilson briefly argued that it should become an independent state or be incorporated into Yugoslavia. A stalemate in negotiations was broken when the brigand poet and nationalist politician Gabriele D'Annunzio occupied the city to annex it to Italy. He maintained a grip on the city for fifteen months until the Italian military forced D'Annunzio and his troops to leave and it was declared an independent city-state in 1920.

As Dominique Reill has shown, however, underneath their apparent sympathy for Italian rule, the people of Fiume were less motivated by nationalism or by the soaring rhetoric of their poet-leader than by an active desire for Imperial continuity. The Kingdom of Hungary had provided the city considerable local autonomy, respected the city's multinational character, and enabled the port to develop an important economic role linking the hinterland to the Adriatic and global economy. In the aftermath of the First World War, many citizens of Fiume—whatever language they spoke—imagined that their best chance of retaining these Imperial advantages lay with the Italian Empire rather than with the new and untested Yugoslavia.[8]

---

[7] "Auf der Fahrt der Frieden entgegen," *Neue Freie Presse*, May 12, 1919, 1.

[8] Dominique Kirchner Reill, *The Fiume Crisis: Life in the Wake of the Habsburg Empire* (Cambridge, MA: Harvard University Press, 2020).

Sometimes the Allies did hold elections or plebiscites to determine the new borders, but this practice was problematic because the plebiscites could contradict territorial promises that had already been made. Moreover, people did not necessarily vote based on nationalism or language, but rather on the basis of history, local tradition, and economic commercial considerations. More than 60 percent of the Slovene-speaking population of Southern Carinthia, for example, voted to join Austria rather than Yugoslavia in a 1920 plebiscite. In Silesia, to the north, meanwhile, many Polish speakers preferred to remain in Germany rather than join the new Polish state. Their votes, like the resistance of the people of Fiume, reflected their uncertainty about the future of the new states, as well as a desire to maintain accustomed economic, social, and political networks that would have been disrupted by annexation.[9]

When the frontiers of the new states were not determined by armed occupations, the Allies themselves made decisions based more on political or economic concerns rather than the principle of "national self-determination." They called together teams of "experts," including geographers and historians, who were supposed to "scientifically" make recommendations about the new frontiers of Europe. One of Woodrow Wilson's most influential advisors, geographer Isaiah Bowman, was confident that he could impose national order on the multinational lands. He advocated drawing frontiers based on linguistic majorities, balanced by economic considerations, and simply expecting minorities to assimilate.[10]

In determining the shape of Czechoslovakia, for example, the Allies decided to assign territories inhabited by over 3 million German-speaking people to the new state, rather than let them unite with Austria, because this heavily industrialized region was seen as key to Czechoslovakia's economic viability. For similar reasons, territory transferred from Hungary to Czechoslovakia included 850,000 Magyar speakers. The city of Pressburg/Poszony, one of Hungary's ancient capitals, was given to Slovakia to serve as its new capital. Unfortunately, Pressburg had hardly any Slovak speakers. The new regime could not even find a historically Slavic name to give to the city, although informally it had been called Prešporok by some. For a while they planned to name it after Wilson, Wilsonovo Město. The new state finally invented a Slavic-sounding name, Bratislava, for the Slovak capital.[11]

As the terms of the Treaty were publicized, the winners celebrated and the losers protested. But the local protests that accompanied the dissolution of the Habsburg state did not necessarily align with the nationalist priorities of new state leaders. As we saw in chapter 6, as the Habsburg state crumbled in the

---

[9] Brendan Karch, "Plebiscites and Postwar Legitimacy," in *Beyond Versailles*, 16–37.
[10] Leonard V. Smith, *Sovereignty at the Paris Peace Conference of 1919* (Oxford: Oxford University Press, 2018), chap. 3.
[11] Peter Bugge, "The Making of a Slovak City: The Czechoslovak Renaming of Pressburg/Pozsony/Prešporok, 1918–19," *Austrian History Yearbook* 35 (January 2004): 205–27.

summer of 1918, authority had often devolved to or been seized by local elites. And at the local level, as Gábor Egry has shown, there was more space for cooperation across linguistic or national divides, as the primary concern of leaders was to establish order and to secure the material existence of populations that were hungry, angry, and exhausted. Protesters often indiscriminately targeted anything associated with the old regime, regardless of nationality. In Transylvania, for example, which was awarded to Romania, but had significant Magyar-speaking and German-speaking minorities, looters attacked state officials and propertyholders without much regard for their nationality. Local national councils often cared more about social issues such as land reform than national issues. Even their ideas about the meaning of "self-determination"—including whether it would be achieved within a Hungarian or Romanian state, varied tremendously. While this transitional period was brief, there was simply no consensus about what comprised the "national interest."[12]

When the dust settled, losers argued that the new frontiers in Habsburg Central Europe were arbitrary and political. This simultaneously gave them hope that political protests might result in a revision of Europe's map. Both the celebrations and the protests sometimes became violent. Celebration often involved an assault on the material culture associated with the Habsburg Empire. Revelers tore Imperial eagles and images of Francis Joseph from the walls of schools and railway stations and government offices and destroyed them or consigned them to cellars. In Prague, they swiftly renamed streets and town squares, took down German signs, and toppled statues associated with the Habsburg regime, such as the seventeenth-century Marian column in the Old Town Square (a move not appreciated by Czechoslovakia's substantial Catholic populations in Slovakia, Moravia, and Silesia).[13] But we should not assume that all members of minority groups were hostile to the symbols and leaders of new states. In Czechoslovakia, for example, Jewish, German, and Hungarian-speaking members of so-called "activist" parties, those that cooperated with the new government, often venerated new president Thomas Masaryk as a protector of minorities, a symbolic successor to Francis Joseph. And many members of national minority groups in Romania pledged their loyalty to the Romanian King. In interwar Poland, meanwhile Józef Piłsudski was seen by many minority groups as a defender of a multinational vision of Poland dating back to the Polish-Lithuanian Commonwealth.[14]

The material culture of the former Habsburg Empire could not easily or entirely be displaced locally. A Joseph Roth novella, *The Bust of the Emperor*, conveys the significance of former Imperial symbols to people's sense of home. Count

---

[12] Gábor Egry, "Negotiating Post-imperial Transition: Local Societies and Nationalizing States in Central Europe," in *Embers of Empire*, 15–42.

[13] Nancy Merriwether Wingfield, *Flag Wars and Stone Saints: How the Bohemian Lands Became Czech* (Cambridge, MA: Harvard University Press, 2007); Morelon, *Streetscapes*, chap. 6.

[14] Egry, "Negotiating Post-imperial Transition," 26.

Figure 7.2 Removing German signs in Prague, 1918.
Source: https://commons.wikimedia.org/wiki/File:Removing_german_signs_in_1918_from_Rosicky.png

Morstin, a Habsburg aristocrat and Austrian patriot, had always been comforted by the shared material culture of the Empire: "Everywhere the gendarmes wore the same cap with a feather or the same mud-colored helmet with a golden knob and the gleaming double eagle of the Habsburgs; everywhere the doors of the Imperial tobacco monopoly's shops were painted with black and yellow diagonal stripes." The familiar, standardized coffee shops, uniforms, and architecture unified a land known for its diversity and gave him a sense of being at home wherever he traveled.[15] After the Empire's collapse, the Count was plagued by a sense of loss, and by existential questions about the meaning of home.

> "Now, thought he, since this village belongs to Poland and not to Austria, is it still my home? What, in fact, is a home? Is not the distinctive uniform of the gendarmes and custom officers, familiar to us since childhood, just as much "home" as the fir and the pine, the pond and the meadow, the cloud and the brook? But if the gendarmes and customs officers are different and fir, pine, brook, and pond remain the same, is that still home?[16]

In response to this quandary, he resolved to live as though "there had been no war and no Polish Republic; as though the Emperor had not been long laid to rest

---

[15] Joseph Roth, "The Bust of the Emperor," in Roth, *Three Novellas* (New York: Overlook Press, 2003), 45–6.
[16] Roth, "The Bust of the Emperor," 61–3.

in the Kapuzinergraft, as though this village still belonged to the territory of the old Monarchy." He reinstalled a bust of the Emperor Francis Joseph in the entryway of his home, until Polish officials forced him to remove it, at which point he organized a ceremonial burial of the bust. A rabbi, an Orthodox priest, and a Catholic priest led the procession, another symbol of the survival of a now invisible multicultural society in the new Polish nation-state.

Many Central Europeans reacted far more violently than did the fictional Count to decisions made in Paris. They mobilized in the streets, sent appeals to their governments, to the delegates at Versailles, and directly to President Wilson. On January 27, 1919 German nationalist demonstrators in the south Styrian town of Maribor/Marburg, now under the command of the Slovene military, tried to meet with a group of traveling experts sent out by Wilson to investigate where exactly the border should be drawn between the new Kingdom of Serbs, Croats, and Slovenes, and German Austria. In an incident whose exact origin remains unclear today, Slovene troops fired on the crowd, killing at least nine and wounding several more. Afterwards, the commission wrote that it could not determine where the border ought to be drawn, since the Slovene- and German-speaking populations were highly mixed, and as we saw in similar cases, many Slovene speakers apparently hoped to maintain their traditional commercial relations with Austria to the north.[17] In neighboring Carinthia, before the Paris planners could hold the 1920 plebiscite mentioned above, the region saw considerable fighting between nationalist paramilitary groups on both sides.

Discontented with the Paris settlements, protesters engaged in intense propaganda wars, publicizing their arguments for revising state borders in pamphlets, articles, maps, and books written in English and French and addressed to an international public.[18] They framed their grievances in Wilsonian terms, highlighting the hypocrisy of the Allies. German nationalists were often most vocal in voicing their discontent. The most disgruntled issued apocalyptic warnings. In Graz, for example, German nationalists telegraphed to Wilson to express their outrage at the terms of the peace treaty, which "will make us a nation of slaves, deprive us of every possible means of making a living and strike a blow to the face to the most basic human rights."[19] A telegram from the Austrian Christian Social Party and German Freedom Party in May 1919 proclaimed its opposition to the "enserfment" of the German-Austrian people. "Where are the principles of humanity and justice, where are Wilson's fourteen points, which were guaranteed to us as a basis for peace?" They warned, "We will not allow ourselves with our wives and children to be sentenced to death or eternal economic slavery, but

---

[17] Pieter M. Judson, *Guardians of the Nation: Activists on the Language Frontiers of Imperial Austria* (Cambridge, MA: Harvard University Press, 2006), 237.
[18] See especially Case, *Between States*, 39–40.
[19] Kundgebung in Graz gegen den Friedensvertragsentwurf, June 14, 1919, AdR, AAng, BKA-AA, St. Germain, Karton 6, OestA.

demand fairness, humanity, and justice. If the Entente wants to prepare a grave for us, all of Europe will be destroyed with us." The frequency with which protesters used the term "slavery" was not coincidental. As Larry Wolff has shown, Wilson, a Southern segregationist, liked to imagine himself as the Abraham Lincoln of East Central Europe, "emancipating" Habsburg subjects from "slavery." Central Europeans thus talked back to Wilson using a language of slavery and emancipation.[20]

A rhetoric of postcolonial emancipation shaped the economic, cultural, and political policies of the Habsburg successor states. Ironically, however, this same rhetoric simultaneously undermined the sovereignty of these fledgling states. For if, as nationalists claimed, the nations of East Central Europe had suffered under Habsburg oppression for close to five hundred years, they now suffered from the stigma of political immaturity. Like the peoples in the Middle East whom the Peace Conference subjected to Mandate status, Western diplomats could easily conclude that East Europeans were insufficiently "mature" for complete self-rule. They required the benevolent control of European powers to help steer them on a path to eventual independence. But as Natasha Wheatley has shown, the nationalist leaders who crowded the negotiating table in Paris in 1919 insisted that Hungary, Czechoslovakia, and Poland were not "new" states at all. Rather, their leaders insisted, they were "old" states whose sovereignty was finally being resurrected. Similar arguments would be made later in the twentieth century by leaders demanding independence from European colonialism.[21]

Nonetheless, the semi-independent status of the successor states was concretely embedded in the Minorities Treaties that the great powers required them to sign in exchange for their independence or territorial aggrandizement. These treaties obliged signatories to protect national minorities within their borders and to submit to external scrutiny by a League of Nations Committee. The idea of creating a supranational institution to protect minority rights was not in itself problematic. After all, the Imperial Austrian state and institutions like the common military had served similar functions. Indeed, the technical terms of the minority protections treaties were often taken directly from Austrian nationality law, ensuring legal continuity. For example, following Austrian judicial decisions, the treaties typically specified that a minority community that comprised 20 percent of the population was entitled to a public elementary school in its language.[22]

The problem was that the League of Nations imposed these treaties only on states in eastern and southeastern Europe, but not on the great powers

---

[20] Wolff, *Woodrow Wilson and the Reimagining of Eastern Europe*.
[21] Natasha Wheatley, *The Life and Death of States: Central Europe and the Transformation of Modern Sovereignty* (Princeton: Princeton University Press, 2023).
[22] On Minority Rights and the League, see Carol Fink, *Defending the Rights of Others: The Great Powers, the Jews, and International Minority Protection, 1878-1938* (Cambridge: Cambridge University Press, 2016).

themselves. Italy did not have to sign a treaty guaranteeing rights to the German-, Slovene-, or Croatian-speakers it had gained along with new territories in the north and east. Britain was not required to sign international treaties guaranteeing such rights to Ireland (let alone its other colonial subjects), and France was not obliged to guarantee any rights to the German-speaking minority in Alsace-Lorraine or the subjects of its large empire. And the United States—which failed to ratify the Paris treaties—certainly did not sign any treaties guaranteeing rights to Black Americans, to other domestic minorities, or to the subjects of its empire in the Philippines.

The blatant hypocrisy of the great powers was not lost on the citizens of the new Central and East European nation-states. Before the war had even ended, a Viennese newspaper speculated that the Allies would be as eager as the Central Powers for peace, given their own "minority problems," writing, "The Irish and Indian questions plague the British global empire no less than the Czech and South Slav questions plague us."[23] But when in 1922 Lithuania proposed that all member states of the League of Nations adopt universal standards of minority protection, a French delegate responded, "France has no minorities." Armed with an ethnographic map, a Romanian delegate contested this claim, only to receive the reply: "Minorities only exist where there is a Treaty."[24]

According to contemporary logic, members of minority groups in Western Europe or the United States did not need protection because those societies were fully civilized and fully democratized. East Europeans, by contrast, could not be fully trusted with self-government. One of the most influential players at Versailles, Jan Smuts, President of South Africa, argued that a mandate system applied to Europe could function to train Eastern Europeans for full sovereignty. "The peoples left behind by the decomposition of Russia, Austria, and Turkey are mostly untrained politically; many of them are either incapable or deficient in the power of self-government," he insisted.[25]

There was, however, a glaring problem with enforcing minority treaties—a problem that had vexed Habsburg lawmakers well before 1914: it was not always self-evident who belonged to a minority group in the first place. In regions in which many people were flexible, indifferent to nationalism, or opportunistic, it could be difficult to tell who belonged to which national community. Many citizens lived in bilingual households. Many people who spoke Czech or Slovene or Polish considered themselves to be Germans and vice versa, for social or cultural reasons, or were more attached to a regional or local community than to a national one. This issue created a pressing problem: how to classify people in a

---

[23] "Ein neuer Schritt zum Frieden," September 15, 1918, *Neues Wiener Tagblatt*, 1.
[24] Tara Zahra, "The 'Minority Problem' and National Classification in the French and Czechoslovak Borderlands," *Contemporary European History* 17, no. 2 (2008): 138.
[25] Quoted in Margaret MacMillan, *Paris 1919: Six Months That Changed the World* (New York: Random House, 2002), 99.

context in which nationality often determined access to political rights, resources, and citizenship?

For example, when Czechoslovakia conducted its first census in 1920, the government wanted to count as many Czechoslovaks and as few Germans and Hungarians as possible to boost the new nation-state's legitimacy domestically and internationally. There would be no need for minority rights if there were no minorities. But even when all Czechs and Slovaks were counted together, they still only made up two thirds of the population of the state. So Czech authorities set out to close German schools, confiscate the property of German nobles, and make it difficult for members of minority groups to retain their jobs as civil servants. They also forcibly classified people, especially children, as members of the Czech nation. These practices built on policies and techniques used to "objectively" determine an individual's nationality in the Austrian Empire, but were now radicalized and supported by the state.

If census-takers suspected that citizens were lying about their "true" nationality, they had the right to launch investigations, interrogate witnesses, and officially reclassify people as Czechs based on so-called "objective characteristics." These characteristics included factors such as which newspapers individuals subscribed to, where they went to school, and with whom they socialized, as well as languages spoken and the nationality of parents. Similar policies were introduced in other successor states. In Southern Styria, for example, Yugoslav authorities asserted that many individuals who identified themselves as Germans were actually "Germanized Slovenes." While German children technically continued to enjoy a minority right to attend German elementary schools in Yugoslavia, local authorities were empowered to investigate and dispute any individual's claim to be a German. Moreover, the state ruled that a family's Slovene last name automatically meant Slovene nationality, so that children with Slovene-sounding family names had to attend Slovene schools, regardless of their self-identification as Germans.[26]

Another irony of the politics of "minority rights" is that it was sometimes used against minority groups. In linguistically mixed regions of Czechoslovakia, for example, Czech nationalists continued to claim that Czechs were an oppressed minority, demanding that the government take even more radical measures against their German neighbors. In making these demands, local nationalists often used the rhetoric of postcolonial nationalism. In one request for state support, the National Union of Northern Bohemia insisted, "No small number of our brothers still suffer under the rule of foreign colonists!" Even in

---

[26] See Arnold Suppan, "Zur Lage der Deutschen in Slowenien zwischen 1918 und 1938: Demographie—Recht—Gesellschaft—Politik," and Andrej Vovko, "Das Minderheitenschulwesen in Slowenien im Zeitabschnitt des alten Jugoslawiens," in *Geschichte der Deutschen im Bereich der heutigen Slowenien 1848–1941/Zgodovina Nemcev na Območju Današnje Slovenije 1848–1941*, ed. Helmut Rumpler and Arnold Suppan (Vienna: Verlag für Geschichte und Politik, 1988).

Prague, Czech nationalists in the 1920s complained about seeing "Austrianness everywhere."[27]

In borderland territories that were stigmatized as "backwards" and/or nationally or politically unreliable, several of the successor states undertook civilizing missions of their own. In interwar Poland, Kathryn Ciancia has shown how border guards, settlers, teachers, local officials, and even boy scouts streamed into Volhynia, recently annexed from the USSR, to "modernize" and "civilize" the region. They debated whether the Ukrainians and Jews that inhabited the region were mature enough to handle democratic participation.[28] Armies of bureaucrats, experts, and teachers were also dispatched from Prague to rural Slovakia and to Subcarpathian Rus, where locals often viewed them as colonial invaders.

Across East Central Europe, meanwhile, the extreme social deprivation of the final years of the war had radicalized populations, and the Russian Revolution had expanded the realm of possible outcomes. In Yugoslavia, radicalized soldiers returning from captivity in Russia—many of them peasant conscripts—battled for control of the state with ex-Habsburg officers on the radical right. In the fall of 1918 these so-called "Green Cadres" attacked the property of nobles and bureaucrats, prompting the recently established Zagreb National Council of Slovenes, Croats, and Serbs to implore them, "Don't destroy, don't burn down, don't kill, since you are destroying and burning that which is yours, soldiers!"[29]

In Hungary, the battle for control of the state began with revolution and the establishment of a short-lived Republic led by Mihály Károlyi on October 30–1, 1918. That regime was overthrown only four months later, and replaced by a Communist dictatorship under Béla Kun, which maintained its grip on power from March to June of 1919. Many Hungarians saw the Communists as their best hope for defending Hungary against the invasion of Romanian and Czechoslovak armies. Many men joined Bela Kun's Red Army for this reason, even if they were not actually Bolsheviks. Others were mobilized into the Red Army by local trade unions, or simply through the absorption of old Habsburg regiments into the Red Army. The Hungarian Bolsheviks effectively turned the tables on the invaders and attempted to take back Slovak and Transylvanian territory that had been lost at the end of the war.[30]

This revolution was brutal, however. Feminist and pacifist Rosika Schwimmer described "public hangings on Budapest's large squares, attended by tens of

---

[27] Národní hnutí, Provolání, November 8, 1921, carton 9, Národní jednota severočeská (NJS), NA. See also memo to Ministry of Education, December 1921, carton 13, NJS, NA. On "Austrianness everywhere," Morelon, *Streetscapes*, chap. 6.

[28] Kathryn Ciancia, *On Civilization's Edge: A Polish Borderland in the Interwar World* (Oxford: Oxford University Press, 2021).

[29] John Paul Newman, "Post-imperial and Postwar Violence in the South Slav Lands, 1917–1923," *Contemporary European History* 19, no. 3 (August 2010): 249–65, quotation, 254.

[30] Tamás Révész, "A National Army Under the Red Banner? The Mobilisation of the Hungarian Red Army in 1919," *Contemporary European History* 31 (2022): 71–84.

Figure 7.3 Proclamation of Hungarian Soviet Republic, 1919.
Source: https://www.alamy.com/march-1919-the-proclamation-of-hungarian-republic-now-turned-over-to-hungarian-bolsheviki-apparent-from-the-dispatches-received-of-the-proclamation-of-a-new-hungarian-government-inviting-the-workmen-and-peasants-of-bohemia-serbia-rumania-romania-and-croatia-to-form-an-armed-alliance-against-aristocracy-landowners-and-dynasties-that-cout-kayrolyi-provisional-president-of-the-republic-has-turned-the-country-over-to-the-bolsheviki-anger-over-the-decision-of-paris-peace-conference-and-thereby-plunging-these-people-into-a-war-against-the-entente-image227004129.html?imageid=E53FEF14-81D3-453D-B40E-B28CAAB9CA1F&p=307105&pn=1&searchId=9a026ba3869d1abc16f258252223499c&searchtype=0

thousands of people...house-searches, a militarism lubricated with all the ointments of the old system, women going wild and serving unquestioningly, and all of that in the name of the most noble, beautiful axioms of humanity!"[31] But what came next was even worse. When Romanians broke through Hungarian lines on the June 30, Béla Kun fled. A counterrevolutionary movement seized power and unleashed its own reign of terror on Socialists, Jews, and internationalists in Hungary. This counterrevolution formed part of a transnational, anti-Communist, paramilitary movement.[32]

Joseph Marcus of the American Joint Distribution Committee (JDC) traveled to Hungary in the spring of 1921. In 130 unflinching pages he described countless

---

[31] Rosika Schwimmer to Clara Ragaz, December 21, 1919, Box 121, Rosika Schwimmer Papers, NYPL.
[32] On the revolution and counterrevolution in Budapest see Paul A. Hanebrink, *In Defense of Christian Hungary: Religion, Nationalism and Antisemitism; 1890–1944* (Ithaca, NY: Cornell University Press, 2006); Robert Gerwarth and John N. Horne, eds., *War in Peace: Paramilitary Violence in Europe After the Great War* (Oxford: Oxford University Press, 2012); Eliza Ablovatski, *Revolution and Political Violence in Central Europe: The Deluge of 1919*, Studies in the Social and Cultural History of Modern Warfare (Cambridge: Cambridge University Press, 2023).

Figure 7.4 Romanian troops enter Budapest, 1919.
Source: https://archive.org/details/outlawsdiary02tormuoft/page/n7/mode/2up?view=theater; https://commons.wikimedia.org/wiki/File:Tropas-rumanas-ocupan-budapest-1919--outlawsdiary02tormuoft.png

atrocities of the new right-wing regime. Around twelve to thirteen corpses were being fished out of the Danube each day:

> Many of them have the hands or feet tied with bullets or wires; many bear the marks of torture or bullet wounds. The police are forced to issue a statement that the deceased had committed suicide. And when a newspaper dares to question the possibility of persons committing suicide with their hands and feet tied, or by first filling their abdomen with rags, or similar acts, the paper is punished by the Minister of Interior.

Many Jews were arbitrarily interned in camps. Marcus visited a camp in Zalaegerszag that housed over 1,100 men, women, and children. He found many prisoners naked and starving, along with evidence of arbitrary beatings, torture, and rape. Altogether, an estimated 1,500–2,000 people died in the counterrevolution.[33]

For individuals who found themselves on the wrong side of a new state border, or on the wrong side of a new government, flight was the only alternative. Approximately 9.5 million people in Europe were classified as refugees in 1926. Many were victims of "national self-determination" in the Habsburg successor

---

[33] Joseph Marcus, "Is There White Terror in Hungary?" June 5, 1921, JDC Archive, NY AR1921_011915.

states. Around 200,000 people fled Romania for Hungary from Transylvania, for example. Refugees had a difficult time, however, integrating into a society that was itself decimated by war, and they often formed powerful revisionist lobbies.[34]

The League of Nations' High Commission for Refugees, under the leadership of diplomat and arctic explorer Fridtjof Nansen, was established in 1921 as the first international effort to assist the unprecedented number of refugees. The Nansen system provided stateless refugees with documents, the so-called "Nansen passports." The "refugee" and "stateless person" were thus born in international law.[35]

Building on wartime developments, both nationality and citizenship were more important than ever. Article 80 of the 1918 Treaty of St. Germain, the so-called Option Clause, was intended to address situations in which an individual's citizenship and nationality were not aligned: essentially allowing individuals to voluntarily "unmix" themselves. It enabled citizens of the former Habsburg Empire who differed "by race and language" from the majority population to "opt" for citizenship in another successor state, so long as that state was populated by "persons speaking the same language and having the same race." In practice, self-identified Germans were most likely to take advantage of the clause. Approximately 180,000 German families (totaling 540,000 people) from the former Austrian crownlands opted to become citizens of the First Austrian Republic.

Questions of citizenship and national classification were also of immediate relevance to members of the former Imperial civil service, whose applications for recognition, continued employment, or pensions flooded the Austrian government after 1918. As John Deak has shown, a legal understanding of citizenship based on residence conflicted with an emerging conception of rights and citizenship based on ethnicity. In practice, authorities often relied on longstanding practices of classification based on so-called "objective" national characteristics to determine which employees were entitled to keep their jobs and which would be purged.[36]

Many individuals who attempted to opt for citizenship in another state were unsuccessful. Recent work by Dominique Kirchner Reill, Ivan Jeličić, and Francesca Rolandi has shown that the Imperial institution of *Heimatrecht* or pertinency was frequently used to exclude people from citizenship in the successor states. Authorities in several successor states used one's local pertinency before 1914 as a basis for determining state or national citizenship after 1918. Since the majority of people did not have *Heimatrecht* where they actually lived, they had

---

[34] Case, *Between States*, 27–8.
[35] Bruno Cabanes, *The Great War and the Origins of Humanitarianism, 1918–24* (Cambridge, MA: Cambridge University Press, 2014).
[36] John Deak, "Fashioning the Rest: National Ascription in Austria after the First World War," in *Beyond Versailles*, 124–38.

to apply for it in order to become citizens of the new states. Unsurprisingly, local officials were inclined to reject applications from individuals who were considered undesirable, including national minorities, Communists, poor people, and pensioners.[37] Hungary systematically denied citizenship to Jews and Socialists, for example.

The problem was so great that in 1922, Italy convened a Conference of the Successor States in Rome, where delegates agreed that in cases of contested citizenship, applicants should have the right to appeal to a Court of Arbitration comprising representatives of the states concerned and one neutral party. If no decision was reached, the place of birth or last place of domicile was to be decisive. But the convention was only adopted by Italy and Austria, and never enforced. The problem was complicated by the fact that the successor states—building again on old Imperial laws regulating *Heimatrecht* and citizenship—required lengthy residence and extensive documentation to be naturalized (ten years in Austria, twenty in Czechoslovakia, according to a law passed in July 1926).

In some cases, stateless individuals were deported back and forth across state borders, leaving them in a permanent state of insecurity and illegality. For example, a 14-year-old stateless orphan who had arrived in Austria with his father as a refugee in 1914 was picked up selling things on the street and deported to Czechoslovakia in the 1920s. He was caught there, imprisoned, and sent back to Austria, and then back to Czechoslovakia again. Mathilde Herschkowitz, a Jewish seamstress from Szatmar, in Transylvania, lived in Hungary for fifteeen years with her husband, a Hungarian tailor. When her husband died, she was deported to Romania, but the Romanian government deported her back to Budapest, where she lived with her three children in fear of being caught and deported again. A social worker familiar with her case concluded, "She can only be saved if a Hungarian citizen would marry her."[38]

It is no coincidence that many of these stateless people were former Jewish refugees displaced during the war. Despite the minority treaties, Jews were targeted throughout the Habsburg successor states as emblems of the old Imperial order, and as representatives of a form of "cosmopolitanism" or globalism that no one wanted.[39]

The status of Jewish refugees was particularly precarious in Vienna. At the end of the war, Viennese police estimated that 100,000 refugees remained in the capital city. As of September of 1918, Austrian welfare agencies reported that they were

---

[37] Dominique Kirchner Reill, Ivan Jeličić, and Francesca Rolandi, "Redefining Citizenship after Empire: The Rights to Welfare, to Work, and to Remain in a Post-Habsburg World," *Journal of Modern History* 94, no. 2 (June 2022): 326–62.

[38] Cadbury, "The Problem of the 'Staatenlosen' from the Humanitarian Side," 12–22 (p. 21), and Anna Askeanazy, "The Problem of Statelessness," in *The Problem of Statelessness* (Geneva: Imprimeries Populaires, 1930), 3–11.

[39] On Jews as targets of anti-global politics after the First World War, see Tara Zahra, *Against the World: Anti-Globalism and Mass Politics Between the World Wars* (New York: W.W. Norton, 2023).

providing state assistance to 326,261 refugees, including 68,286 Jews. Almost immediately after the establishment of the new Republic, state officials mobilized to prevent these refugees from becoming Austrian citizens. On September 10, 1919, the Austrian Interior Ministry issued a decree stipulating that "foreign" refugees were to clear out of Austria within ten days. Police plastered the city of Vienna with posters declaring that refugees who ignored the decree would be subject to criminal proceedings and deportation. In practice, transport and financial difficulties meant that the threat of deportation was rarely carried out. Poland was not eager to have its Jewish citizens return home and refused to issue the visas and travel documents necessary for repatriation. Since Austria refused to naturalize them and Poland refused to take them back, these Jews were effectively rendered stateless.[40]

The exclusion of Jews from Austrian citizenship was consolidated in racial terms by the Austrian interpretation of the Option clause, as work by Gerald Stourzh has shown. In 1921, the Austrian Supreme Court decided to define "race" as an "inborn, inherent, physically and psychically determined quality," that "cannot be removed at will or changed according to preference."[41] On the basis of this judgment, the Austrian Ministry of the Interior, then under the leadership of *Grossdeutsche Volkspartei* member and rabid anti-Semite Leopold Waber, proceeded to reject almost all Jews from the Austrian successor states who attempted to opt for Austrian citizenship—around 75,000 people. The League of Nations Minority Council ultimately supported Austria's decision, ruling that "Austria is fully justified, based on local and international law, to exclude Eastern Jews. This should however take place with consideration of humanitarian principles."[42]

Pogroms, boycotts, and expulsions made the same point by other means: Jews did not belong in the successor states. In Hungary, alongside the rampage of murders, internments, beatings, and torture directed at Jews during the counterrevolution, the right-wing government issued an edict (no. 20,000) on September 30, 1920, expelling all Jews who had arrived in the country since 1914 on the grounds that these "unwanted foreigners" were harmful to the economy and represented "a great danger to the peace of the state."[43]

Like the Austrian expulsion order, this one targeted Galician, Russian, and Polish Jews who had arrived in Hungary as refugees during the war.[44] The Horthy regime also passed a *numerus clausus* law in 1920 to limit the number of Jews in

---

[40] Oskar Besenböck, "Die Frage der jüdischen Option in Österreich, 1919–21," (PhD diss., University of Vienna, 1992), 46–55.
[41] Stourzh, "Ethnic Attribution in Late Imperial Austria," 175, footnote 33, our translation. For the entire text of the court's decision, see Erkenntnis z. 2973 ex 1921, Verwaltungsgerichtshof, June 9, 1921, reprinted in Besenböck, "Die Frage der jüdischen Option," 166–75.
[42] Besenböck, "Die Frage der jüdischen Option," 134.
[43] JDC Archive, New York 1919–21, Hungary, General, 1921. NY_AR1921_01280.
[44] Marcus, "Is There White Terror in Hungary?," 87–8.

Hungarian universities to 6 percent, effectively defining Jews as a non-Hungarian minority.[45]

Ironically, while Jews in Hungary were being attacked and excluded from the Hungarian and German-Austrian nations, Czech and Slovak Jews were targeted on the grounds that they had supported the Hungarian or German cause. As we saw in chapter 6, assaults on Jewish property and people were widespread in Czechoslovakia in the fall of 1918. This violence was linked to an association of Jews with the German community, but also reflected ongoing social tensions around resources such as food and housing, and the decline of state authority. In Prague, for example, Czech legionnaires publicly evicted Jewish refugee families from apartments to install legionnaire families in their place.[46]

In Slovakia, American JDC official Henry Alsberg found around 40,000 Slovak Jews in a state of total destitution after the armistice, exacerbated by the fact that they were "being actively boycotted by the non-Jewish population." Local Slovak populations often depicted these refugees as welfare parasites. The exasperated chief of police in the Slovak border town of Bardejov complained, "They are Orthodox, not one family makes a living doing productive work, they are all only hawkers, racketeering, smuggling across the border to Poland. The town is in an impoverished state because of them; all business is in their hands."[47]

In Poland there was an initial period of cooperation between Jewish leaders and the various local committees and authorities that stepped into the place of the former Habsburg state. In the final months of nominal Habsburg rule, Zionists had organized Jewish militias for the self-defense of the Jewish population, in partnership with local Polish authorities in Western Galicia. In the contested eastern borderlands of Galicia, meanwhile, Jewish units pledged their neutrality in the escalating conflict between the Polish and Ukrainian national forces. But as Jan Rybak shows, this moment of cooperation quickly ended when military reinforcements and marauders from outside these local regions began to arrive on the scene. At this point, pogroms erupted across the state, and locals often joined in the violence.[48]

The death toll is disputed, but historians conservatively estimate that between 40,000 and 100,000 Jews died as a result of anti-Semitic violence between 1918 and 1921, more than 600,000 were displaced, and millions of homes and businesses burned, destroyed, or looted.[49] One of the most infamous outbreaks of anti-Semitic violence occurred in Lviv/Lemberg/L'vov in 1918, during the war

---

[45] Hanebrink, "Transnational Culture War."
[46] Morelon, *Streetscapes*, chap. 6.
[47] Cited in Rebekah Klein-Pejsova, *Mapping Jewish Loyalties in Interwar Slovakia* (Bloomington, IN: Indiana University Press, 2015), 38.
[48] Rybak, *Everyday Zionism in East-Central Europe*, 166–84.
[49] Jeffrey Veidlinger, *In the Midst of Civilized Europe: The Pogroms of 1918–1921 and the Onset of the Holocaust* (New York: Henry Holt, 2021), 5, 24–5.

between Polish and Ukrainian national forces to determine Poland's postwar borders. The large Jewish population of the city was caught in the middle of the violent struggle between Polish and Ukrainian nationalists. The incoming Polish army and local Poles saw Jewish neutrality and Jewish self-defense as support for Ukrainians and killed at least seventy-three Jews in a gruesome three-day pogrom in the city between November 21 and 23, 1918. Despite efforts by Zionist militias to defend local Jews, 7,000 Jewish families were victimized by the violence, with 2,000 left homeless and more than five hundred shops and businesses destroyed.[50] Jews were also murdered and assaulted in Kielce, Pinsk, Lida, Wilna, Kolbuszowa, Czestochowa, and Minsk. In several cases, locals participated in plunder and violence that was initially instigated by outsiders. In Pinsk, on April 5, 1919, a group of Jews who had assembled to discuss the distribution of relief funds was robbed and taken prisoner. Out of the group, thirty-five Jews were summarily executed without trial on flimsy accusations of being Bolsheviks, while the remainder were "stripped and beaten by the prison guards so severely that several of them were bed-ridden for weeks," according to the American investigation led by Henry Morgenthau.[51]

Given these circumstances, it is not surprising that many Jews attempted to flee Eastern Europe. But one reason that Europe faced such a severe refugee crisis in the 1920s and 30s was that the United States, which had welcomed millions of immigrants before the First World War, instituted new immigration restrictions. In the United States, the 1924 Johnson-Reed Act created a quota system that discriminated heavily against migrants from Eastern and southern Europe on racial grounds. The number of people leaving East Central Europe declined dramatically. The new system allowed only 3,078 Czechoslovak citizens to legally immigrate to the United States in 1924, for example, less than one tenth of the number of Czechs and Slovaks who applied for emigration passports to the United States that year. The Polish quota in 1924 was only 25,800, even as more than 100,000 Poles per year requested emigration visas to the United States in the early 1920s, many hoping to join family members who were already overseas.[52]

The emergence of a refugee crisis in interwar Europe was not only a product of xenophobia in the West, however. It reflected a broader collapse of transatlantic migration networks, as states of both emigration and immigration rushed to secure their borders. Within Europe, France was the only country that actively recruited large numbers of migrant workers between the wars. But the Habsburg

---

[50] William W. Hagen, *Anti-Jewish Violence in Poland, 1914–1920* (Cambridge: Cambridge University Press, 2018), 156.
[51] Mission of the United States to Poland, JDC Archives, 1919–1921 New York Collection, Poland, Discrimination and Persecution, 1919–21.
[52] Mezinárodní ženský kongres ve Washingtoně, vystěhovalecká otázka, January 7, 1925. Carton 3798, Ministerstvo sociální péče (MSP), NA; no author, *L'émigration polonaise, son importance et son organisation* (Warsaw, 1922), 10.

successor states actively recruited emigrants to return home to contribute to the project of nation-building. Thomas Masaryk toured the United States, hoping to convince Czech-Americans that they could "make America in Czechoslovakia." Many officials painted prewar emigration as a symptom of economic and social backwardness that would be overcome in the promised land of the nation-state. In 1923 Leopold Caro, a Polish economist and lawyer, declared, "We should not permit emigration, especially permanent emigration, from our country. When, before the Great War, masses of our peasants were forced to emigrate to other parts of the world and place their labor at the disposal of foreign countries—this was the shame of our people."[53] Preventing migration thus formed a part of the "postcolonial" politics of the interwar nation-states.

Migration policy also reflected new demographic realities. An unprecedented number of citizens had been slaughtered in battle during the First World War. Austria-Hungary lost at least 1,200,000 soldiers and 120,000 civilians in military actions, and another 467,000 to starvation or disease as the Spanish flu ravaged the population in 1918. These demographic losses, along with the pressing need for labor, transformed human beings into what one emigration expert called the nation's "most valuable commodity."[54] The International Labor Organization explained in 1922, "The emigrant is now considered as part and parcel of the human capital of the nation, and governments desire to use this capital in the interests of the nation, and for purposes which have no direct connection with the interests of the emigrant himself."[55]

The leaders of the successor states did not, however, value all emigrants equally. New nationalist leaders generally hoped to prevent the emigration of citizens who were considered "desirable" from a nationalist perspective, while encouraging the departure of national and religious minorities.[56] Through the emigration of national and linguistic minorities and the return of nationally "reliable" and "productive" citizens from abroad, government officials hoped to transform their multinational states into more homogenous nation-states. In Poland, for example, new passport restrictions in 1920 hindered the emigration of ethnic Poles. But the Polish Interior Ministry simultaneously decreed that Jews should be encouraged to emigrate "in the interest of the Polish Republic."[57]

---

[53] Leopold Caro, *Ku nowej Polsce* (Lwow: Księgarni nauczycielskiej, 1923), 13.
[54] Jan Žilka, "Několik myšlenik o naší vystěhovalecké politice," *Československé emigrace* 3, no. 6 (June 1928): 1.
[55] International Labor Organization, *The International Emigration Commission* (Geneva, 1922), 89.
[56] Tara Zahra, *The Great Departure: Mass Migration from Eastern Europe and the Making of the Free World* (New York: W.W. Norton, 2017), chap. 3.
[57] Wydanie paszportów zagranicznych do Ameryki obywatelstom polskim wyznanie mojzeszowego, May 19, 1920; Opis Ministerstwo spraw wewnętrznych, June 28, 1920, W sprawie wydawania paszportów do Ameryki, Sig. 411, Starostwo Grodskie Krakowie, Archiwum państowe w krakowie (APKr).

At the same time, ironically, Austria, Hungary, and Italy encouraged German, Magyar, and Italian minority populations in neighboring countries to stay put, so that they would later be able to make revisionist claims on lost territory.

For equally cynical reasons, East European governments tended to look favorably upon Zionism and Jewish nationalism. In Czechoslovakia, the state officially recognized Jews as a national community and offered Jewish citizens the option of declaring themselves members of the Jewish nationality on the censuses of 1921 and 1930. Czechoslovak officials (along with Zionists) hoped that German-speaking Jews would choose to identify as Jews rather than Germans. The Polish government also expressed its support for the Zionist cause throughout the interwar period, declaring its "special interest in the emigration of the Jews from Poland" as early as 1919.[58]

The decline in mass migration and the violence directed toward Jews and other national minorities after the First World War reflected a broader politics of economic and political anti-globalism. Before the war, the Habsburg Empire had been the largest region in Europe for the free movement of humans and goods. The Empire's collapse transformed that single zone into seven different economic and political units (Austria, Hungary, Romania, Czechoslovakia, Yugoslavia, Poland, Italy). None of these countries could meet its population's needs with domestic production, but all imagined that achieving national independence required severing economic ties of dependence with neighbors. Hungary increased tariffs up to 50 percent for finished goods; Yugoslavia up to 170 percent. Trade between Austria and the Bohemian lands (now Czechoslovakia), regions once economically interdependent, decreased by 50 percent.[59] Moving goods across the Atlantic was often easier than getting them across these regional frontiers. For example, the volume of goods transported by railway from the port of Trieste to Central Europe declined by more than two thirds from its 1913 level after the war. The *Sudbahn* railway line that had linked Trieste to Vienna now ran through three different states which were at odds with one another. The railway company proposed an international management to prevent the three states from engaging in a tariff war and blocking the flow of goods, to the benefit all. But the

---

[58] Czechoslovak Zionism was not, however, primarily oriented toward emigration to Palestine. On Zionism and the interwar Czechoslovak census, see Tatjana Lichtenstein, *Zionists in Interwar Czechoslovakia: Minority Nationalism and the Politics of Belonging* (Bloomington: Indiana University Press, 2016); On Zionism in interwar Poland, see Ezra Mendelsohn, *Zionism in Poland. The Formative Years, 1915–1926* (New Haven: Yale University Press, 1981), 112.

[59] On economic policies in interwar East Central Europe, see Tibor Iván Berend and György Ránki, *Economic Development in East-Central Europe in the 19th and 20th Centuries* (New York: Columbia University Press, 1974); Jan Kofman, *Economic Nationalism and Development: Central and Eastern Europe Between the Two World Wars* (Boulder, CO: Westview Press, 1997); Christoph Kreutzmüller, Michael Wildt, and Mosheh Tsimerman, eds., *National Economies: Volks-Wirtschaft, Racism and Economy in Europe Between the Wars (1918–1939/45)* (Newcastle upon Tyne: Cambridge Scholars Publishing, 2015).

idea was ultimately rejected by governments concerned above all with maintaining sovereignty.[60]

To address these economic issues, representatives of seven Habsburg successor states met in Porto Rosa in November 1921. They signed a convention in which they agreed "to take all measures to abolish the special obstacles affecting the regular passenger and goods traffic in Central Europe, especially as traffic over the railway system of the succession states." Yet barriers remained, particularly since there was not yet a uniform set of regulations regarding passports and visas. Only in 1922 did representatives of the successor states gather in Graz to attempt to standardize the passport system in the region.[61]

In this context, some Central Europeans sought salvation in new political forms, such as federation, that would renew economic cooperation between former Habsburg lands. Oskár Jászi, the Minister of Nationalities under the short-lived Karolyi regime in Hungary, called for a "United States of the Danube" with free trade between its members and a shared foreign and military policy. Visions of a Danube Federation had circulated since 1848. His model was something like the United States or Switzerland. Such a union would possess "such a wealth of natural, climatological, and ethnographic resources," that autarky, what he imagined to be "an intrinsic test of a viable polity," would be attainable to a greater extent there than in almost any other polity in world history. For Jászi, the choices were clear: "Federation or war!... Only the complete freedom of economic circulation, the complete unity of military and international functions, the communion of the organs of state consciousness which typifies federations is capable of... creating lasting peace."[62]

These ideas were of course not Jászi's alone. Hundreds of ordinary people sent petitions and proposals to the new Ministry for National Minorities. Many of them outlined their own visions for guaranteeing national "self-determination," evoking Wilsonian language to support their claims. One petitioner even suggested that Hungary should become the 49th U.S. state, a plan which would supposedly safeguard Hungary's autonomy while enabling it to benefit from American military protection and economic resources. More commonly, however, petitioners

---

[60] "Cronaca della città. Stato d'animo," *Il Piccolo*, April 4, 1920. On relationships between Trieste and the hinterland, see Marco Bresciani and Klaus Richter, "Trieste and Danzig After the Great War: Imperial Collapse, Narratives of Loss, Reconfigured Globalization," *The Journal of Modern History* 95, no. 3 (September 1, 2023): 557–95.

[61] United Nations Archive, Geneva, R1121_14_18427, The Porto Rosa Conference on Transit Questions. On passports and visas, see Peter Becker and Natasha Wheatley, eds., "Remaking Mobility: International Conferences and the Emergence of the Modern Passport System," in *Remaking Central Europe: The League of Nations and the Former Habsburg Lands* (Oxford: Oxford University Press, 2020), 193–213.

[62] Oszkár Jászi and Stefan von Hartenstein, *Der Zusammenbruch des Dualismus und die Zukunft der Donaustaaten* (Vienna: Manz, 1918), 46, 49, 96; for an overview of federative ideas in East Central Europe, see Holly Case, "The Strange Politics of Federative Ideas in East-Central Europe," *Journal of Modern History* 85, no. 4 (2013): 833–66.

supported a United States of Europe, or variations on both federalist and nonterritorial visions of national autonomy, ideas that seemed relevant to the new context of 1918, in which there were both Hungarians in other states (such as Romania) and in which Hungary also had a large population of minorities.[63]

Other Austrians reimagined Habsburg economic integration on an even broader scale. Aristocrat Richard N. Coudenhove-Kalergi, founder of the pan-Europe movement, promoted a free trade union that extended well beyond Central Europe, to include Africa. It was intended to revive trade relations within Europe and to put Europe on a more equal footing with the United States, which many Europeans envied and feared (including Hitler) precisely because of its vast hinterland, its capacity for self-sufficiency. Coudenhove, a white supremacist, warned that in the absence of such a federation, Europe was doomed to become an "economic colony of America," and that European workers would be "enslaved by American capital."[64]

To newly empowered leaders in Belgrade, Bucharest, and Prague, however, the Danube Federation sounded suspiciously like the former Habsburg Empire. They had no interest in resuscitating it.[65] But if formal federalist schemes enjoyed only limited success, other efforts were more successful. Behind the scenes, trade relations between the Habsburg successor states did pick up again in the 1920s. Austria bought coal from Czechoslovakia and Poland; Viennese trading houses handled Czech and Polish exports, and by 1929, at least 25 percent of Austrian trade was flowing to or from Czechoslovakia, Hungary, and Poland. This was in part thanks to the regional and international connections and outlook of Viennese bankers and entrepreneurs, who remained connected to one another and invested in economic cooperation.[66] But these steps toward greater regional exchange were crushed by the Great Depression, which pushed the economies of southeastern Europe into relations of dependence with Germany and destroyed Imperial trade networks once and for all.[67]

---

[63] On these petitions, see Anna Adorjáni, "Interpreting Non-Territorial Autonomy in Late Habsburg Hungary (1848–1918)," (PhD diss. University of Vienna, 2023), 202, 249–55.

[64] Richard Coudenhove-Kalergi, "Das Paneuropaische Manifest," in *Kampf um Paneuropa, aus dem 1. Jahrgang von Paneuropa* (Vienna: Paneuropa Verlag, 1925), 9. On Pan-Europe see Sven Beckert, "American Danger: United States Empire, Eurafrica, and the Territorialization of Industrial Capitalism, 1870–1950," *The American Historical Review* 122, no. 4 (October 1, 2017): 1137–70; Katherine Sorrels, *Cosmopolitan Outsiders: Imperial Inclusion, National Exclusion, and the Pan-European Idea, 1900–1930* (New York: Palgrave Macmillan, 2016). Lucile Dreidemy and Eric Burton, "Collective Colonialism for European Integration. The Rise of the Paneuropean Movement in Post-imperial Austria," in *Integration and Collaborative Imperialism in Modern Europe*, ed. Bernhard Schär and Mikko Toivanen (London: Bloomsbury, 2023).

[65] István Bethlen, *The Treaty of Trianon and European Peace: Four Lectures Delivered in London in November 1933* (London: Longmans & Green, 1934), 152, 177–82.

[66] Andreas Weigl, "Beggar-Thy-Neighbour vs. Danube Basin Strategy: Habsburg Economic Networks in Interwar Europe," *Religions* 7, no. 11 (November 3, 2016): 129.

[67] Stephen G. Gross, *Export Empire: German Soft Power in Southeastern Europe, 1890–1945*, New Studies in European History (Cambridge: Cambridge University Press, 2015).

Imperial legacies did not simply "trickle down" through the policies of the successor states in their borderlands or heartlands. They also "trickled up" into new international institutions and norms. As Natasha Wheatley argues, Central Europe was a "Ground Zero" for the construction of the new international order after the First World War.[68] Having knocked Humpty-Dumpty off the wall in 1918, the Allies—through the League of Nations and other international organizations—attempted to put the pieces back together in the 1920s, recreating economic and political ties that had been dissolved at the end of the war. In realms as varied as economics and finance, hunger and food, migration, minority rights and statelessness, the control of epidemics, and the traffic in drugs and sex, these organizations attempted to reconnect the shards of shattered Imperial and international networks.[69]

The challenges of economic fragmentation in Central Europe also produced new ideas. In the realm of trade and economic policy, Quinn Slobodian has shown that Austrian economists responded to the collapse of the Habsburg Empire and the postwar threat to the free movement of goods and capital by developing what are now often referred to as "neoliberal" economic policies and institutions. These "globalists" hoped to "protect" or insulate markets from the vagaries of democratic politics, and especially from the protectionist and anti-globalist policies of democratically elected governments.[70]

Fears of Bolshevism also fueled the postwar wave of internationalism in the successor states. In Austria, revolution seemed imminent. Arthur Salter described the country's economic situation in 1922: "There seemed no escape from destitution, starvation, riots and perhaps revolution, with incalculable foreign consequences."[71] That year the League of Nations Economic and Financial Committee, led by Salter, stepped in to bail Austria out of its financial abyss with a package of loans for reconstruction. Ignaz Seipel, Austria's chancellor, played on fears of revolution in his appeals to the Allies and the League for assistance. In a speech to the League's general Assembly in 1922, he warned that if the international community did not act, "it would mean the creation of a vacuum in the middle of Europe, a vacuum with monstrous suction that would pull in Austria's neighbors and would disrupt the balance of power among them that had only been established with great skill."[72]

---

[68] Natasha Wheatley, "Central Europe as Ground Zero of the New International Order," *Slavic Review* 78, no. 4 (2019): 900–11.

[69] Becker and Wheatley, eds., *Remaking Central Europe*.

[70] Quinn Slobodian, *Globalists: The End of Empire and the Birth of Neoliberalism* (Cambridge, MA: Harvard University Press, 2018).

[71] Sir Arthur Salter, "The Reconstruction of Austria," *Foreign Affairs* 2, no. 4 (June 15, 1924): 632.

[72] Cited in John Deak, "Dismantling Empire: Ignaz Seipel and Austria's Financial Crisis," in *From Empire to Republic: Post-World War I Austria*, ed. Günter Bischof, Fritz Plasser, and Peter Berger (New Orleans: University of New Orleans Press, 2010), 123–41 (p. 135).

For several years the Austrian government had been printing money to pay its expenses and debts, resulting in the total collapse of the crown. The state was supported primarily by charity. The League's program to reconstruct Austria's finances provided $130,000,000 in loans to meet its deficits from 1922 to 1924. The loans came at a high cost, however. The League required the Austrian government to open its books to a League commissioner, and to implement austerity measures according to the dictates of outside auditors, including cutting social spending, raising taxes, and firing almost 100,000 civil servants. This kind of external financial control had previously been attempted only in colonial contexts. This humiliation was not lost on League officials nor on Austrians.[73]

While League officials later remembered the Austrian reconstruction mission as a great success story, other countries disagreed. As Jamie Martin has shown, they increasingly declined the League's offers of financial assistance, repelled by the stink of colonialism. Portugal, Liberia, Poland, Mexico, India, and China all refused offers of League loans. These forms of intervention also represented a model for the forms of supranational intervention into the finances of a sovereign state that would later be adapted by the International Monetary Fund. In many ways, the League and other international institutions perpetuated the Imperial power of the British Empire between the wars.[74]

Yet we cannot reduce the goals of the League and other international and humanitarian organizations in East Central Europe solely to maintaining or establishing Imperial or colonial power. Nor did these internationalists simply attempt to re-establish a globalized "World of Yesterday." The League also assisted in the construction of new nation-states and forms of national infrastructure and helped in some cases to reinforce national sovereignty rather than undermine it. Internationalists thus attempted to create a new architecture for internationalism and globalism that would be more sustainable in a world of sovereign nation-states. This was partly because League agencies were staffed and sometimes run by Central Europeans with their own state-building agendas.[75]

---

[73] On the League reconstruction of Austria, see Nathan Marcus, *Austrian Reconstruction and the Collapse of Global Finance, 1921–1931* (Cambridge, MA: Harvard University Press, 2018); Patricia Clavin, *Securing the World Economy: The Reinvention of the League of Nations, 1920–1946* (Oxford: Oxford University Press, 2013); Patricia Clavin, "The Austrian Hunger Crisis and the Genesis of International Organization after the First World War," *International Affairs (Royal Institute of International Affairs 1944–)* 90, no. 2 (2014): 265–78; Jamie Martin, *The Meddlers: Sovereignty, Empire, and the Birth of Global Economic Governance* (Cambridge, MA: Harvard University Press, 2022), chap. 2. On the ways that the financial reconstruction impacted the bureaucracy, see Deak, "Dismantling Empire," 135–8.

[74] Martin, *The Meddlers*, chap. 2; Susan Pedersen, *The Guardians: The League of Nations and the Crisis of Empire* (Oxford: Oxford University Press, 2015); Mark Mazower, *Governing the World: The History of an Idea, 1815 to the Present* (New York: Penguin Press, 2013); Mark Mazower, *No Enchanted Palace: The End of Empire and the Ideological Origins of the United Nations* (Princeton: Princeton University Press, 2009).

[75] Sara Silverstein, "Reinventing International Health in East Central Europe: The League of Nations, State Sovereignty, and Universal Health," in Becker and Wheatley, eds., *Remaking Central Europe*, 71–98.

Despite these innovations, and despite the rhetoric of revolutionary change, countless legal, political, and social continuities survived in Central Europe. The Habsburg Empire fell, but Imperial institutions, laws, and social and political hierarchies lived on. When the Czech National Council took charge of the Bohemian government in October 1918 and declared the new state of Czech-Slovakia, the first law they passed ruled that: "all previous provincial and Imperial laws and regulations remain for the time being in effect." This was not simply because the state's leaders wanted to prevent anarchy or revolution, but because Czech nationalists felt invested in the institutions of the Imperial state. After all, they had already helped to create and staff several of these institutions from the ground up. In that sense, much of their Czech administration had already existed within the framework of the Habsburg Empire. Alois Rašín, a prominent member of the National Committee, later recalled, "The basic purpose of this law was to prevent any anarchic situation from developing so that our whole state administration would remain and continue on October 29 as if there has been no revolution at all."[76]

Several of the successor states faced the significant challenge of unifying diverse legal and administrative systems inherited from different states. For example, in the new Polish state, created out of former Austrian, German, and Russian territories, there were multiple currencies, railroad systems, and three legal systems until 1932. Romania had to somehow standardize systems inherited from Austria, Russia, and Hungary, while Czechoslovakia had to contend with forms of provincial administrations inherited from both Austria and Hungary. Yugoslavia maintained special education legal and education systems for Muslim citizens, systems it inherited from both the Ottoman and Habsburg Empires.[77] It took years to achieve goals of integration and unification, and in some cases local and regional discrepancies remained. These discrepancies made it challenging to simply transfer bureaucrats from one district to another—local knowledge was essential.[78]

At the local level, a shortage of qualified personnel meant that there was significant continuity in the ranks of public servants, regardless of nationality. This was particularly true in Romania, where a dearth of Romanian applicants meant that Hungarian and German speakers often kept their jobs in the postal service and other government offices. This uncomfortable reality for nationalists was also the subject of recurring complaints in Czechoslovakia, where radicals complained about the high number of civil servants who had served in Viennese ministries who now occupied high positions in the new state.[79] In

---

[76] Quoted in Judson, *The Habsburg Empire*, 433–4.
[77] Emily Greble, *Muslims and the Making of Modern Europe* (Oxford: Oxford University Press, 2021).
[78] Egry, "Negotiating Post-imperial Transition," 22.
[79] Martin Klečacky, "Převzetí moci. Státní správa v počátcích Československé republiky 1918–1920 na příkladu Čech," *Český časopis historický* 116, no. 3 (2018): 693–732; Morelon, *Streetscapes*, 272.

Czechoslovakia, however, Hungarian railway and postal workers were gradually—though not entirely—replaced.[80]

Significant continuities remained in terms of economic and social inequalities as well. In Transylvania, Máté Rigó has shown, elite Jewish, Hungarian, and German industrialists—all minorities in "Greater" Romania—managed to hold on to considerable economic and social power, despite the nationalizing and nationalist rhetoric of state leaders. This was partly because of the absence of a significant Romanian middle class, and in part because these members of minority groups had valuable connections to essential trading partners outside of Romania. They ironically managed to profit from protectionist policies to maintain their wealth.[81]

Meanwhile, land reform was halting. Significant reallocations of land took place in interwar Yugoslavia, where 1.6 million hectares were redistributed to 535,600 families between 1919 and 1934; and in Romania, where 6.3 million hectares were expropriated, of which 3.8 million were reallocated to peasant landholders. But in Poland and Hungary, initial promises of radical reform were never carried out, due to the entrenched power of conservative landowners. By 1935, in Hungary, 43 percent of land remained tied to large estates, and in Poland only 25 percent of land attached to large estates was ever expropriated. In Czechoslovakia, as well, significant territory was taken from Hungarian and German landowners and parceled out to soldiers of the Czech Legion or to emigrants returning from abroad, but the pace of reform was quite slow and incremental.[82]

Even if continuity, as much as rupture, defined the post-Imperial era, the implications of the Habsburg Empire's demise were tremendous, and spilled over well beyond Europe's borders. In particular, the language of "self-determination" that framed the revolutions—but also had significant antecedents in the Empire—gave hope to discontented Imperial subjects everywhere, as they appropriated Wilson's rhetoric to demand an end to colonial subjugation. Without the collapse of the Habsburg Monarchy, anti-colonial nationalists elsewhere might not have been able to imagine a post-Imperial future, and might not have been so bitterly disappointed when the great powers decided that only (some) "white" Europeans were ready for (qualified, supervised) national self-determination.[83]

Many challenges faced by interwar nation-builders would also plague decolonization efforts in the later twentieth century: tensions between a rhetoric of revolutionary change and the realities of legal and social continuity; the

---

[80] Egry, "Negotiating Post-imperial Transition," 22–6.

[81] Máté Rigó, "The Long First World War and the Survival of Business Elites in East-Central Europe: Transylvania's Industrial Boom and the Enrichment of Economic Elites," *European Review of History: Revue Européenne d'histoire* 24, no. 2 (March 4, 2017): 250–72; Rigó, *Capitalism in Chaos*.

[82] On land reform and its limitations, see Berend and Ránki, *Economic Development*, 186–93.

[83] Erez Manela, *The Wilsonian Moment: Self-Determination and the International Origins of Anti-Colonial Nationalism* (Oxford: Oxford University Press, 2007).

challenge of carving viable economic and political units out of large, economically interdependent empires; and tensions between individual and collective national rights in states that were religiously and linguistically diverse—between an understanding of "democracy" premised upon national homogeneity and one that respected minority rights.[84]

The consequences of the Empire's dissolution reverberated for decades, not only in the memoirs of Habsburg nostalgists. Robert Gerwarth has argued that the "vanquished" powers of the Great War inflicted the greatest havoc on Europe in the twentieth century. It was in the east and south, including the former Habsburg lands, where bitterness and anger festered about the terms of the Versailles Treaty; where bloody revolutions were followed by even bloodier counterrevolutions; and where the most extreme and violent ideologies and practices of the twentieth century took root: Bolshevism, fascism, Nazism, Communism; ethnic cleansing; political violence and terrorism on the right and left.[85]

These ideologies reflected a revolt against empire, globalism, and against diversity itself. But they were also the product of continuities; of high expectations and disappointed hopes. Many citizens of the former Habsburg Empire genuinely believed that their new states would usher in a new era of democracy along with self-determination, although by the late 1920s democracy had already begun to lose its luster in most successor states. Nor were the legacies of the war all negative. The successor states made some very tangible gains, including the extension of suffrage to women, new forms of economic development, the expansion of welfare states, and new rights for workers. Several of these achievements built on wartime institutions or on precedents from the late Imperial era. But within a framework of nationalist democracy, in which rights generally accrued to members of a privileged national collective rather than to individuals, these gains often came at the expense of those excluded from the national community. Those legacies echoed on in many of the wars and nationalist conflicts that characterized the twentieth century down to the very end.

The Great War and the Transformation of Habsburg Central Europe. Pieter M. Judson & Tara Zahra, Oxford University Press. © Pieter M. Judson & Tara Zahra 2025. DOI: 10.1093/9780191842306.003.0008

---

[84] On the problems of post-1945 postcolonial nationalist claims and their Habsburg antecedents, Natasha Wheatley, *The Life and Death of States: Central Europe and the Transformation of Modern Sovereignty* (Princeton: Princeton University Press, 2023).

[85] Gerwarth, *The Vanquished.*

Conclusion

Continuities, Legacies, Memories

Long after the Habsburg Empire disappeared, the language of empire remained ubiquitous in Central Europe. But what is striking is the extent to which it was used in contradictory ways. On the one hand the new governments of East Central Europe insisted on the need to overcome the legacy of empire in their relationship to former national enemies, while on the other hand they perpetuated Imperial laws, institutions, and practices. They distanced themselves from empire, claiming that it had rested on an antidemocratic form of rule, while at the same time that they set out to "civilize" and "nationalize" their own Imperial borderlands. They ostentatiously commemorated their wartime victories even though much of the male population had fought on the side of the defeated military.

In light of such chaos, it is not surprising that Austrian-Jewish writers like Joseph Roth and Stefan Zweig wrote nostalgically about the Habsburg Empire in the decades after its collapse, seeing it as emblematic of a certain ideal of multinational coexistence. But on the ground, what could be remembered and how depended a lot on where you were situated.

For example, in a comparison of the postwar Austrian Tyrol, the South Tyrol (annexed by Italy from Austria after the war) and the Trentino region (which also became a part of Italy), Laurence Cole has shown that different cultures of memory emerged within constraints set by the postwar Italian and Austrian states. In the South Tyrol, German-speakers who had fought in the Habsburg army mourned their defeat, but the Italian government, which celebrated the region's annexation to Italy as a victory, suppressed collective forms of commemoration. The Italian government also celebrated its acquisition of the Trentino. This left members of the local population whose men had fought in the Habsburg army to mourn their losses privately, with small local memorials that focused on the comradeship of the soldiers and avoided attributing any grand Imperial or national significance to their sacrifices. Only in the Austrian Tyrol were Habsburg veterans publicly commemorated, in rituals that emphasized the heroism of Austrian soldiers and the tragedy of their losses.[1]

The example of the Tyrol reveals a broader pattern. There was often no unified culture of memory in the Habsburg successor states and many gaps separated

---

[1] Laurence Cole, "Divided Land, Diverging Narratives: Memory Cultures of the Great War in Successor Regions of Tyrol," in *Sacrifice and Rebirth*, ed. Mark Cornwall and John Paul Newman (2016), 256–83.

official and popular memories of the war and the Empire. In most of the successor states veterans had fought on the "wrong side" of the war. Unless they belonged to a very small minority of soldiers who had deserted to the Allies before the war's end, they did not receive compensation for their wartime injuries or support for their dependants. Family members of fallen veterans were also prevented from publicly commemorating or mourning their losses, even in cemeteries. Any recognition of the sacrifice of these veterans would have been seen as a betrayal of the new nation-states which construed the Habsburg military and state as its "enemy." But privately, and locally, veterans and their families often sought ways to remember their service to and experiences in the Imperial army.[2]

Since the 1980s, many historians have come to share a more positive appraisal of the Empire and its legacy. This has been partly a product of more critical approaches to nationalism and the nation-state in the wake of the Yugoslav wars, as well as the constructivist and transnational "turns" in historical studies. As historians, we have become increasingly skeptical about the alleged stability and "naturalness" of national identification at the level of the individual, and wary of positioning nations or nation-states either as the presumed containers or subjects of history, or as the best vehicles for guaranteeing economic prosperity and political democracy. Meanwhile, in the last decade the world has moved in the opposite direction, one that often cultivates strong forms of ethnic nationalism. The resurgence of populist nationalist governments and movements in Europe, now directed against immigrants, refugees, Jews, and supranational institutions like the European Union, has endowed the Habsburg Empire with new relevance as a potential model of a multinational, multilingual, multiethnic state, however flawed.

Where does the history of the First World War in Habsburg Central Europe sit within this broad reassessment?

It might be tempting to write about the Empire's dissolution as a product of outside forces that cynically used the ideal of "national self-determination" in order to sow dissent. In other words, far from being an anachronistic state in decline, we could see the Habsburg Empire as a state interrupted by war and dismembered by outsiders. This is a powerful counternarrative to the story told by the interwar nationalists themselves. To them, an anachronistic and oppressive empire was doomed to fail long before 1914, both by its inability to accommodate the nationalist movements it sought to suppress, and by its alleged economic, social, and political backwardness. But without down playing the cynicism and hypocrisy of the Allies, it is clear that shifting the blame also risks romanticizing the Empire and underestimating its weaknesses as well as the agency and mistakes of its own governments in its pursuit of victory.

Another way of positioning the war in the history of the Habsburg Empire is to emphasize, as scholars have more recently done, a process of social breakdown

---

[2] See collected essays in Cornwall and Newman, *Sacrifice and Rebirth*.

that was partly of the state's own making. This is a story of internal collapse and conflict not necessarily linked to longstanding nationalist tensions (though the war certainly exacerbated such tensions), but to poor decision-making, mismanaged resources and opportunities, the abandonment of legal norms, and the suppression of social and political conflict. Equally important, we should remember that these elements were all part of a general European crisis—many of the same threats to stability and survival plagued each of Europe's combatant states, and some of them managed to survive while others did not. Survival, moreover, was not necessarily evidence of a more democratic or egalitarian political culture. For example, food appeared on the tables of British citizens in the metropole at the expense of colonial subjects, as massive supplies of rice, wheat, and legumes grown in India were diverted to London. While prices skyrocketed and people starved in Calcutta, there was no rationing in Britain until 1918.[3]

As we have argued, the Habsburg Empire imploded during the war not so much because of an excess of nationalist feeling, but because the state betrayed its own commitment to its citizens and to the very rule of law. The wartime regime constantly demonstrated its mistrust for the Empire's own citizens, and those citizens returned that mistrust with dividends. This dynamic played out in refugee camps, internment camps, and POW camps, but also in schools, censorship offices, in markets, and on the streets. The state's original effort to use the war to strengthen Imperial loyalties ultimately backfired when some groups were treated with intense suspicion or as "uncivilized" people in need of reeducation. The military could not shake its paranoid perception that subversion was everywhere—especially perpetuated by "suspect" nationalities such as Serbs, Ukrainians, and Italians, but also through democratic participation itself. This was partly a matter of self-defense. Officials constantly blamed suspect nationalities for military defeats and incompetence. In a larger sense by emphasizing national differences in its policies, the military provoked the very conflict among national groups it sought to suppress, by openly favoring some and viciously persecuting others.

But it was not only military authorities which contributed to the state's downfall, in a struggle that pitted the "bad" military against the "good" civil service. As the civil governments struggled to provide for citizens, their bureaucrats at all levels—often in desperate circumstances—also chose to sort Austrians and Hungarians into national groups—whether in refugee camps or in providing welfare benefits. They delegated authority to nationalist associations, and to local and regional governments that were better equipped to handle the crisis on the ground. In doing so, they devolved the power and legitimacy of government to local and regional—and nationalist—"peripheries." These "peripheries," in places

---

[3] Stefan Goebel, "Cities," in *The Cambridge History of the First World War*, ed. J. M. Winter (Cambridge: Cambridge University Press, 2014); S. Chattopadhyay, "War, Migration and Alienation in Colonial Calcutta: The Remaking of Muzaffar Ahmad," *History Workshop Journal* 64, no. 1 (January 1, 2007): 214–16.

like Prague, Cracow, Lemberg/L'viv/Lwów, Pressburg/Poszony, or Zagreb, would become new "centers" of the postwar successor states.

In many ways, Austria-Hungary was defeated by its own ambition during the war—ambitions to mobilize, manage, and deploy the Empire's vast resources quickly and fairly, to expand the rights of citizenship, to provide for refugees, and to monitor and secure popular loyalties. As much as local officials wanted to provide food for the population, however, they were simply unable to obtain it. As much as they wanted to create organized and sanitary camps for refugees, the resources were not there to do so. And these "failures" had a lasting impact. The Empire set the terms of its own destruction with wartime policies that deepened national divisions and resentments. But it also invented new forms of population policies and political mobilization that carried on in the interwar successor states.

In this light, the war no longer seems like a mere coda or final chapter in the history of the Habsburg Empire. It was, rather, essential to the foundation of a new order, one that radiated far beyond the borders of the former Empire itself. This is a common way of thinking about the First World War in the history of Western Europe and other parts of the world, but less common in the history of the Habsburg lands, where the war is typically seen as an ending point, rather than a beginning or a middle. The nationalist narratives of the interwar era denied continuities between the Habsburg Empire and the successor states because doing so would be to concede that the radical "decolonization" promised by interwar nation-builders was incomplete. But ironically, a more optimistic narrative about the viability of the Habsburg Empire also tends to downplay continuities across the divide of the war. In this view, the Empire's promise was destroyed by the Paris System of 1918, replaced by states that became breeding grounds for the political radicalism and genocidal violence of the twentieth century.

Thinking about the war as a beginning as well as an ending helps us to avoid both extremes of romanticizing the Habsburg Empire or demonizing it as a "prison of nations." Instead of focusing on the question of Imperial collapse, we have attempted to put the subject of wartime social and political transformation at the center of the story. During the First World War, Habsburg authorities, experts, and citizens in all regions and at all levels (Imperial, regional, local) were innovators. Experts and local administrators developed new approaches, desperate to try to solve vexing wartime social problems. Citizens, too, demanded new rights or new forms of welfare, using a common language of wartime sacrifice and mutual obligation. Nothing that developed during or after the war was woven from scratch, but Habsburg authorities and citizens developed new practices, ideas, and institutions that had a profound impact on the rest of the century.

The Great War and the Transformation of Habsburg Central Europe. Pieter M. Judson & Tara Zahra, Oxford University Press. © Pieter M. Judson & Tara Zahra 2025. DOI: 10.1093/9780191842306.003.0009

Index

For the benefit of digital users, indexed terms that span two pages (e.g., 52–53) may, on occasion, appear on only one of those pages.

Adler, Friedrich 123
    amnesty 135
Adriatic coast 15, 17, 19–21, 59–60, 131, 137, 156
Aehrenthal, Alois Count Lexa von 17–19
Africa 7, 19–20, 162
agriculture and food production 16, 42–4, 71
Albania 56, 59, 62–3, 65–7
    Austro–Hungarian occupation of 73–4, 76–7
    establishment of 21
    under Ottoman rule 13–14
Alexandria, Egypt (POW camp) 99
Allied naval blockade 31–2, 36, 75–6, 111
Alsace-Lorraine 131–2, 143, 161–2
Alsberg, Henry 170
American Joint Distribution Committee 116, 165–6, 170
Andrássy, Count Julius 15, 26, 121
Anschluss (annexation to Germany)
    Austrian support for 156
anti-Semitism 45–6, 74, 90–1, 135–6, 147–8, 164–71, 182
Apponyi, Albert 154–5
Archduke Friedrich 124–6
Archduke Otto 126–7
Armeeoberkommando (AOK) (Austro-Hungarian High Command) 25–6, 63, 70–6, 87–8, 93–4
Armistice of November 11, 1918 151
Armistice of Villa Giusti (1918) 5–6, 150–1
Attems, Count 40–1
Austria-Hungary
    enduring influence of 153, 158–61, 167, 174–80
    great power status of 24–5, 27
    internal dissolution of 2, 115, 136, 142–3, 147–51
    multinational character of 65–6, 89–90
    proposals for federalization of 64, 138, 146–51
    proposals for trialism in 18, 28, 146
    rule of law in 6, 12, 24–7, 66, 75, 104, 183,
        see also militarization of society
    structure of 9–11, 64, 75–6
    successor states to 4, 152–6, 161–8

Austrian Christian Social Party 149–50, 155–6, 160–1
Austrian Defense Ministry 108–9
Austrian Ministry of the Interior 144–5
Austrian parliament
    approval of emergency war legislation 25
    lack of influence on decision for war 8–9
    reopening of 127, 138–9
    shut down of 35
Austrian Republic 168–9
    financial reconstruction of 177
Austrian Social Democratic Party 47, 123, 128–30, 149–50, 155–6
Austro-German alliance 61, 64, 71–2, 75, 124, 130–1, 133, 140–1, 144
Austro-Hungarian Foreign Ministry 12, 19, 28–9

Balkan Wars (1912–13) 19–23, 25–6, 28–30, 62
Balkans 13, 15–16, 33, 56–7, 59
    prewar political situation 13–15, 17
Banat 22–3
Bardolff, Carl von 20
Belgium 69, 131–2
Belgrade 57, 59, 176
Belgrade,
Belluno 73
Beneš, Edvard 132–3
Berchtold, Leopold 28
Berlin Treaty 18–19
Besserabia 154
black market 45–6, 74, 90, 135–6
Black Sea 13, 18
Bohemia 34, 41, 47–8, 92, 149–50, 153–6
Bolsheviks 100, 119–20, 144–5
    Hungarian 164
Bolsheviks
    influence on Austria-Hungary 93, 122–3
Bosnia and Herzegovina 25–7, 29–30, 40–1, 51, 148–9
    and Zagreb treason trial 24
    Habsburg civilization mission in 15–17
    Austrian occupation and annexation of 4, 14–19, 25–6, 64

Bowman, Isaiah 157
Boyer, John 149–50
Brandström, Elsa 96–7
Bratislava, *see* Pressburg/Poszony
Britain 13, 17–18, 60, 132, 143–4, 161–2
Brno/Brünn 81
Brociner, Marco 80
Brück an der Leitha (refugee camp) 91–2
Brusilov, Aleksei 60
    and the Brusilov offensive 60–1
Bucharest 61, 74, 176
Budapest 44, 47–8, 52–3, 75, 136, 149, 153
Budisavljević, Vladimir 40–1
Bukovina 2–3, 37, 56–7, 78, 154
Bulgaria 13–14, 17, 19–23, 29, 59, 61, 65–6, 154
Bülow, Bernhard von 18
Burghauser, Wolfgang 87
Burián 146

Caporetto/Kobarid 56, 62, 73
Carinthia 157, 160
Carnegie Foundation 76
Caro, Leopold 171–2
Carpathian Mountains 58, 78, 90, 94
Cattaro/Kotor 40–1
Cena, Nickolaus 40
censorship 3–4, 25–6, 35, 37, 42–3, 52–99, 116, 135
charity 112–15
Charles I 63–4, 75, 140, 143–4, 146–7, 149–51
    ascension to the throne of 124, 126–7
    desire for peace 124, 131–5
    exile and abdication 151
    reforms of 135–9
Chelm
    Ukrainian demands for 140
children 4, 33, 43–4, 49, 55, 78, 88–9, 111, 135–6, *see also* orphans
    in refugee camps 88
citizenship 4, 9–10, 89–90, 103–18, 167–8
    divided loyalties 104–8
    entitlements and duties of 103–6, 116–18
Clark, Christopher 21
Clary, Governor of Styria 39
Clemenceau, Georges 143
Cole, Laurence 181
communism, *see* Bolsheviks, Russian Revolution (October 1917)
Cornwall, Mark 24, 50–1, 144–5
Coudenhove-Kalergi, Richard N. 175
Cracow 72–3, 147–8, 153
Croat nationalism 15–40, 115
Croatia 18, 24, 39–40, 148–9
Croatian-speaking populations 93–4, 138, 161–2

Czech nationalism 23, 39, 41, 53–4, 115–16, 138, 147, 153–4
Czech nationalists
    alleged disloyalty of 41–2
Czechoslovakia 4, 41–2, 92, 110, 157–8, 161, 168, 170–5, 178–9
    establishment of 150–1, 153–8
    plans for the creation of 145–6
Czechs 37–8, 93–4
Czernin, Ottokar 126–8, 131–2, 134, 140–1
Czestochowa 170–1

D'Annunzio, Gabriele 156
Dalmatia 2–3, 40–1, 148–9
Dardanelle straits 13, 18
Daszkiewiczowa, Ludwika 112
Davis, Belinda 112
Deák, István 11, 58
Deak, John 24–5, 167
democracy 2, 4, 24–5, 157, 179–80
denunciation 39, 41–2, 45–6, 69, 103–4
deportation 69–70, 168–9
desertion 70, 93–4, 120, 137, 142–4
Diller, Erich Baron 71
disease 46, 57, 88, 98
Dobruja 154

Easter Rebellion (1916) 119–20
Eastern Front 33, 71, 79–80
Eckartsau 151
education 15–16, 49–51, 71, 88–90, 108
Egry, Gábor 157–8
emergency war measures, *see* militarization of society
émigré and exiled nationalists 132–3, 144–6
Empress Zita 125–7, 132, 143
ethnic cleansing 2, 4, 21–2

Falkenhayn, Erich von 61
family
    perceived threats to 108–9
Farkas, Mózes 76
Ferenczi, Emerich/Imre 114
Fiume 156
food crisis 4, 36, 42–6, 55, 72–3, 92–3, 104, 134–42, 146–7, *see also* hunger
forced labor 62, 67, 73
Fourteen Points 132–3
France 13, 17, 30, 60, 69, 132, 143–4, 161–2, 171–2
Francis Ferdinand 11–12, 20, 28–9, 67, 126–7
    assassination of 1–2, 7, 29–30
Franz Conrad von Hötzendorf 11–12, 20, 27–30, 33–4, 52, 69–70, 93–4, 137, 144
    dismissal of 124–6

Franz Joseph I 7–12, 15–16, 20, 28, 41, 56–7, 60–4, 109, 158–60
  death of 123–4
  fraternization 97–8
Freud, Sigmund 103

Galántai, József 40
Galicia 2–3, 19–20, 23, 31–2, 36–9, 56–8, 60, 65–7, 69–73, 92, 130–1, 138–40
  Habsburg loss of authority over 147–8
Galician Front 33–4, 36, 42–3, 57
gender 109, *see also* women
  transformation of roles 121
General Lukachich 149
German nationalism 103, 115–16, 135, 155, 160
German-Austria 155–6, 160–1
German-Austria (establishment of) 149–50
German-speaking populations 39, 149–50, 155–8, 160–2, 181
Germany 13, 17, 20, 28–30, 36–62, 64–5, 71–2
  as ally of Austria-Hungary, *see* Austro-German alliance
  war financing strategy 51
  war propaganda strategy 52
Gerwarth, Robert 180
Gmünd [refugee camp] 91–2
Graz 47, 52–3, 70, 81, 160–1, 174
Greece 13–14, 17, 19–22, 59
guerilla warfare 67–8
Gumz, Jonathan 24–5, 67

Habsburg military elite 11, 13, 21, 32, 41, 56–7, 59–61, 64, 66–7, 71–2, 93–4
  authoritarian views of 11, 24–7, 33
  paranoia of 8, 19–25
  pro-war attitudes of 19, 25–6, 28–30
  paranoia of 144–5
Hague Conventions (1899 and 1907) 94–6
Healy, Maureen 42, 47, 54–5, 104, 112, 123
Herschkowitz, Mathilde 168
Hindenburg Program 129
Hindenburg, Paul von 141, 143–4
Hoen, Maximilian von 54–5
Hofmannsthal, Hugo von 64–5
Hohenburg, Duchess Sophie von 1
Hoyos, Count 29
Hsia, Ke-Chin 114
Hungarian parliament 148–9
Hungarian Social Democratic Party 129–30
Hungarian-speaking populations 61, 93–4
Hungary 15, 20, 22–4, 26–8, 39–40, 44, 60–1, 64, 67, 69, 72, 88, 90–1, 139, 146, 156, 161, 164, 169–70, 178–9
  as a rump state 154–5

Counterrevolution 164–7, 169–70
  dissolution of 148–9
  economic policy during war 75–6
  under Béla Kun 164–5
hunger 5–6, 67, 108–9, 147–8, 157–8, *see also* food crisis

Iłża 73
India 162, 182–3
infant mortality 86, 88
inflation 31, 74, 114, 142, 176
Innsbruck (war art exhibition) 52–3
Interior Ministry 70, 81, 85, 88
internment of civilians 62, 67–70
Ireland 161–2
Istanbul/Constantinople 13, 19–20, 77, 131
Istria 86
Italian Front 60, 73, 85, 91, 134, 153
Italian nationalism 70, 115
Italian-speaking populations 37–8, 70, 93–4, 97–8
Italy 13, 19–21, 23–5, 41, 56, 59–62, 65–6, 70, 73–4, 132, 134, 143–4, 168, 181
  declaration of war on Austria-Hungary 80
  postwar expansion 156
Izvolsky, Alexander 18–19

Jászi, Oskár 174
Jeličić, Ivan 167–8
Jews 13–14, 65–7, 71–3, 80, 116, 158, 168–9
  as refugees 45–6, 90–2, 168–71
Jičín (refugee camp) 91–2
Jiu Valley (coal reserves) 61
July Crisis 28–30

Kaiser Wilhelm 54–5
Kállay, Benjamin 16–17
Kalwoda, Johannes 40–1
Karlovy Vary/Carlsbad 103–4
Károlyi, Mihaily 149
Karst region 60
Kaunas/Kovno 58
Kepisz, Slanisław, *see* Daszkiewiczowa, Ludwika
Kerchnawe, Hugo 65, 76
Khabarovsk 97
Kielce 71, 170–1
Kingdom of Serbs, Croats, and Slovenes, *see* Yugoslav state
Kobarid/Caporetto (Battle of) 134, 142–3
Kohn, Hans 97
Kolbuszowa 170–1
Konrad, R.M. 112
Korošec 146–7
Kosovo 14

Kramář, Karel 41–2
Kriegsüberwachungsamt (KÜA) 25–6, 37, 47
Krobatkin, Alexander 39–40
Kronenbitter, Günther 19
Kučera, Rudolf 47–8
Kun, Béla 164
Kyiv 140–1

L'viv/Lwów/Lemberg 36, 54–5, 58, 72–3, 94, 153–4, 170–1
labor conditions 47–9, 55, 65–6, 89
labor strikes 46–7, 120, 129–30, 136–8, 140–3
labor unions 46–7, 55
Lammasch, Heinrich 146
League of Nations 161–2, 167, 169, 176
Lein, Richard 41–2
liberals 121
Libya 19–20
Lida 170–1
Linz 70, 81, 97–8
Lithuania 162
Ljubljana/Laibach 147, 154
Łódź 72
Lower Austria 48–9, 135–6
Lublin 71, 73, 140

Macedonia 13–14, 17–22, 59
malnutrition 44, 46, 91–2
Maribor/Marburg 81, 154, 160
Marin, Irina 40
Masaryk, Thomas 158, 171–2
Mataja, Heinrich 115
Matis, Herbert 34–5
Mauro, Nelly 91–2
Mediterranean 13, 18
militarization of society 25–7, 32–3, 35, 40, 44, 46–7, 63, 66–7, 69–71, 87–8, 93–4, 104–21
Ministry of Social Welfare 115–16, 139–40
Minorities Treaties 161–4
Minsk 170–1
Mitzka, Rudolf 76
mobilization 6, 9, 19–20, 29–33, 37, 51–2, 55–7, 108
Moldavia 13–14
Montenegro 17, 19–20, 29–30, 40–1, 56, 59, 62–3, 65–6, 69
Moravia 18, 149–50, 155–6
Morelon, Claire 41, 54–5, 150
Morganthau, Henry 170–1
Moscow 119
Mount Lovćen 69
Mucha, Alphons 15–16
Müller-Guttenbrunn, Adam 103
Muslims 13–14, 21–2, 65–6
mutiny 120, 137, 142–3

Nagyvárad 90
Nansen passports 167
Nansen, Fridtjof 167
nationalism 2, 24, 37–8, 40–1, 69, 97, 100, 102, 115, 139–40, 146–7, 152–6, 183–4
nationalist associations 4, 36, 39–41, 53–4, 67, 115

occupation 5, 15–17, 56–7, 62–8, 71–3, 76, 78, 80, 87–8
  of Ukraine 141–2
  resource exploitation 62–3, 72–3
  variation between regions 63, 71
Omsk 94–6, 98
orphans 113
Orthodox Christians 13–15, 21–3
Ottoman Empire 13–22, 178
Ottoman Empire (Young Turk Movement in) 15, 17–18

Pachmann, Lothar Ritter von 64–5
pan-Slavism 41
paramilitary groups 5–6, 14, 21–2
paranoia 37–8, 71, 85
  of Habsburg state 100–1
Paris Exhibition (1900) 15–16
Paris Peace Conferences 2, 68–9, 160
Pašić, Nikola 145–6
passports 103–4
patriotism for Habsburg Empire 3–4, 7–8, 16–18, 23–5, 27, 41, 53–4, 89–90, 93, 105
peasants 31, 141–2
Petar I (King of Serbia) 24
Petrograd 96, 119
Piave offensive 144–5
Pilsen/Plzeň 47–8
Piłsudski, Josef 138–9, 154, 158
Pinsk 170–1
Pittsburgh Agreement 145–6
Pizzini, Enrico 96–7
Plzen/Pilsen 47
Pogorelz, Olga 81
Pola/Pula 91–2
Poland 62–3, 67, 71–3, 75–6, 92, 138–9, 154, 161, 170, 176
Poland 178–9
  Congress Poland 56, 64–6, 71–2
  occupation of 71–4
Polish nationalism 71–2, 115, 130–1, 138–40, 170–1
Polish-speaking populations 24, 64, 66, 71–3, 170
Polish–Ukrainian War (1919) 154
Porto Rosa Conference 174
postwar federation proposals 174–5
postwar migration policies 171–4
Potiorek, Oskar 40–1

POWs 58, 85, 93–102, 111–12, 183
  effect on masculinity 94–7
  forced labor 97–8
  recreational activities 94–6
  resentments of 99–101
  return of 100, 137
  stigma of capture 93–4
  treatment in Italy 99
  treatment in Russia 94, 97–8
  unequal treatment 94–6, 98–100
Prague 5, 41, 45, 47–8, 52–4, 81, 88, 90, 150, 152, 158, 176
Pressburg/Poszony (Bratislava) 47, 157
profiteering 44–5, 76
Prohászka, Ottokár 91
propaganda 50–2, 54–5, 62, 68–9, 144–6
prostitution 67, 88
Prussia 71–2
Przemyśl 36, 147–8
Pula/Pola 51

Rachamimov, Iris 94–6
Radom 71
railways 71, 77, 81
Rašín, Alois 41–2, 178
rationing 31–2, 43–4, 91–2
Rauchensteiner, Manfried 57
Red Cross 23, 53–4, 96, 99–100, 110
refugee camps 78–9, 81–93
refugees 2, 5, 21–2, 37, 45–6, 59, 78–93, 110, 167–72
  social composition and segregation of 80–1, 86–7
Reill, Dominique Kirchner 156, 167–8
Reiss, Rudolph Archibald 68–9
Renner, Karl 129
requisitioning 26, 72–3
revolution
  fears of 120–1, 127–8, 135, 144–5
  hopes for 122–3
Rigó, Máté 61, 75–6, 179
riots 45, 73, 120
Roda, Alexander 38–9
Rolandi, Francesca 167–8
Roma 13–14
  internment of 87–8
Romania 13–14, 17, 20–4, 28–9, 56, 60–2, 64–6, 157–8, 178–9
Romania
  Central Powers occupation of 74
  invasion of Transylvania 154
Romanian nationalism 148–9
Romanian-speaking populations 37–8, 40, 61, 66, 74–98
Rösetbaumer, Chaja 92
Roth, Joseph 90, 158–9, 181

rumor 37, 42–3, 45, 55, 94
Russia 10–11, 13, 15, 18–22, 28–31, 56–8, 60–2, 66–7, 71–2, 74, 97–8, 130–1, 162, 178
  alliance with Serbia 12, 15, 17–19
  Habsburg view of 20, 29–30
  pre-war strategy 13–14, 20–3
Russian Revolution (1905) 17–18
Russian Revolution (March 1917) 119–20
Russian Revolution (October 1917) 100, 116–20, 127–8, 130
Russo-Japanese War (1904–5) 17–18, 22–3, 56–7
Ruthenes 37–40, 69–72, 74, 93–4
Rybak, Jan 147–8, 170

Salonica 59
Salter, Arthur 176
Salzburg 52–3, 70
Sarajevo 1–2, 29, 37, 67
Schapp, Max 78
Scheer, Tamara 25–6, 47, 63
Schwarz-Hiller, Rudolf 93
Schwimmer, Rosika 153
Seipel, Ignaz 176
self-determination 2, 133, 154, 156–8, 160–1
Serb nationalism 14–16, 21–4, 39–40, 69
Serbia 12–25, 28–9, 31, 56–7, 59, 62–9, 73–4, 87–8, 131
  Austro-Hungarian decision for war against 14–15, 28–9
  Austro-Hungarian occupation of 73, 75–6
Serb-speaking populations 37–40, 67, 69, 71, 93–4, 97–8, 138
Shmidlap, William 103–4
Silesia 2–3, 149–50, 155–6
Sixtus Affair 131–5, 143–4
Škoda works 34–5, 47–8
Slavic-speaking populations 13–15, 25, 28, 98
Slobodian, Quinn 176
Slovak nationalism 23, 145–6, 148–9
Slovakia 158, 170
Slovene nationalism 23, 146–7, 154
Slovene-speaking populations 138, 148–9, 160–2
Slovenia (in Habsburg Empire) 18, 60
Smuts, Jan 162
social democracy 128–30
Social Democratic Party of Austria 128–30
socialism 47, 55, 121, 123, 135, 138–9, 149–51
South Slav populations 126–7
Sperber, Manès 66–7
St. Pölten 70
stateless people 2, 167–9
Steinklamm (refugee camp) 91–2
Stergar, Rok 146–7
Stourzh, Gerald 169

Stürgkh, Karl Count 28, 39, 52, 113–14
    assassination of 123
Styria 39
Sultan Abdulhamid II 17–18

Thrace 19–21
Tisza 124–8
Tisza, István 20, 28–9, 39–40, 52, 60–1, 91
Tisza, István
    assassination of 149
trade unions 35, 128–30
Transylvania 22–3, 28–9, 60–1, 74, 76, 154, 157–8, 179
Treaty of Berlin (1878) 15, 18
Treaty of Brest–Litovsk (1918) 56, 58, 119, 122, 132, 137–43
Treaty of Constantinople (1913) 20–1
Treaty of London (1915) 60, 156
Treaty of St. Germain (1919) 167
Treaty of St. Germain (1919) (Option clause) 167, 169
Treaty of Trianon (1920) 154–5
Treviso 73
Trieste 46, 51, 81, 100
Triple Alliance 20, 28–9
Trotsky, Leon 140–1
Turkey 162
Tyrol 60, 131, 155–6, 181

Udine 73
Udyński, Baron Karl Heinold von 113–14
Ukraine 56, 140–2, 154
Ukrainian nationalism 130–1, 138–9, 170–1
Ukrainian People's Republic 140
Ukrainian-speaking populations 23–4, 72, 91–2, 97–8, 170
United States of America 7, 103, 107, 116–18, 122, 175
    and treatment of minorities 161–2
    as a model for Europe 171–2, 174–5
    Austro-Hungarian citizens in 106–8
    declaration of war on Germany and Austria Hungary 132–3
    immigrant communities in 105–8, 122
    immigration restrictions in 107, 171
    policies towards minority groups 161–2
    recognition of Czechoslovakia 150
    troops on the Western Front 143–4
    war aims of 132–3
USSR 140–1, 154
Ustí nad Labem/Aussig 88

Venezia 73
veterans 6, 85, 110, 112–15, 121, 127, 153, 181–2
    state support of wounded 113–15

Vicenza 73
Victor Emmanuel, King of Italy 96–7
Vienna 37, 47, 75, 81, 88, 90–2, 116, 123, 149–50, 153, 155–6, 165–6, 168–70
    arrival of refugees 80
    civil–military conflict over occupation policies 72–3
    War Exhibition at Prater Park 52–4
    wartime food supply 43–4
    wartime public opinion in 42
Vilnius 58, 170–1
Vizhnitsa 78
Vojvodina 148–9
von Rogozski, Kasimir 72–3

Wallachia 13–14
war crimes 68–9
    allegations against Serbs 67
    Austro-Hungarian denial of 68–9
War Ministry 37, 46–7
Warsaw 58, 72, 152
wartime economy 31, 33–7, 46–7, 75–6, 137
Watson, Alexander 133
Wehrmann statues 51
Weisskirchner, Richard 110
Welfare Ministry 135
welfare state 4, 55, 81, 85, 103–18, 168–9
    and gender 105, 110
    and national segregation 115–18
    escalating demands for relief 110
    wartime expansion of 89–90, 93, 104, 128, 135–6
Western Front 58, 68, 79–80, 98–141, 143–4, 151
Wheatley, Natasha 161, 176
widows 51, 67, 113
Wilhelm II 135
Wilson, Woodrow 132–3, 150, 152, 156–7
Wolff, Larry 132–3, 160–1
women 31–3, 43–4, 48–51, 54, 88–9, 97–8, 111–12, 135–6
    employment in wartime 47–9, 88
    gender and citizenship 105, 110, 112
Women's Auxiliary Service 112
workers 4, 31–2, 34, 36, 46–9, 73, 80, 97–8, 119, 127–30, 136–8

Yovanovitch, Voyslav M. 68
Yugoslav state 18, 68–9, 145–6, 154, 156–7, 160, 179

Zablotow 66–7, 92
Zagreb/Agram 24, 52–3, 148–9, 152–3
Zionism 74, 170–1, 173
Zweig, Stefan 37, 65, 181

The manufacturer's authorised representative in the EU for product safety is Oxford University Press España S.A. of el Parque Empresarial San Fernando de Henares, Avenida de Castilla, 2 – 28830 Madrid (www.oup.es/en or product.safety@oup.com). OUP España S.A. also acts as importer into Spain of products made by the manufacturer.

www.ingramcontent.com/pod-product-compliance
Ingram Content Group UK Ltd.
Pitfield, Milton Keynes, MK11 3LW, UK
UKHW021105100326
468845UK00005B/951